FLAVOUR

Ottolenghi
FLAVOUR

Yotam Ottolenghi   Ixta Belfrage

with Tara Wigley
Photography by Jonathan Lovekin

EBURY
PRESS

CONTENTS

INTRODUCTION

I have never been shy about my love of vegetables. I have been singing the praises of cauliflowers, tomatoes, lemons and my old friend the mighty aubergine for over a decade. I have done this on my own – in cookery demos, on book tours and in the pages of books and magazines; and I have done this in a group, in lively discussions with colleagues in the restaurants and in the test kitchen. It's become my mission to present vegetables in new and exciting ways and I have embraced it with nothing but enthusiasm.

Still, in the spirit of openness, I must confess to a small niggling doubt that creeps in now and then: how many more ways are there to roast a cauliflower, to slice a tomato, to squeeze a lemon or to fry an aubergine? How many more secrets are there to be discovered in a handful of lentils or a bowl of polenta?

The answer, I am delighted to report, is many. My journey of discovery into the world of vegetables – by which I mean anything, really, which originates from a plant – has taken me in all sorts of directions that I simply hadn't imagined. If my first vegetable book, *PLENTY*, was the honeymoon period, a great big party where certain vegetables – peppers, tomatoes, aubergines, mushrooms – got a whole chapter to themselves, *PLENTY MORE* was all about process; recipes were divided into the ways in which the vegetables were treated: mashed or tossed or grilled and so forth. *FLAVOUR* is the third book in the series: it's about understanding what makes vegetables distinct and, accordingly, devising ways in which their flavours can be ramped up and tasted afresh; it's about creating flavour bombs, especially designed for veg. This is done in three ways.

PROCESS, PAIRING, PRODUCE

The first is to do with some basic *processes* that happen to vegetables when they are cooked, or to some key ingredients that they are cooked with. The second is about *pairing*: what you match a vegetable with to draw out one of its distinct qualities. The third is to do with the *produce* itself: the sheer depth of flavour that certain ingredients naturally possess that allows them to play a starring role in a dish, more or less by themselves, or to prop up and brightly illuminate other vegetables.

So, after *PLENTY* and *PLENTY MORE*, *FLAVOUR* is '*PLENTY 3*', if you like, or *P3*, with the three 'p's (process, pairing and produce) being the key concepts for explaining what makes certain vegetable dishes taste so good. Let me give you some examples to illustrate this, using some of my favourite ingredients: celeriac (to demonstrate process), tamarind and lime (to think about pairing) and mushrooms (to show how it can be just the produce itself doing the work).

First, *process*. Three recipes in this book involve cooking celeriac whole for more than two hours, then dressing and serving it in different ways. During the initial cooking of the celeriac, and before any other ingredient is added, something truly magical happens. Much of the water in the celeriac evaporates, its flesh turns from white to golden-brown and it becomes sweeter and richer. This browning and caramelising, which happens to many veg (and non-veg) when they are cooked in a certain way, is a key process that teases out flavour from them. Whatever you choose to do to the celeriac after this is less

HOW MANY MORE WAYS ARE THERE TO FRY AN AUBERGINE? THE ANSWER, I AM DELIGHTED TO REPORT, IS MANY

important. Indeed, you don't need to do anything more to it at all, if you don't want to; the browning process is such a flavour bomb that it's heavenly eaten at this stage, cut into wedges and served with a squeeze of lemon or a dollop of crème fraîche. Other processes which have a similarly terrific effect are charring, ageing (which is mostly done to ingredients well before they reach your kitchen) and infusing, all of which transform and elevate vegetables to great heights.

Illustrating my concept of *pairing* is a little less straightforward because every time you cook you obviously pair ingredients together. What I have done, though, is identify four basic pairings – acidity, heat (as in spicy heat), fat and sweetness – which are fundamental. Introducing one or more of these key pairings to a dish has the effect of showing the vegetables (or fruit) they are partnered with in a completely new light. The ASPARAGUS SALAD WITH TAMARIND AND LIME (P. 171) is a great example. Many argue that asparagus is so magnificent – with a subtle, yet refined flavour – that it doesn't need to be paired with anything really, except some oil or butter and possibly a poached egg. I have made this same point myself in the not so distant past. What I have learned more recently, though, is that asparagus can actually stand its ground also when paired with robust and purportedly dominant ingredients. It does this particularly well when the paired element is complex

and multi-layered. In the salad I mentioned, raw asparagus is paired with three sources of acidity, each with its own particular characteristics: lime juice, vinegar and tamarind. All these layers and iterations of sour come together in a single harmony which heightens and alters the taste of raw asparagus in a way that really opens your eyes to the vegetables.

The third concept is to do with *produce*. Vegetables, famously, are not as good at imparting flavour as meat and fish are, because of their high water content and the low levels of fat and protein they contain. Some, though, are absolutely brilliant at it. Our SPICY MUSHROOM LASAGNE (P. 228) is living proof of the power of this particular veg to carry the weight of a whole complex dish on its own little shoulders, giving any meat a good run for its money. Not many vegetables can do this, delicious as they may be, but since mushrooms are bursting with umami – that satisfying savoury flavour which makes tomatoes, soy sauce, cheese and many other ingredients so impactful – they are perfectly capable of providing ample flavour and some serious texture to give vegetarian dishes a very solid core. Other plant-based ingredients that show similarly impressive skills are alliums (onions and garlic), nuts and seeds, and fruit. All four are the types of produce that you can rely on to do some seriously hard work for you in your kitchen.

While making a delicious recipe can be simple, great cooking is never the result of one element in isolation – it is the interplay of different types of *processes*, *pairings* and *produce* in one dish that elevates and makes it exquisite. Using the lasagne example again, this dish clearly heavily relies on mushroom umami (produce), but it also benefits greatly from an interplay of different fats (pairing) and the complex art of ageing cheese (process). The structure of the book, in which each chapter highlights one particular kind of process, pairing or produce, is, therefore, not there to undermine or deny the existence of many other elements in a recipe; its purpose is to highlight the USP of a dish, a particular element at the core that makes it particularly delicious or special.

FLEXITARIANISM

With the challenge to ramp up flavour in vegetables and take it to new heights, I've used every possible tool available in the kitchen. For me, and the way I cook and eat, this includes ingredients such as anchovies, fish sauce and Parmesan which are not, of course, often used in recipe books in which vegetables play the starring role. Though I totally understand why that is the case, with many people following an exact vegetarian or vegan diet, I have decided to appeal to the widest group of vegetable lovers possible.

I find that more and more people are looking to brand their own individual kind of vegetable eating. Yes, many define themselves as vegetarian or vegan, but there is also a certain fluidity which characterises the current approach to how we feed ourselves. You find vegans in all but eggs, those who eat seafood but won't touch milk because of the predicament of dairy cows, some who

IF YOU WANT TO WIN MORE PEOPLE OVER TO THE VEG CAMP, THERE IS NO WORSE WAY TO GO ABOUT IT THAN DEMAND THAT THEY GO COLD TURKEY

exclude only proteins which are particularly harmful to the environment; there are pescatarians, beegans (vegans that eat honey) and lacto-vegetarians (abstaining from meat and eggs). There are also 'lapsed' vegans or vegetarians: those who have given up a strict regime but have taken away with them the joys and skills of cooking a great meat-free meal.

My own approach to vegetables has always been pragmatic and inclusive. If you want to win more people over to the veg camp, there is no worse way to go about it than demand that they go cold turkey (excuse the pun). If an animal-based aromatic ingredient (we are not talking prime cuts of meat here, or a bluefin tuna steak) does an outstanding job at 'helping' a vegetable taste particularly delicious, I will definitely use it for the benefit of those who are happy to eat it. At the same time, I will also offer various alternatives to animal products (and dairy products, whenever I can) so that everyone can join in.

This flexitarian approach to cooking and eating acknowledges the diversity of the people we are and the variety of choices we make. From the 100 recipes in the book, 45 are strictly vegan and another 17 are easily 'veganised'. Whatever your own preference might be, I feel confident that you will find good reasons to join in my celebration of all the flavours vegetables have to offer.

My confidence here is based on my knowledge of vegetables after years of cooking and writing about them, during which I have never ceased to be surprised. It is grounded in my love of vegetables and my understanding of how versatile they are, how receptive they are to different cooking practices, how chameleon-like is their ability to take on flavour and metamorphose themselves from one dish to the next.

And thus, a simple cauliflower, to use a favourite example, can reinvent itself in every book and in many chapters, showing up once as a seductive Levantine fritter, then grilled and engaged with saffron and raisins, only to return disguised as bulgur in a modern take on tabbouleh, followed by an

SIMPLY 'MAGICAL', TO BORROW A TERM FAVOURED BY MY FIVE-YEAR-OLD SON

incarnation as a glamorous savoury cake, a meaty steak, dressed as (coronation) chicken, or simply served whole, grilled yet totally unadorned, with only its natural splendour to call its virtues. This is how wide the range and how wondrous the potential of every single vegetable. Simply 'magical', to borrow a term favoured by my five-year-old son.

IXTA

Much as vegetables have this supernatural ability to be turned into an endless smörgåsbord of delicious food, it takes a focused creative effort to unravel this potential. In other words, the umpteenth way to cook the beloved cauliflower didn't just present itself out of thin air. It was a result of trial and (many an) error, mixing and matching cauliflower with other components on the plate, of constantly looking for exciting new ingredients for it to be paired with, and generally, being super sensitive to the processes that happen in the pan, or the roasting tray or the serving platter.

The people leading this creative process are, naturally, crucial to the particular route it will take. So, if you have already managed to spot a lime or two in places where lemons would appear in previous Ottolenghi books, or noticed a range of Mexican and other chillies peppered all over these pages,

THE UMPTEENTH WAY TO COOK THE BELOVED CAULIFLOWER DIDN'T JUST PRESENT ITSELF OUT OF THIN AIR

or if you came across quick pickles and infused oils used to give dishes a finishing touch – you have identified the fingerprints of Ixta Belfrage, who's had those same fingers on the vegetable pulse for the last couple of years and helped shape the recipes in this book in a particular way.

Ixta is one of the most detail-obsessed chefs I know (and I have met a few of those over the years), with an unusual talent both for making the most spectacular versions of familiar dishes (see that LASAGNE again, P. 228) and for putting together an unusual set of components and effortlessly creating a totally new masterpiece (see, or, rather, go make, the SWEET AND SOUR SPROUTS WITH CHESTNUTS AND GRAPES, P. 93).

Ixta's journey into the world of food, which is evident in so many of the dishes here, was, a bit like mine, anything but straightforward. Despite growing up mostly in London, she spent much of her early years in different corners of the globe, eating, observing and just soaking up some wonderful food traditions and flavours.

If you talked to Ixta, she'd be happy to tell you about her friend's grandfather, Ferruccio – who, in a corner of Tuscany, makes the best lasagne in the world, and passed a few secrets on to her. She would talk about her grandfather's home, near Mexico City, where she keenly watched chiles rellenos (stuffed peppers) being prepared. She'd mention Brazil, where her mother is from and where she fell for pirão (cassava flour porridge), mocequa (fish stew) and fried cassava chips, and she'd definitely tell you about Christmas holidays in France and that most glorious of apple pies, pastis Gascon.

SHE TEACHES ME SOMETHING NEW EVERY SINGLE DAY. AND FOR THIS, I AM UTTERLY GRATEFUL

After all that, you'd be right to assume that cooking would be Ixta's first port of call in her professional life. Yet on her way there, she managed, among other things, to start a foundation course in art, go to university in Rio, move to Australia for three years and work as a door-to-door power and gas sales person, become a travel agent and come back to London and study design.

It took Ixta's sister finally asking the obvious question one day – 'Why the f*** aren't you a chef?' – for the penny to finally drop, which it did with a loud bang. After that, this self-taught, highly observant person, who spent her childhood, adolescence and young adulthood absorbing techniques and flavours like a sponge, set out on an accelerated route which included running her own small catering operation, setting up a market stall in London, where she sold tacos (of course), and, finally, applying for a job at NOPI.

When, less than a year later, she arrived in my test kitchen – with no formal training and a modest amount of experience, but with a mountain of knowledge, creativity and talent – I soon understood that I could more or less leave Ixta to her own devices. Cooking her own food, which is deeply rooted in the cultures she has soaked up over the years, while also brilliantly incorporating the language of contemporary cooking, she teaches me something new every single day. And for this, I am utterly grateful.

TARA

The power of a good recipe to expose the hidden potential in an ingredient and show it in a new and wonderful light is the greatest joy of my profession. It's what keeps Ixta and me going, trying to explore further, to look at every possible iteration, to wrack our brains until we finally hit on something which is both delicious and truly special.

Good cookbooks do the same thing with a set of dishes. They take them, just like raw ingredients, and piece together a narrative; they give a compelling account that makes sense and touches the spot, like a perfectly balanced stew or a trifle with just the right proportions of creamy to fruity to boozy.

Telling a story in such a way is a difficult task which takes a particular and rare talent. Tara Wigley, who has worked on all but two of the eight cookbooks that have come out of the Ottolenghi family, has this talent in ladlefuls. With her deep insight into both the human palate and the Ottolenghi flavour palette, she'd always managed to turn our recipes into much more than a set of instructions for recreating dishes at home. She gave them a context and put ideas behind them; she assembled them in particular ways that made them make sense and made people want to prepare them.

In this book, Tara took one short look at the recipes and instantly isolated and identified what Ixta and I hopelessly struggled to figure out. She gave our vague ideas names, helped us structure the book, and then she put together the introductions to the three main sections which provide the book with its theoretical basis. To that effect, the story which is unearthed here, through recipes, has been brought to light thanks to Tara.

YOTAM OTTOLENGHI

FLAVOUR'S 20 INGREDIENTS

We conclude this introductory section with a list of *FLAVOUR*'s essential ingredients. By 'essential', we don't suggest that you necessarily need to go out and buy them all before you start cooking, or that you just can't do without them. In fact, you will be able to reproduce many of the dishes here without a single one of these ingredients. What we mean is that the twenty ingredients we highlight, as well as popping up regularly on the pages alongside our beloved vegetables, also capture the essence of this book, its particular spirit. If you open a jar or a bag of any of these ingredients, edge your nose close and have a little sniff, you should be able to smell *FLAVOUR*.

Since we champion veg and the numerous ways in which you can dial up their flavour that one extra notch, it is no surprise that many of our essentials are aged or fermented. In fact, there is a whole section (P. 93–113) dedicated to dishes which rely on aged ingredients to make them as delicious and special as they are. There is also a long introduction (P. 33–5) explaining the super-power of ageing and how it generates layers of flavour. Aged ingredients are shortcuts to jars of flavour which, we believe, should sit on every kitchen shelf.

As well as umami-rich ferments, chillies form another strong grouping on our list of essentials. Though celebrated for their spiciness (see the CHILLI HEAT section, P. 196–211, and introduction, P. 127–9), our chillies do much more than that. They bring with them to the table a whole set of sub-flavours and fine aromas that you simply can't find elsewhere, a different kind of sweet, smoky, leathery, chocolatey or tart. They also have an incredible ability to marry together with other flavours to create a new, singular harmony. We always think of the combination of garlic, ginger and chilli, which sits at the heart of so many dishes, and try to imagine it without the chilli. Impossible.

Chillies, like ferments, run across cultures like busy diplomats. Practically every region in the world to which we are drawn has its own unique take on chilli sauce, or oil, or marinade. A little bottle or jar with deep scarlet liquid inside signifies a flavour bomb of a very particular kind.

In *FLAVOUR*, Mexico is where we frequently go for our fix of chilli heat. This has as much to do with the incredible range of chillies that come out of this country as it does with Ixta's childhood memories of Mexico and her infatuation with its food.

Chillies, as well as masa harina, hibiscus flowers and all the clever feasts that you can create with them, are the latest additions to the ever-expanding Ottolenghi pantry. We urge you to try them out, but please don't ditch the old favourites. Some of them – rose harissa, black garlic, Aleppo chillies – are on this list; others – tahini, za'atar, preserved lemons, pomegranate molasses – aren't, but they are dotted throughout the recipes, busily doing their now-familiar magic.

Aleppo chilli is a dried and flaked chilli, common in Turkey and Syria, named after the city of Aleppo. While the flakes themselves are dark red, they impart a bright red colour when infused. We use Aleppo chilli to add medium heat to lots of sauces and marinades, such as our NAM JIM (P. 202), NAM PRIK (P. 44), RAYU (P. 237) and CHAMOY (P. 187). It's also great in salad sprinkles (see KOHLRABI 'NOODLE' SALAD, P. 260). You can find Aleppo chilli in some supermarkets, but better yet, visit a Middle Eastern grocer, where you can get large bags of the stuff under the name 'pul biber' for a fraction of the price. Use half the amount of regular chilli flakes, as a substitute.

Ancho chilli is the dried version of the poblano chilli. Poblanos are green when fresh, and become very dark red when dried, developing fruity and sweet notes with mild to medium levels of heat. We use them in both sweet and savoury contexts here – see TANGERINE AND ANCHO CHILLI FLAN (P. 278) and BLACK BEANS WITH COCONUT, CHILLI AND LIME (P. 86).

Anchovies don't need much of an introduction, but we should note that we do mean those that have been aged in salt, rather than marinated or pickled, and we would urge you to get anchovies kept in olive oil, rather than sunflower oil. Anchovies give a savoury depth to the dishes you add them to. They are only particularly fishy if you use a fair amount. We are aware that vegetarians and vegans don't eat anchovies, so they are

optional in all the recipes. They can be substituted with extra seasoning, and by that we mean anything from salt, miso and soy sauce to finely chopped olives and capers.

Black garlic is garlic that has been gently heated for 2–3 weeks, causing the Maillard reaction (see more on P. 28) to render it black, sweet and a bit liquorice-y, with notes of balsamic vinegar. It brings a distinctive sweetness to the OLIVE OIL FLATBREADS (P. 246) and the DIRTY RICE (P. 252).

Black lime is a lime that has been sun-dried until it has lost all its water and turned rock hard. Popular in the Persian Gulf, it is intensely sour and gives dishes a uniquely earthy and slightly bitter type of acidity. There are different versions across the region, with different names, such as Omani limes, Iranian limes and noomi basra, and they can range in colour from blond to dark brown to black. You can use any of them in our recipes, but we prefer the small black limes. You can harness the lime's flavour in different ways: pierce holes in it and add it to a broth or stew to impart milder flavour, or soak and finely chop the whole lot to add an intense hit of earthy acidity. You can find them online or in Middle Eastern grocers.

Cascabel chillies are, we think, the best dried chillies out there. We've used them in countless dishes in our restaurant, ROVI – the BUTTER BEANS IN SMOKED CASCABEL OIL (P. 41) for one – and in the rub for our OYSTER MUSHROOM TACOS (P. 238). On first inspection they are black, but if you hold them up to the light, they are in fact a deep and seductive red. They are sweet, nutty and mildly chocolatey, which makes them work wonderfully in both sweet and savoury contexts (try using them instead of ancho chillies in the TANGERINE AND ANCHO CHILLI FLAN, P. 278).

Chipotle chilli is the dried and smoked version of the jalapeño chilli. It gives medium heat and is, unsurprisingly, smoky. We steep chipotle flakes in warm oil for a very quick but extremely effective chilli oil to drizzle over CHEESE TAMALES (P. 158), and blitz them into a coating for peanuts, which play a starring role in the RADISH AND CUCUMBER SALAD (P. 263).

Fish sauce is a Southeast Asian condiment made from fermented fish. Unsurprisingly, it is extremely funky, and although we love it, we can appreciate that not everyone does. Own-brand supermarket varieties aren't always top quality, so do try to get your hands on the real deal; Squid Brand (which interestingly contains no squid) is very good, and is readily available in any Asian supermarket. Fish sauce is totally optional in all recipes. It's comparable in salt levels to light soy sauce, which can be used in its place. You may want to add less light soy sauce, however, if the recipe already contains soy sauce.

Gochujang chilli paste is a Korean fermented paste made from chillies, glutinous rice and soya beans, making it complex, hot, sweet and savoury all at once. Do try to get your hands on the real-deal Korean brands (O'food, for example), which have a serious depth to them, compared to the often dull own-brands sold in supermarkets. Gochujang is available in most Asian supermarkets, but if you can only get the supermarket stuff, taste before you add – you may need to double the amount if it's lacking in colour, body or flavour.

Ground cardamom has been an Ottolenghi pantry staple for a while because we love using it in both sweet and savoury contexts. We sell it in our webstore but, otherwise, it's still quite hard to come by. You can make your own, however, by starting with whole cardamom pods, discarding the papery shells and grinding the seeds to a fine powder. You'll be happy to have the ready-ground stuff when making our CARDAMOM TOFU (P. 172), though, as it requires a fair amount.

Hibiscus flowers are used widely in Mexico to flavour all sorts of foods and drinks. They are floral and tart, comparable in taste to cranberries, and impart an almost instant bright pink hue to anything they infuse. Dried hibiscus flowers are available in many health food shops and online, although we tend to use hibiscus tea bags, as they are more readily available. We use hibiscus to add an extra level of face-puckering acidity to our LEMON SORBET (P. 289), and to add tartness and vibrant colour to our PICKLED ONIONS (P. 158).

Jarred butter beans, specifically Brindisa Navarrico butter beans, prove that not all pre-cooked butter beans are created equal. If you are not going to cook butter beans from scratch, these 'judiónes' – *giant* butter beans – are just as soft, creamy and *perfectly* seasoned. Do try to source them to use in the BKEILA STEW (P. 75), or to steep in a wonderfully smoky CASCABEL OIL (P. 41). Tinned butter beans are, of course, a fine alternative.

Mango pickle is a hot, sharp and textured pickle, used widely in South and Southeast Asia, the dominant spice in which is fenugreek. It shouldn't be confused with mango chutney, which is often cloyingly sweet. We use a hot variety in our STUFFED AUBERGINE ROLLS (P. 152) and our CHICKPEA PANCAKES WITH MANGO PICKLE YOGHURT (P. 91).

Masa harina is a flour made from nixtamalised corn. Nixtamalisation is an ancient Aztec process by which corn is soaked and cooked in an alkaline solution before being washed and hulled. This helps with turning it into flour and boosts its nutritional value. Masa harina is used in Mexico and other parts of Central and South America to make tortillas (try our OYSTER MUSHROOM TACOS, P. 238) and tamales (try our CHEESE TAMALES, P. 158), among other things. It's important to remember that it is not interchangeable with cornflour or polenta. You can find it at Whole Foods, most health food shops and online.

Miso is a Japanese seasoning made by fermenting soya beans (but also sometimes rice or barley) with salt and koji, which is rice that has been inoculated with mould spores, making it sound far less delicious than it actually is. Miso is the embodiment of umami (SEE P. 35); it's sweet, salty and meaty all at once, and can single-handedly give an incredible depth of flavour to anything you add it to. We use white miso paste in our recipes because it has the perfect balance of sweet, salty and savoury that we're after. The aptly named Miso Tasty brand is our go-to. Try to avoid using sweet white miso paste; it is, unsurprisingly, much too *sweet* for savoury recipes.

Red bell pepper flakes are the dried flakes of what Australians would call 'capsicums', Americans would call 'bell peppers' and the British would simply (or rather confusingly) call 'peppers'. You can find bell pepper flakes in most supermarkets. Unlike chilli flakes, red bell pepper flakes are mild and sweet rather than hot, and impart a bright red colour when soaked.

Rice vinegar is made from fermented rice grains and is widely used in China, Japan and Southeast Asia. Rice vinegar is milder, sweeter and less acidic than distilled Western vinegars, so we often use it in situations that call for a more subtle and rounded hit of acidity. Our TAHINI AND SOY DRESSING (P. 113), for example, benefits from the use of rice vinegar, as does the dressing in our TOMATO AND PLUM SALAD (P.267).

Rose harissa is a version of the popular North African chilli paste containing rose petals. We use a fantastic, richly spiced but not terribly hot version by Belazu. It's not available everywhere, though, and own-brand supermarket varieties tend not to be very good. As an alternative, we opt for the Tunisian variety by Le Phare du Cap Bon (which you're likely to find internationally in a yellow and blue tube or tin). It won't have the rose flavour but this wouldn't really disrupt any of our recipes. The only things to watch are the level of heat, which is much higher in Tunisian products, and the fact that they don't contain as much oil. Our advice is to taste your harissa before you add it, increasing or decreasing the amount you use depending on how hot and strong you like things, and to add a bit of olive oil if you think the dish needs it. As a general rule, you'll probably want to use about a third of the amount of Tunisian chilli paste when rose harissa is called for.

Shaoxing is a wine fermented from rice. It is mildly sweet and subtly funky, similar in taste to pale dry sherry, which can be used in its place if necessary. It's quite easy to get hold of, though, and available in many supermarkets as well as in Asian supermarkets. It adds a particularly wonderful musty aroma to the CAPONATA (P. 135), SWEET AND SOUR SPROUTS WITH CHESTNUTS AND GRAPES (P. 93), and GRILLED FIGS (P. 110).

Tamarind paste is extracted from the sweet-sour pulp of the pod-like tamarind fruit. It's indigenous to tropical Africa, but popular throughout Asia, South America and the Middle East. Commercial products can be a bit tricky for home cooks because they vary greatly in concentration. Generally, they are sharper and more intense than the paste you extract yourself from a block of tamarind because they have citric acid added to them, so you'll have to double the amount the recipe calls for when making it yourself. To do that, mix a lemon-sized piece – roughly 120g – with some lukewarm water, about 60ml. After a few minutes, use your hands to mix everything together, adding a little more water if needed, so that the pulp falls away from the seeds and fibre. Pass it through a fine sieve, discarding the seeds and fibre, and store the thick paste in the fridge for up to a month.

A NOTE ON INGREDIENTS

Unless otherwise specified, all eggs are large, all butter is unsalted, all olive oil is extra virgin. Vegetables are trimmed, and garlic, onions and shallots are peeled (keep the trimmings and peelings to make stock). Garlic cloves are regular in size. Chillies have their stalks removed and are used with their seeds, although of course you can remove the seeds if you prefer less heat.

Salt is table salt, but we often also call for flaked sea salt, especially when finishing dishes. Black pepper is freshly cracked (never ground).

Parsley is flat-leaf, and both curry leaves and kaffir lime leaves are fresh, rather than dried.

Yoghurt, crème fraîche and cream are all plain and full-fat, and can always be replaced by dairy-free alternatives, to keep things vegan.

A NOTE ON TOASTING NUTS AND SEEDS

We toast nuts and seeds in an oven preheated to 160°C fan, spread out on a baking tray and stirred halfway through. Flaked almonds and sesame seeds take 6–7 minutes. Pine nuts, walnuts and pistachios take around 8 minutes and whole almonds and hazelnuts take 8–10 minutes.

A NOTE ON TEMPERATURES AND MEASUREMENTS

All recipes have been tested in a fan-assisted oven. If cooking in a conventional oven, temperatures should be increased by 10°C–20°C, depending on your oven. Hobs and ovens all vary in how well they convect heat, so look out for visual descriptions in the method, rather than only relying on timings, to achieve desired results.

Teaspoon and tablespoon measurements vary by region. In this book 1 teaspoon = 5ml and 1 tablespoon = 15ml.

A NOTE ON CLING FILM, PARCHMENT AND FOIL

All efforts have been made to minimise our use of single-use materials. Parchment and foil can often be reused, rather than discarded, and reusable food wraps can be used in place of cling film.

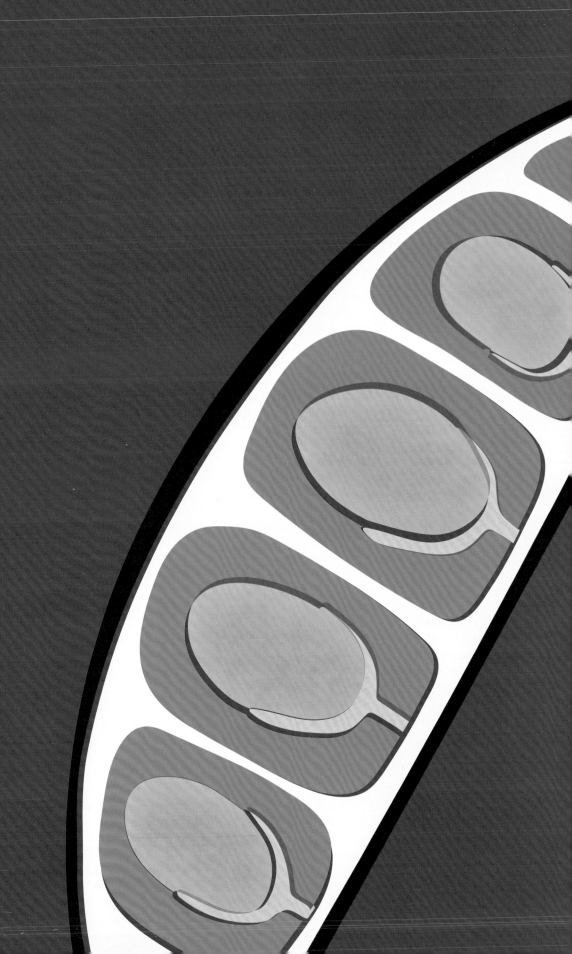

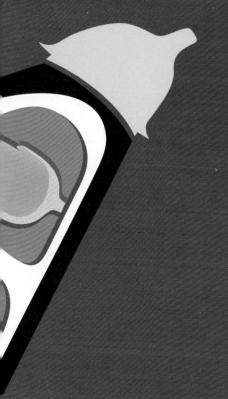

PROCESS

One of the ways to ramp up flavour in a vegetable is to subject it to a process before or during cooking. In *FLAVOUR*, we've homed in on four processes: *charring*, *browning*, *infusing* and *ageing*. These demonstrate how the application of heat, smoke or the passage of time to a vegetable or other ingredient can dramatically change, draw out or intensify its flavour. They show, in short, how flavour can be dialled up to make things even more tasty.

Recipes have been grouped according to the main process undertaken, but there's often more than one thing going on in the same dish. Although the oil and beans in the BUTTER BEANS IN SMOKED CASCABEL OIL (P. 41), as just one example, are *infused* by a pack of punchy aromatics, it's the deep *charring* of these aromatics in the first place that makes the dish stand out. Such is the very nature of vegetables: varied, versatile, brilliant vegetables that come in all shapes and sizes, and can be prepared in a huge variety of ways. Nevertheless, it's useful – when thinking about how flavour can get ramped up in a vegetable – to have a look at each process, one at a time.

CHARRING

In the beginning, there was fire. We are not talking about the dawn of time. We're thinking, for now, about Yotam's first memory of 'cooking'. It was a potato, tossed into a bonfire along with a few onions, on the Jewish holiday of Lag BaOmer, when spiritual light is celebrated by setting real lights across the land. Despite *his* best intentions, though, his spiritual awakening wasn't ignited by the lights but by the humble potato: a little ball of char, singeing his eight-year-old fingers as he peeled away its thick black skin. The steamy flesh, soft and billowy, speckled with black and tasting deep and sweet and smoky, was worth every blister on both his thumbs. This was an epic revelation.

SUCH IS THE POWER OF HEAT, SMOKE AND SOME NEAT BLACK STRIPES

Another big 'first', cooking-wise, was during the early days of Ottolenghi, when a simple salad of chargrilled broccoli, with slivers of garlic and red chilli, swiftly and firmly embedded itself on the menu. More than a decade on, it's still there. Our customers – many of whom tell us that they didn't really eat broccoli until they started charring it – won't let us take it off. For many, the experience of what broccoli *can* taste like is a revelation. Such is the power of heat, smoke and some neat black stripes.

So, what's the secret behind this charring process?

The science is relatively simple to understand. The direct application of heat to the outside of the ingredient is creating a chemical change. On a cellular level, amino acids and sugars are rearranging themselves nicely. This leads to a concentration of flavours which, in turn, imparts a delicious complexity, bitterness and sweetness. On top of that, there's a 'bonus' aroma which comes from the smoke that's emitted as the skin singes and which is impossible to resist.

The degree to which these things are all imparted depends on the nature of what is being charred (its size, its water content, its sugar levels), how long it is left on the heat, and how much cooking it gets elsewhere before or after it hits the grill. Some vegetables, like the 'famous' broccoli – but also cauliflower and Brussels sprouts, for example – need a bit of pre-grilling help, cooking-wise. We like boiling them quickly in water to allow heat to get to the core, before drying them well and throwing them on the grill with a bit of oil. Other vegetables benefit from being chargrilled in the pan first and then finished off in the oven. These tend to be the more robust, hard vegetables, such as pumpkin, sweet potato, beetroot and some cabbages.

At the other end of the scale, things like mangetout and other green peas and beans (see SLOW-COOKED CHARRED GREEN BEANS, P. 49), thin slices of fennel, tomatoes, or ribbons of courgette, don't need anything beyond the charring. They can just get a lick of oil and go straight on to the pan for a few seconds with no further cooking. As a general rule of thumb, things which can be eaten as they are, uncooked, can just get this kiss from the pan to reach their full smoky potential without any additional cooking or marinating. Sweet firm fruit also work well, as in the GRILLED PEACHES AND RUNNER BEANS (P. 37).

Post-grill, it's very effective to throw the still-hot charred vegetables into a bath of aromatics and oil, where the smokiness will infuse the oil that will, in turn, become a more potent dressing as a result of this interaction. At the same time, the vegetable itself is more prone to absorb the aromas of garlic, lime, or whatever it happens to sit with in the liquid while it's fresh off the pan. This double win is what happens to the mushrooms in the CONFIT GARLIC HUMMUS WITH GRILLED MUSHROOMS (P. 234).

A griddle pan is brilliant at charring and burning vegetables that sit at the centre of a dish – the char marks as badges of honour for an ingredient well initiated – but it is also a useful tool in infusing aromatics and other highly flavoured components with a smoky scent that they carry on with them wherever they are applied. Many sauces, salsas, flavoured oils and marinades will start with the charring of ingredients such as chillies, ginger, garlic, citrus zest, hard herbs and spices before allowing them to spread their smoky goodness all around. A Marie Rose sauce used for dipping ROMANO PEPPER SCHNITZELS (P. 146), for example, escapes the fate of becoming the cloying sweet mayo of the famous prawn cocktail by the addition of well-scorched, deeply smoked tomatoes and chillies.

Kit-wise, the magical effects of charring can be brought about fairly modestly. You can use a simple frying or sauté pan to achieve some great basic charring, which we often do when neat char marks aren't called for and the cooking carries on after this initial stage. In most cases, though, and if you don't have a barbecue to hand, investing in a heavy, cast iron, ridged griddle pan is highly recommended. This will hold heat well and allow you to scorch your vegetables at temperatures which aren't easily reached in home kitchens. It will stand the test of time and shouldn't warp or break under intense heat.

Beyond the pan, though, you just need some long-handled tongs, making it much easier to handle and turn whatever is on the grill. Good ventilation is also key: open the windows! Open the doors! Turn on the extraction!

Lastly, one other way worth mentioning if you want to get a deep-charred and smoky aroma into your food, and doing it 'as nature intended', is simply sitting your vegetables directly on the flame of the stove itself. Though we don't call for this method outright in any of our recipes (it involves a fair bit of stove-scrubbing when it's time to clean up), it works really well with some vegetables, saving you time and achieving an even deeper flavour than when

GOOD VENTILATION IS ALSO KEY: OPEN THE WINDOWS! OPEN THE DOORS! TURN ON THE EXTRACTION!

using a pan. Peppers can benefit from this treatment (see CHARRED PEPPERS AND FRESH CORN POLENTA, P. 140), but aubergines are where you really want to experiment with a 15-minute lie-down over an open flame. Your HERB AND BURNT AUBERGINE SOUP (P. 42), your ICEBERG WEDGES WITH SMOKY AUBERGINE CREAM (P. 38) and every baba ganoush you make from here on will thank you for it.

BROWNING

If charring is brought about by applying direct heat to the outside of an ingredient, then how is browning different? The clue is in the name. The instruction to 'roast a celeriac until its skin is golden-brown' will conjure a certain image: an enticing one. 'Char a pepper until its skin is black all over and collapsing', on the other hand, and the image is different. But then, these skins are used for different things. You'll want to snack on the golden-brown crusty skin of the celeriac. The charred skin of the pepper, meanwhile, can be peeled off and thrown away.

Browning is the name we give to the process that happens when we cook our celeriac. It's the same transformation, really, that takes place every time we toast bread, roast coffee beans or brown butter. As with charring, the science is pretty easy to understand. It's to do with the effect of heat on the sugars,

WHAT BROWNING MEANS, FOR THE HOME COOK, IS THAT THINGS SMELL BETTER, TASTE MORE COMPLEX

proteins and amino acids in the food. Once cooking starts and temperature increases, these sugars, proteins and amino acids don't keep to themselves. Rather, they all react to produce a huge array of flavour chemicals, aromas and colours. What browning means, for the home cook, is that things smell better, taste more complex and change colour, often from pale to golden-brown. Bread becomes malty, crunchy and darker; coffee beans become richer, more robust and deepen in colour; butter becomes nutty, rich and golden-brown.

In order for browning to take place, the temperature needs to be over the boiling point of water. The process generally starts happening around 110°C. A little bit of acidity and low-to-average water content are also conducive. When a vegetable is steamed or boiled, the conditions needed for browning will never occur. Steamed or boiled cauliflower florets will never taste like more than hot cauliflower florets. Roast the same florets in a hot oven, however, and they will undergo a transformation. Complex flavours that didn't exist are now there: notes that are nutty, creamy, sweet and nuanced.

What cooks call browning, food scientists call the Maillard reaction. It's called Maillard after the early twentieth-century French scientist, Louis-Camille Maillard, who discovered it. It's called a reaction because, in addition to requiring heat to get started, the process also produces heat. In this intense heat, the building blocks of proteins, in the presence of carbohydrates, keep rearranging themselves. The process becomes more complex as the products of each reaction get involved in their own reactions, creating thousands of different flavour and aroma molecules. The aromas you smell when cooking – deep savoury aromas that don't exist in the food's raw state – is the Maillard reaction at work.

Sweet vegetables, like beetroot and celeriac, for example, or swede and plantain, benefit particularly well from this process. The application of heat to them intensifies the sugars even further. The result can be something crusty and sweet on the outside and then almost caramel-like on the inside, tender and delicious. Yotam will never forget the first time a celeriac was roasted whole at work, testing recipes for the NOPI restaurant cookbook.

FLAVOUR EXPLODES WHEN IT'S BROWNED, FLYING INTO ALL SORTS OF NEW PLACES

Coming out of the oven after three hours of roasting, it was cut into twelve wedges and served with a squeeze of lemon. It was devoured whole in mere minutes! We've had similar 'complaints' from people who have, for the same sweet reason, been known to demolish an entire cauliflower or swede by themselves. In its raw form one person would be hard pushed to snack on a whole cauliflower head. Flavour explodes when it's browned, though, flying into all sorts of new places.

When cutting up vegetables to roast, rather than roasting them whole, there are a couple of practical things to keep in mind. The first is not to overcrowd the tray: if things are crammed too close together there will be no space for steam to escape and the vegetables will 'weep'. Spread them out nice and evenly, and the conditions will be perfect for browning. Keep an eye on them in the oven: rotate the tray halfway through cooking and give everything a gentle stir. Also, don't combine vegetables with very different sugar levels (or starch or water content) on the same tray: you don't want to be roasting slices of watery courgette, for example, with cubes of sugary squash. This will lead to uneven cooking: some veg will steam, others will weep, others will burn: none will be happy.

It's not just vegetables, sweet or otherwise, which can be transformed by the Maillard reaction. So can any ingredient that contains a combination of sugar, protein and carbohydrates. All these elements need to be there for the reaction to take place. The reason olive oil does not caramelise or brown in the way that butter does (in the HASSELBACK BEETROOT WITH LIME LEAF BUTTER, P. 50, for example), is that the oil is a pure fat; butter on the other hand also contains water, milk protein and whey solids. It's these solids which brown when unsalted butter is gently heated and whose colour and flavour change. These are the 'brown bits' which lead to the creation of the nutty, sweet, toasty brown butter. The flavour is wonderful: caramel-like and rich, just what a dish of steamed (and therefore *not* browned) CURRIED CARROT MASH (P. 67) needs, for example, to elevate it to the flavour bomb world we're spending time in.

Apart from roasting vegetables, as we have discussed, other cooking methods that will bring about the Maillard reaction are sautéeing, pan-frying, searing, grilling, baking, toasting and so on. Anything stewed, steamed or simmered won't reach 100°C+ and so, will never be Maillard. Anything fried, on the other hand, always will be.

Two practical notes to end on. The first is to do with taking things off the heat before they're fully done. The second is to do with putting things on the heat before you're fully ready.

First, things like slivers of garlic or chilli which are frying, or nuts and seeds which are toasting, need to come away from the heat slightly before they are done if you are leaving them in the oil (or on the tray in the case of the nuts). The residual heat from the oil in the pan or the tray will continue to cook

IT'S NO LONGER JUST AN ONION: IT'S THE SAVOURY, SWEET PROMISE OF A DELICIOUS MEAL JUST AROUND THE CORNER

what's in or on it. If you have taken things as far as you want them to go, then just make sure you transfer them elsewhere to cool. A kitchen paper-lined plate, in the case of the garlic, using a slotted spoon, or to a separate tray in the case of the nuts.

The second is perhaps more of a secret than a practical tip. Either way, if you are ever running late getting a meal to the table and the crowds are rousing, never forget that the raw onion sitting on your counter is your ultimate weapon in deception. A raw onion will only ever look, smell and taste like a raw onion. Quickly chop it up, though, put it into a hot pan with some oil, let it take on some colour and it becomes something else entirely. It's no longer just an onion: it's the savoury, sweet promise of a delicious meal *just* around the corner.

INFUSING

If browning is a fairly complex chemical process, and charring is a bold one, then infusing – by contrast – is all rather gentle and straightforward. It's what takes place when an aromatic is added to a liquid and heat and time are applied. We do it every morning when we make a cup of tea. The aromatic can take all sorts of forms – hard herbs, dried spices, fresh botanicals, alliums – as can the type of liquid, degree of heat and length of time things are left to steep. Vegetable oil, olive oil, high heat, low heat, two minutes on the heat, two hours off the heat – these are all variables that can be adjusted, depending on what level of infusion you're after.

Beyond the morning cup of tea, infusions are a wonderfully useful, economic and effective process to lean on in the kitchen throughout the day. For one thing, they can quickly root a dish in a specific area and cuisine. Just as tea leaves have the power to transport us to Darjeeling, Ceylon, Assam and beyond, the combination of ingredients in an infusion can take a dish all over

THE COMBINATION OF INGREDIENTS IN AN INFUSION CAN TAKE A DISH ALL OVER THE WORLD

the world. The garlic, onion, rosemary, thyme, green chilli and olive oil used in the WHITE BEAN MASH (P. 76), for example, takes the dish straight to the Mediterranean. The curry leaves, mustard seeds and chillies of the PAPPA AL POMODORO WITH LIME AND MUSTARD SEEDS (P. 85), on the other hand, evoke the warmth of the Indian subcontinent.

As well as taking a dish to far-flung lands, infusions are also an economical way of getting there. The kit is simple: a saucepan, a source of heat, a wooden spoon to stir, a slotted spoon to lift things out. The ingredients are often humble: garlic, onions, dried spices, lemon peel, fresh or dried chillies. There's something nice and democratic, as well, about the fact that infusions travel in packs. This is not about the elevation of one ingredient – as with the mighty aubergine which, once charred, gets to steal the show – but about the coming together, mingling and exchange of flavour between groups of everyday ingredients. It's about the sum being greater than the individual parts, and about the magical transformation ingredients can go through with a bit of time, heat and oil.

The type of oil you use to heat the aromatics depends on what you're after. Sunflower oil, with its neutral taste and higher smoking point, is what you need when you don't want the identity of the oil itself to impact too much on a dish, flavour- or body-wise. This is what you want when you are making a MAYONNAISE (P. 89), for example. More often than not, though, we go for olive oil, because it tastes so good and because of its viscosity and great mouth-feel.

The 'magical transformation' referred to above can be harnessed in different ways for a dish. Sometimes it's all about the exchange of flavour at the heart of the infusing process. This is when the aromatics infuse the oil they're heated in, which can then be used in all sorts of ways: a curry leaf oil which is used to make the mayonnaise for the OVEN CHIPS (P. 89), for example, or for drizzling over a MELON AND BUFFALO MOZZARELLA SALAD (P. 80) before serving. Sometimes it's about the look, as well as the taste. Our HUMMUS WITH LEMON, FRIED GARLIC AND CHILLI (P. 79) is transformed from rather dull to glistening green and red, thanks to the coriander and chillies that get to bathe in hot olive oil. And texture can also be a factor, when aromatics which have been made crisp through frying can, once they've done their work infusing the oil, be lifted out with a slotted spoon, set aside and used later to garnish a dish. Quickly fried curry or kaffir lime leaves, strips of ginger and chilli, slivers of garlic, sprigs of rosemary or thyme: these all look fantastic sitting on top of a WHITE BEAN MASH (P. 76) or a plate of BLACK BEANS (P. 86), as well as bringing an interesting textural contrast when it comes to eating.

Sometimes, of course, it's about all three things: about the exchange of flavour, the look of the aromatics and the contrast in texture they provide. But not all the recipes do this, of course. With the CHILLED AVOCADO SOUP WITH CRUNCHY GARLIC OIL (P. 82), for example, the soup element is totally distinct from the garlic and cumin oil that gets drizzled over it. The contrast is part of the point, though, or what makes the dish work well: the chilled, fresh soup jolted out of its summer slumber by a lick of punchy, crunchy oil which has been infused with a mix of garlic, cumin seeds and coriander seeds.

Part of the crunch in this oil here is brought about by finely chopped garlic. Chopping it, rather than crushing it smooth or cooking the cloves whole, makes for these individual pops of garlic throughout the infusion. To disperse the taste of garlic more evenly throughout a dish the cloves need to be crushed, as happens in the marinade which the CUCUMBER SALAD (P. 113) sits in, for example. Other times a dish can handle whole slices of garlic, fried until golden-brown. As well as infusing the oil that's then used in a dish, the fried slices can also be used as garnish and eaten, as in the LEEKS WITH MISO AND CHIVE SALSA (P. 257). And then there are all the times in which we confit a whole garlic head by slicing the top off, drizzling it with oil, wrapping it in foil and cooking it in the oven until soft and mellow and beautifully brown. A whole head of garlic, slow-cooked, in hummus, along with all the garlic-infused oil that comes with it (P. 234)? An enthused – and totally infused – 'yes please', from us!

AGEING

After a day in the test kitchen, with all the charring and browning and infusing that can go on, Yotam's supper at home tends to be small and simple. More often than not, he'll just have a glass of red wine with a wedge of Parmesan or a square or two of dark chocolate. This isn't much, but it is enough because what wine, Parmesan and chocolate all have in common is that they've all had their flavours dialled up by a process of ageing and so it doesn't take much of them to satisfy the taste buds.

Before refrigeration was commonplace, food was aged as a means to preserve it. Covering things in salt or brine or shutting off the air supply to let ingredients ferment meant that the shelf life of an ingredient could be extended beyond the time or season naturally available to it. All means of preservation had one ultimate end: to create an inhospitable environment for the bacteria that cause food to spoil. If all cooking is about transformation – about a certain kind of alchemy – then the process of ageing has something particularly magic about it, as the change happens from within. Other cooking processes – including the charring, browning and infusing we've looked at – require the introduction of heat to the equation for the transformation to take place. Ageing, on the other hand, relies only on biology for the organic matter to be transformed from one state to another (more interesting and nutritious) state. As the organic matter decays and ferments, energy is self-generated and

IF ALL COOKING IS ABOUT TRANSFORMATION THEN THE PROCESS OF AGEING HAS SOMETHING PARTICULARLY MAGIC ABOUT IT

created from within. Whether it's milk to cheese, grapes to wine, rice to sake, barley seeds to beer, cabbage to kimchi, soya beans to miso and soy sauce: these ingredients all come into being, ingeniously, by the fermenter's careful management of rot.

Necessity may have been the mother of invention and this harnessing of the process of decay for edible ends might all be fantastic but it's not the reason (now that we all have fridges to keep food fresh) these 'aged' ingredients have stayed around. For some, these foods are consumed and celebrated primarily for their health-bringing properties. The links between fermented kombucha or kimchi and gut health, for example, are becoming increasingly well known. For us, however, the pull is always – it always has been and always will be – about flavour: about the big, bold, beautiful and often 'funky' flavours that are frequently the by-product of the ageing process.

Luckily for anyone who wants to hit the high flavour notes without having to work too hard, the definition of ageing in this section refers to the use of ingredients in which the process of ageing has already been undertaken, by the producer. This is in contrast to recipes which might have started, for example, with the instruction to start fermenting or curing or salting or preserving or pickling things in the first place. Doing these things at home is easy, rewarding, delicious and fun, but they all require planning and lead time. There are lots of brilliant recipes, people and books who can teach and inspire you to make your own cultures, starters and kombuchas. The remit of these recipes, on the other hand, is about getting big flavours on the table in much less time and with, proportionately, much less work.

So a drum roll, please, for the ingredients which do so much of the work here: the mature Parmesan or tangy pecorino, for example, the salted anchovies, fermented miso or gochujang chilli paste; soy sauce, Chinkiang vinegar or Shaoxing rice wine.

Starting with the two Italian hard cheeses, it's interesting to look, initially, at the differences between them. Parmesan is made from cow's milk and pecorino from sheep's milk. From the outset, therefore, Parmesan will always be creamier and less 'tangy' than the sheep's pecorino. The difference, however, is also one of age. Parmesan is always mature – either 'vecchio', if eaten

THESE RECIPES ARE ABOUT GETTING BIG FLAVOURS ON THE TABLE IN MUCH LESS TIME AND WITH MUCH LESS WORK

around twelve or eighteen months old – or else, if it's aged for more like two years, 'stravecchio' or very mature. This very mature Parmesan is wonderfully savoury: rich, nutty and creamy. It punches well above its weight, bringing heft and body to the otherwise light SPRING VEGETABLES IN PARMESAN BROTH (P. 109).

Pecorino, on the other hand, is ready to be eaten at distinctly different stages. Young pecorino – 'fresco' – is firm but creamy and moist. Milky and light in flavour, it is delicate enough to be pulled apart by hand and dotted over all sorts of leafy salads. Half-aged or fully aged pecorino, on the other hand ('semi-stagionato' or 'stagionato') is more mature: robust, sharper and more pronounced in flavour. This is the sort of pecorino you want to snack on, with a glass of red wine, but it can also be grated and added to a dish such as ZA'ATAR CACIO E PEPE (P. 104), for example.

If the hard cheeses form one group of 'aged' ingredients in this section, then 'fermented Asian' ingredients loosely form another. Miso, soy sauce, Shaoxing rice wine, rice vinegar, gochujang paste: these are all things which start with one ingredient – soya beans, rice, chillies – and then, through the process of fermentation, are broken down and preserved for use in the kitchen in an altogether different way. The process allows these ingredients to be used throughout the year but also enables us to consume much more of them – particularly soya beans – because our digestive system can extract nutrients way more efficiently from them in this broken-down state.

Necessity and digestion notwithstanding, the reason these ingredients play such a large role in our pantry comes back, again – of course! – to flavour. Play the word association game with soy sauce and miso, and it won't take long to hit upon the apotheosis of savoury flavour: umami. Umami, roughly translating as 'deliciousness' in Japanese, has been recognised as the fully fledged 'fifth' taste since the early twentieth century, when a chemist named Kikunae Ikeda discovered, in Japan, that the white crystals which form on dried kombu contain large amounts of glutamate. Ikeda's discovery was that the savoury taste of this molecule was something other than the hitherto recognised tastes of sweet, sour, bitter and salt. It became the fifth taste. A bit like salt, glutamate draws out – or dials up – the flavour of food but, unlike salt, does not have a distinctive taste of its own. For the home cook, this means that the ability to be able to inject some seriously savoury flavour into one's cooking is easily and quickly there.

When using aged ingredients in your everyday cooking, keep in mind the fact that their flavour is big and bold so a small amount goes a long way towards ramping up flavour. Keep in mind, too, that anything so inherently big and bold in savoury flavour needs to be balanced out with something fresh or zesty, young or sweet. You'll see this interplay at work in the recipes here: a lemon or lime salsa, for example, to bring a smack of citrus to the PARMESAN BROTH (P. 109) or the POTATO AND GOCHUJANG BRAISED EGGS (P. 99). Sweet fresh grapes are needed with the SWEET AND SOUR SPROUTS (P. 93), to balance out the soy sauce, and strips of lemon skin are there with the GRILLED FIGS (P. 110), once they've been baked with the soy sauce, Shaoxing rice wine and Chinkiang vinegar. As always, cooking and putting together ingredients is about balance. Aged ingredients are undoubtedly the kind of flavour bombs you want to stock your larder with, but, for us, lemons and limes are still sitting there in a great big bowl, ready to be squeezed and zested.

SERVES FOUR
As a starter or as part
of a spread

CALVIN'S GRILLED PEACHES AND RUNNER BEANS

400g runner beans, stringy edges removed and halved widthways at an angle

3 tbsp olive oil, plus extra for greasing

2 ripe (but firm) peaches, pitted and cut into ½cm-thick slices (200g)

5g mint leaves, roughly torn

¾ tbsp lemon juice

80g young and creamy rindless goat's cheese, roughly broken into 4cm pieces

20g ready-roasted and salted almonds, roughly chopped

¾ tbsp runny honey

flaked sea salt and black pepper

Ottolenghi's executive chef Calvin Von Niebel first developed this recipe in our test kitchen with beautifully ripe peaches, new season beans, and honey straight from a London rooftop beehive. It was a memorable moment, thanks to the clarity of the flavours and the quality of the ingredients. It is essential that you also seek the best ingredients you can. This dish particularly relies on them, since there is little cooking going on and only a light dressing. Peaches can be substituted with nectarines or apricots and the runner beans with other green bean varieties.

Serve as a starter, with spicy mushroom lasagne (see p. 228) as a main, if you like, and lemon sorbet (see p. 289) for dessert.

1. Toss the beans together with 2 tablespoons of oil and ½ teaspoon of flaked salt. Place a well-greased griddle pan on a high heat and ventilate your kitchen. Once the pan is hot, cook the beans for 3–4 minutes on each side, until you get clear grill marks and the beans are almost cooked. Transfer them to a bowl and cover with a plate for 5–10 minutes, depending on how crunchy you like your vegetables; the residual heat will help soften them.

2. Drizzle the remaining tablespoon of oil over the peach slices and grill for 1–2 minutes on each side, until you get visible grill marks.

3. Toss the beans and peaches together with the mint and transfer to a platter (or plate individually). Season with the lemon juice, a good pinch of flaked salt and a good grind of pepper. Dot the goat's cheese and almonds around the platter, and finish by drizzling over the honey.

SERVES FOUR
As a side or starter

ICEBERG WEDGES WITH SMOKY AUBERGINE CREAM

————————

1 small head of iceberg lettuce (350g), cut into 12 wedges
60ml olive oil
25g Parmesan, finely grated
45g rainbow or breakfast radishes, thinly sliced on a mandolin, if you have one, or by hand
2 small avocados, pitted, peeled and thinly sliced
5g chives, sliced into 1½cm lengths
salt and black pepper

AUBERGINE CREAM
2 medium aubergines (600g)
2½ tbsp lemon juice
1 garlic clove, roughly chopped
50g Greek-style yoghurt
2 tsp Dijon mustard
60ml olive oil, plus extra for greasing

CRUNCHY BITS
1 tbsp olive oil
60g almonds, roughly chopped
100g sourdough, crusts removed and then blitzed into coarse crumbs to get 60g
50g pumpkin seeds
⅓ tsp Urfa chilli flakes (or another variety of chilli flake if you can't get them)

There are bucketfuls of crisp textures in this salad, and one creamy smoky dressing that brings everything together beautifully. The smokiness is achieved in the tried and tested way which has featured in many of our recipes in the past: burning an aubergine over direct heat for a substantial amount of time, until it collapses on itself into a deliciously smoky mess.

This is still our preferred way, but if you wish to avoid all that smoke in your kitchen and hate the sight of a thick layer of charcoal on your griddle pan once you're done, here's another method: preheat the oven to 230°C fan, then halve the aubergines lengthways and cut deep cross-hatches into each cut side. Rub with a little oil, place on a parchment-lined baking tray, cut side up, and roast for 40–45 minutes, until soft and very well browned. Transfer to a large bowl, cover with a large plate and leave to soften for 20 minutes. Scoop the aubergine flesh out into another bowl, discarding the skin, stalks and water.

This salad is inspired by a dish at Aloette, a splendid restaurant in Toronto, Canada.

1. First, make the aubergine cream. Place a well-greased griddle pan on a high heat and ventilate your kitchen. Pierce the aubergines seven or eight times all over and, once the griddle is smoking, grill them, turning two or three times until the outsides have completely charred and the insides have softened, 45–50 minutes. Transfer to a sieve set over a bowl and, once cool enough to handle, remove the flesh, discarding the stems and the charred skin. Measure out 200g of aubergine flesh, reserving any extra for another use. Transfer to a food processor along with the remaining ingredients, ½ teaspoon of salt and a good grind of black pepper, and blitz until completely smooth. Set aside until needed.

2. Meanwhile, make the crunchy bits. Put the oil into a large frying pan on a medium-high heat, then add the almonds and cook, stirring often, for about 2 minutes. Add the breadcrumbs, pumpkin seeds and ¼ teaspoon of salt and cook for 5 minutes more, stirring continuously, until golden. Add the chilli flakes and cook for another 30 seconds. Transfer to a tray and leave to cool completely.

3. To assemble, arrange the iceberg wedges on a large platter. Drizzle with 2 tablespoons of oil and a sprinkle of salt and pepper. Spoon over the aubergine cream, followed by the Parmesan, radish and avocado. Sprinkle lightly with salt and pepper again and drizzle with the remaining 2 tablespoons of olive oil. Top with the chives and a generous amount of crunchy topping, serving any extra alongside.

As an antipasto

1 × 700g jar of good-quality cooked large butter beans, drained (500g) (we use Brindisa Navarrico large butter beans, but you can, of course, use tinned or cook your own)
flaked sea salt

SMOKED CASCABEL OIL
4 dried cascabel chillies, roughly broken in half
5 garlic cloves, skin on and crushed with the side of a knife
2 jalapeños, sliced lengthways (deseeded for less heat)
1 lime: finely shave the skin to get 5 strips, then juice to get 1 tbsp
1 lemon: finely shave the skin to get 5 strips, then juice to get 1 tbsp
½ tbsp coriander seeds, toasted
1 tsp cumin seeds, toasted
400ml olive oil

BUTTER BEANS IN SMOKED CASCABEL OIL

Cascabel chillies are, in our modest opinion, the best dried chillies that money can buy. Fruity, nutty, sweet, slightly smoky and a little bit chocolatey, they tick all the right boxes for us when we're trying to inject vegetables with layers of flavour. In our restaurant ROVI, they are used to flavour mussels or new potatoes and for making these butter beans, which are an antipasto served to customers as they sit down, sprinkled with extra crushed coriander seeds.

Serve the beans as an appetiser or a snack, with some bread and homemade mayo, or mix them with chopped herbs and rocket leaves to make a salad. They are also a very welcome addition to the herb and burnt aubergine soup (p. 42) and the bkeila stew (p. 75). They will keep for up to 2 weeks in a jar in the fridge.

The smoked cascabel oil is a wonderful recipe in its own right, and will keep for up to a month in a glass jar, ready to be spooned over anything from eggs to pasta.

1. Place a large, non-stick frying pan on a high heat and ventilate your kitchen well. Once the pan is smoking, reduce the heat to medium-high. Place the cascabel chillies, garlic, jalapeños, lime skin and lemon skin in the pan and cook until well blackened in places and very fragrant. This will take about 3 minutes for the citrus skins, 4 minutes for the garlic and cascabel chillies and 9 minutes for the jalapeños: use metal tongs to remove them individually from the pan.

2. Put all the charred ingredients into a medium saucepan with the toasted coriander and cumin seeds, lime juice, lemon juice, oil and 2 teaspoons of flaked salt and place on a low heat. Gently cook for about 4 minutes, or until the oil begins to bubble a little, then remove from the heat. Use a pair of tongs or a potato masher to squeeze or crush all the charred ingredients into the oil to release their flavour. Stir in the butter beans and set aside to cool.

3. Once cool, transfer everything to a large jar if refrigerating, or a serving bowl if serving later that day. Leave to infuse for at least 2 hours, or overnight.

HERB AND BURNT AUBERGINE SOUP

3 aubergines, pierced 7 or 8 times all over (750g)

3 tbsp lemon juice

105ml olive oil, plus extra for greasing

2 onions, finely chopped (300g)

6 garlic cloves, crushed

60g coriander, roughly chopped, plus 2 tbsp extra picked leaves to serve

60g parsley, roughly chopped, plus 2 tbsp extra picked leaves to serve

40g dill, roughly chopped, plus 2 tbsp extra picked fronds, to serve

5 spring onions, finely sliced (75g)

2½ tsp ground cinnamon

2½ tsp ground cumin

1 tsp ground turmeric, plus ⅛ tsp

400g baby spinach, finely shredded

500ml vegetable or chicken stock

1 red chilli, thinly sliced into rounds (20g)

2 tsp black mustard seeds

salt and black pepper

This soup draws on both Middle Eastern and Indian cooking techniques: large amounts of herbs are fried to make the base, aubergines are burnt, and the whole thing is finished with an aromatic tempered oil. It's particularly good with our butter beans in smoked cascabel oil (p. 41) spooned on top.

Make the soup up to 2 days before but don't mix the aubergines with the lemon juice and herbs, or top with the tempered oil, until you're ready to serve.

1. Place a well-greased griddle pan on a high heat and ventilate your kitchen. Once the pan is smoking, grill the aubergines, turning two or three times, until the outsides have completely charred and the insides have softened, 45–50 minutes. Don't worry about over-charring the aubergines; the longer they cook, the better. Transfer to a colander set over a bowl and leave to drain for about 30 minutes. Peel the aubergines and discard the stems and skins. Pull apart the flesh into long ribbons and add to a medium bowl with 1 tablespoon of lemon juice, ⅓ teaspoon of salt and a good grind of pepper. Mix, then set aside until needed.

2. While the aubergines are grilling, prepare the soup. Put 60ml of oil into a large saucepan on a medium-high heat. Add the chopped onion and cook, stirring often, until softened and deeply browned, about 12 minutes. Add the garlic and cook for 30 seconds more, until fragrant, then turn the heat to medium-low and add the herbs, spring onions and 3 tablespoons of water. Cook for about 15 minutes, or until deeply green and fragrant, stirring often so the herbs don't catch and burn. Increase the heat to medium-high, add the cinnamon, cumin and 1 teaspoon of turmeric and cook for 30 seconds, then stir in the spinach, stock, 400ml of water, 1¾ teaspoons of salt and a generous grind of black pepper. Bring to the boil, then lower the heat to medium and leave to simmer for about 20 minutes.

3. Remove from the heat, add the remaining 2 tablespoons of lemon juice and use a stick blender to roughly blitz the soup (you don't want it to be completely smooth). Alternatively, blitz half the soup in a blender, then return to the pan with the rest of the soup. Keep warm until ready to serve.

4. For the tempered oil, put the chilli and the remaining 3 tablespoons of oil into a small frying pan on a medium heat. Leave to cook, stirring occasionally, until the chilli becomes translucent and glossy, about 10–12 minutes. Add the mustard seeds and cook for 1 minute more. Stir in the last ⅛ teaspoon of turmeric and immediately pour the mixture into a bowl to stop it cooking further. Set aside.

5. Divide the soup between four bowls. Stir the picked herbs into the aubergine and add to the soup, finishing with a drizzle of the tempered oil.

SERVES SIX
As a side

HISPI CABBAGE WITH NAM PRIK

_____

2 pointed cabbages
(aka hispi or sweetheart cabbage), quartered lengthways (1.6kg)
3 tbsp sunflower oil
5g coriander, finely chopped
1 lime, cut into wedges, to serve
flaked sea salt

NAM PRIK
20g fresh galangal (or ginger, as a substitute), peeled and roughly chopped
1 small garlic clove, peeled
1 tbsp fish sauce (or light soy sauce)
1½ tsp Aleppo chilli flakes (or ¾ tsp regular chilli flakes)
1 tbsp shop-bought tamarind paste, or double if you're extracting it yourself from pulp (see p. 20)
1¼ tsp soft light brown sugar
50g cherry tomatoes
1½ tbsp lime juice
1 tsp sunflower oil

Nam prik (or phrik) is the name of a range of chilli sauces which are at the heart of Thai cooking. Their sharp intensity is the perfect counterpoint to anything grilled, as well as to rice and mild vegetable, meat or fish dishes.

This cabbage is fantastically aromatic. You can serve it as part of a veggie supper with the udon noodles with fried tofu (see p. 202), or the cardamom tofu with lime greens (see p. 172).

The nam prik can be made up to a week before and kept in the fridge, but the cabbage should be grilled not long before serving. *Pictured overleaf.*

1. To make the nam prik, put the galangal and garlic into the small bowl of a food processor and blitz well. Add all the remaining ingredients and pulse until combined and finely chopped but not completely smooth. Transfer to a small bowl and set aside until ready to serve.

2. Toss the cabbage with the oil and 1 teaspoon of flaked salt. Place on a very hot barbecue or griddle pan and grill for 4–5 minutes on each side (i.e. 12–15 minutes in total), until the cabbage softens on the outside, while still retaining a crunch, and you get clear grill marks. Transfer to a platter. Add the coriander to the nam prik and spoon the mixture evenly over the cabbage pieces. Serve either warm or at room temperature, with the lime wedges alongside.

STEAMED AUBERGINES WITH CHARRED CHILLI SALSA

SERVES FOUR
As a side or as part of a spread

2 aubergines (700g)
1–2 spring onions, trimmed and julienned (15g)
1½ tbsp ready-roasted and salted almonds, roughly chopped
1 tbsp coriander leaves, roughly chopped
flaked sea salt

CHARRED CHILLI SALSA
2 large, mild red chillies (30g)
140g Datterini cherry tomatoes (or another ripe, sweet cherry tomato), finely chopped
1½ tsp sherry vinegar, plus ½ tsp to serve

GARLIC AND GINGER OIL
40ml olive oil
2 small garlic cloves, very finely chopped
1 tsp fresh ginger, peeled and very finely chopped

It takes a bit of coaxing to bring people around to steaming aubergines, as opposed to roasting or frying them. Gitai Fisher, who is a colleague in our test kitchen and a fan of aubergines with a bit of a tan on them, was a particularly hard nut to crack. He was brought around after tasting this dish, where the aubergines are, indeed, pale but they are also fantastically silky and have an admirable ability to soak up the aromas of chilli, garlic and ginger like happy sponges.

The charred chilli salsa can be doubled or tripled and kept in a glass jar in the fridge for up to a week, ready to be spooned over scrambled eggs, piled onto tortilla chips, or served alongside grilled tofu or fish.

The aubergines should be steamed just before serving, because they tend to discolour if left to sit around. *Pictured overleaf.*

1. For the salsa, place a frying pan on a high heat. Once the pan is very hot, add the chillies and cook for about 10 minutes, turning a few times until well charred on all sides. Transfer to a small bowl, cover with a saucer and leave to soften for 10 minutes. Deseed one of the chillies (or both, for less heat), then finely chop them, along with the skin. Place in a bowl with the tomatoes, vinegar and ¼ teaspoon of flaked salt, stir together and set aside.

2. For the garlic and ginger oil, put all the ingredients into a small pan with ½ teaspoon of flaked salt and place on the lowest heat. Cook very gently for about 8 minutes, stirring occasionally, until the garlic and ginger soften when mashed with the back of a spoon. Make sure not to heat the oil too much or the garlic will burn: if the oil does start to bubble, just remove it from the heat until it cools.

3. Cut the aubergines into 7cm x 2cm batons, then toss them together with 2 tablespoons of flaked salt in a large bowl. Transfer to a steaming basket (or colander which can sit over a large saucepan) and set aside.

4. Fill a large saucepan with enough water to rise 4cm up the sides. Bring to the boil on a high heat, then place the steamer (or colander) in the pan. Cover with the lid or seal well with foil, to prevent the steam escaping. Reduce the heat to medium and steam for 20–25 minutes, or until the aubergines are very soft but still hold their shape. Lift the steamer off the pan and transfer to the sink to drain for 5 minutes.

5. Transfer the drained aubergines to a large platter, drizzle over the remaining ½ teaspoon of vinegar, and season with ¼ teaspoon of flaked salt. Add the spring onions and gently mix them through. Spoon over the salsa, then drizzle over the garlic and ginger oil. Finish with the almonds and coriander and serve.

SLOW-COOKED CHARRED GREEN BEANS

SERVES FOUR
As a side

500g green beans, trimmed and halved widthways

500g runner beans, stalks trimmed, stringy edges removed and then cut on the diagonal into 3–4 pieces

12 garlic cloves, peeled

1 green chilli, pierced a few times with a small knife (15g)

120ml olive oil

2 onions, finely chopped (300g)

250ml vegetable or chicken stock

2 lemons: finely grate the zest to get 2 tsp, then juice to get 3 tbsp

10g tarragon leaves, roughly chopped

10g dill fronds, roughly chopped

10g parsley leaves, roughly chopped

35g preserved lemon (about 1–2), insides discarded and skin julienned

salt and black pepper

While the tendency with green beans is to steam or blanch them, to ensure they remain bright, green and crunchy, they are also wonderful when cooked longer and a little slower. Given this time, they will soak up the sauce in which they cook, as they do here, while imparting a wonderfully subtle smokiness from the charring.

You can cook the beans the day before, if you want to get ahead, but hold off on adding the lemon zest and juice, and on making the herb salsa, until you're ready to serve.

1. Place a large sauté pan, for which you have a lid, on a high heat. Once the pan is smoking, add a quarter of the beans (both varieties), and cook for about 5 minutes, tossing the pan occasionally, until charred in places. Transfer to a plate or tray and continue in this way with all the beans (do this using two sauté pans if you want to speed up the process). Add the garlic and chilli to the pan and cook in the same way, until charred all over, about 3–4 minutes, then add to the tray with the beans. Set aside the pan to cool slightly.

2. Add 90ml of oil to the pan and place on a medium-high heat. Once hot, add the onions and cook for about 10 minutes, stirring occasionally, until soft and golden-brown. Add the charred beans, garlic and chilli, the stock, 1 ½ teaspoons of salt and a good grind of black pepper. Bring to a simmer, then lower the heat to medium-low and cook for about 20 minutes, covered, until the beans are very soft. Stir through the lemon zest and juice.

3. Put the herbs, preserved lemon, the remaining 2 tablespoons of oil, ¼ teaspoon of salt and plenty of pepper into a small bowl and mix to combine.

4. When ready to serve, stir the herb mixture into the beans, to just incorporate. Serve warm, or at room temperature.

HASSELBACK BEETROOT WITH LIME LEAF BUTTER

8–10 medium-large beetroots (that's about 2 bunches), skin on (1.2kg), or 8–10 ready-cooked beetroots (1kg)
flaked sea salt

LIME LEAF BUTTER
90g unsalted butter
40ml olive oil
5 fresh kaffir lime leaves, roughly chopped
10g fresh ginger, peeled and finely chopped
1 garlic clove, crushed
1 tbsp lime juice, plus 2 tsp to serve

LIME LEAF SALSA
10 fresh kaffir lime leaves, stalks removed and blitzed in a spice grinder (or very finely chopped)
½ tsp fresh ginger, peeled and very finely chopped
½ garlic clove, crushed
½ green chilli, very finely chopped (deseeded for less heat)
1 tbsp coriander leaves, finely chopped
3 tbsp olive oil

YOGHURT CREAM
80ml double cream
90g Greek-style yoghurt

Preparing vegetables hasselback involves slicing them thinly, but not all the way down, so that the slices remain held together at the base, like a fan. This makes them look great, which is a welcome bonus, but the main reason to add this step is the deliciously crispy edges you get all over the surface.

To offset the extra work involved in hasselbacking, you can easily start with shop-bought ready-cooked beetroots (plain, not those kept in vinegar) and save yourself cooking them. If you do end up using raw beets, try to get bunches, and reserve the stems and leaves. These are delicious tossed through salads, or, better yet, use them to make our tempura stems, leaves and herbs (p. 184), along with the charred peppers and fresh corn polenta (p. 140), which make up part of the ROVI spread on p. 303.

If starting from raw, the beetroots can be cooked, peeled and sliced up to 3 days before and kept in the fridge.

Double or triple the lime leaf butter if you like – it will keep in a glass jar in the fridge for up to 2 weeks, ready to ramp up all sorts of roasted vegetables, or to melt over grilled fish. *Pictured overleaf.*

1. Preheat the oven to 220°C fan.

2. Place the beetroots in a baking dish big enough for them to fit in a single layer. Fill the dish with enough water to come 2cm up the sides of the dish. Sprinkle over 1 tablespoon of flaked salt, cover tightly with foil and bake for 1 hour and 20 minutes, or until a knife inserted goes through easily (some larger beetroots may need longer). Discard the water and when cool enough to handle, peel the skin off under cold running water (use gloves so as not to stain your hands). Halve any larger beetroots lengthways. Reduce the oven temperature to 190°C.

3. While the beetroots are cooking, make the lime leaf butter. Put the butter, oil, lime leaves, ginger and garlic into a small saucepan and place on a medium-high heat. Gently cook until the butter melts and begins to bubble, about 4 minutes, then remove from the heat and set aside to infuse for at least 40 minutes. Strain and discard the aromatics, then stir in 1 tablespoon of the lime juice and 1 teaspoon of flaked salt.

4. For the lime leaf salsa, mix all the ingredients together in a small bowl with ¼ teaspoon of flaked salt and set aside.

5. In a medium bowl, whip the cream, yoghurt and a pinch of flaked salt together until light and fluffy, with medium-stiff peaks, about 3 minutes. Refrigerate until ready to use.

6. Once peeled, cut slits in the beetroots at 4mm intervals, stopping about 1cm from the bottom so that the slices stay connected. Place the beetroots on a small parchment-lined baking tray and fan the slices out as much as possible. Spoon the melted butter mixture evenly over and around the beetroots and especially between the slices. Roast for 1¼ hours, easing apart the slices and basting very well with the butter on the tray every 20 minutes or so, until the edges are crisp and caramelised. Set aside to cool for 15 minutes.

7. To serve, spread the yoghurt cream on a platter, then arrange the beetroots on top, spooning the browned butter over and around them. Drizzle over the lime leaf salsa, finish with the remaining 2 teaspoons of lime juice and serve at once.

WHOLE ROASTED CELERIAC THREE WAYS

————

1 large celeriac, hairy roots discarded (no need to peel) and scrubbed clean (900g)
60ml olive oil
flaked sea salt

This simple way of slow-roasting celeriac whole, with nothing but oil and salt, is a method we have explored in the past, serving it simply with a squeeze of lemon or a spoonful of crème fraîche. You can definitely do that with this celeriac. Here, though, this process, in which the starches are converted into sugars (see more on p. 29) that seep out in a wonderful celeriac-flavoured caramel, is harnessed to make three very different celeriac-centred dishes. If you don't get a lot of that aforementioned caramel after roasting, just brush the celeriac with oil and a little maple syrup or honey once it's been cut.

The celeriac is best cooked on the day, but you can roast it the day before if you want to get ahead. You'll need to double the recipe for the celeriac steaks with Café de Paris sauce (p. 60).

1. Preheat the oven to 170°C fan.

2. Pierce the celeriac with a fork all over about 40 times and place on a parchment-lined baking tray. Mix the oil and 1½ teaspoons of flaked salt, then rub the celeriac generously with the oil mixture. Roast for a minimum of 2¼ hours, or up to 2¾ hours, depending on the size of your celeriac, basting every 20 minutes or so, until the celeriac is deeply browned, soft all the way through and oozes a celeriac caramel.

3. Leave to rest for 15 minutes, then cut into either wedges or steaks (depending on the recipe, see p. 55–60), brushing each cut side with the oil and caramel left on the tray (you may need to add a little more oil if there isn't enough to coat the cut sides).

SERVES TWO
As a main or four as a side

1. ROASTED AND PICKLED CELERIAC WITH SWEET CHILLI DRESSING

SERVES TWO
As a main or four as a side

1 **whole roasted celeriac,** cut into 8 wedges (see opposite)
2 **spring onions,** finely sliced at an angle, to serve
5g **picked Thai basil leaves,** to serve
flaked sea salt

PICKLED CELERIAC
1 **medium celeriac,** trimmed, peeled and cut into thin, 6cm-long batons (500g)
3 **celery sticks,** cut into thin 6cm-long batons (120g)
2 **garlic cloves,** skin on and crushed with the side of a knife
3 **limes:** finely shave the skin to get 6 strips, then juice to get 60ml
150ml **rice vinegar**

SWEET CHILLI DRESSING
120ml **sunflower oil**
5 **garlic cloves,** very finely sliced
3 **red chillies,** finely sliced into rounds (30g)
2 **whole star anise**
1½ tbsp **white or black sesame seeds,** or a mixture of both, well toasted
2½ tbsp **maple syrup**
1 tbsp **rice vinegar**
60ml **soy sauce**
2 tbsp **chives,** finely chopped

This dish features celeriac in two very different guises – slow-roasted and pickled – giving it textural contrast and flavour complexity which enables it to take centre stage in a vegetable feast (see p. 303).

You can make the dressing a day ahead, but don't mix in the fried chilli and garlic until you're ready to serve. You'll make more pickle than you need, but it keeps in the fridge for 3 days and is great stuffed into sandwiches and toasties or tossed through a salad. If you don't want to pickle a whole celeriac, use just half and roast the other half, instead. *Pictured overleaf.*

1. Combine all the ingredients for the pickled celeriac with 20g flaked salt in a large bowl and set aside for at least 2 hours, stirring now and then, while you prepare the rest of the dish. You can make this up to 3 days ahead and keep it refrigerated.

2. Heat the sunflower oil for the sweet chilli dressing in a small saucepan on a medium-high heat. Once very hot, add the garlic, chillies and star anise and fry for 2–2½ minutes, stirring to separate the garlic slices, until the garlic is crisp and pale golden (it will continue to colour after you take it out of the oil, so don't take it too far). Strain through a sieve set on top of a small heatproof bowl to collect the oil. Set the fried chilli and garlic aside, to serve. Remove 80ml of the aromatic oil and reserve for another recipe. Combine the remaining 40ml of oil with all the remaining ingredients for the dressing.

3. Preheat the oven to 200°C fan.

4. Place the roasted celeriac wedges on a parchment-lined baking tray, cut side up. Make sure they've been brushed with their cooking oil and celeriac caramel by this point, and if not, brush with some olive oil and a little maple syrup or honey (see opposite). Roast for 20 minutes, or until golden-brown.

5. Arrange the wedges on a large platter and sprinkle with a little flaked salt.

6. Add the fried chilli and garlic to the dressing and spoon over and around the celeriac. Top with 200g of the pickled celeriac mixture, avoiding the pickling liquid, garlic and lime skin. Garnish with the spring onions and Thai basil, and serve.

MAKES SIXTEEN TACOS
To serve four to six

16 whole cabbage leaves, from 1 large pointed cabbage, base trimmed

1 whole roasted celeriac, cut into 16 wedges (see p. 54)

120g soft rindless goat's cheese, roughly broken into 2cm pieces (optional)

2 limes, cut into wedges, to serve

salt

DATE BARBECUE SAUCE
90ml olive oil
1 small banana shallot, finely chopped (30g)
2 garlic cloves, crushed
¼ tsp red chilli flakes
60ml balsamic vinegar
¼ tsp smoked paprika
½ tsp ground cumin
100g pitted dates, roughly chopped
20g black garlic (about 10 cloves)

AROMATIC OIL
90ml olive oil
2 red chillies, finely sliced into rounds
2 garlic cloves, finely chopped (not crushed)
2 tsp coriander seeds, lightly crushed
2 tsp chives, finely chopped

2. CABBAGE 'TACOS' WITH CELERIAC AND DATE BARBECUE SAUCE

This recipe broke a world record by being the first vegetarian dish ever to be selected for the obviously meat-centric barbecue festival, Meatopia. It took a fair bit of pleading to get the organisers to agree to this heretical move, but our celeriac went down a storm with the meat lovers.

The cabbage is a great vessel for the celeriac, but the combination of the celeriac and the very special date barbecue sauce is wonderful in its own right, if you don't want to blanch cabbage leaves.

You'll make more sauce than you need, which is no bad thing. It will keep in the fridge for 3 weeks and can be used in any situation that calls for barbecue sauce.

1. For the barbecue sauce, put 2 tablespoons of oil, the shallot and garlic into a small saucepan on a medium heat. Fry for about 6 minutes, stirring often, until the shallot is soft and golden. Add all the rest of the sauce ingredients except the remaining oil, along with 130ml of water and ½ teaspoon of salt. Bring to a gentle simmer, then turn the heat to medium-low and cook for 8 minutes, or until the dates have softened completely. Leave to cool for 10 minutes, then transfer to a spice grinder or the small bowl of a food processor with the remaining 60ml of oil and blitz to a smooth sauce.

2. For the aromatic oil, put all the ingredients (except the chives) and ¼ teaspoon of salt into a small saucepan on a medium-low heat and gently fry for 8 minutes, until the garlic is soft and fragrant. You may need to turn the heat down if the garlic is colouring too much. Remove from the heat and stir in the chives.

3. Bring a large pot of salted water to the boil. Blanch the cabbage leaves for 30 seconds to 1 minute, until just cooked but still crunchy, then drain very well, transfer to a clean tea towel and carefully pat dry – you don't want the leaves to be at all wet.

4. When you're ready to serve, turn the oven to the highest grill setting. Place the celeriac wedges, spaced apart, on a very large, parchment-lined baking tray (making sure there is no overhanging parchment that could burn). They should have been brushed with their cooking oil and celeriac caramel by this point, but if not, brush with some olive oil and a little maple syrup or honey (see p. 54). Grill on the top shelf of the oven for 6 minutes, until golden-brown. Remove from the oven and brush the wedges with 6 tablespoons (120g) of the barbecue sauce, carefully smothering all sides.

5. To assemble, place a celeriac wedge on each cabbage leaf. Top with the goat's cheese, then drizzle over some of the aromatic oil. Serve hot, with the lime wedges and more sauce alongside.

SERVES FOUR
As a main

3. CELERIAC STEAKS WITH CAFÉ DE PARIS SAUCE

---

2 whole roasted celeriac
(double the recipe
on p. 54), each cut
widthways into 2½cm-
thick steaks
**flaked sea salt and
black pepper**

CAFÉ DE PARIS SAUCE
110g unsalted butter,
cut into 2cm cubes
1 small banana shallot,
finely chopped (25g)
1 garlic clove, crushed
**3 anchovy fillets in olive
oil,** drained and finely
chopped (optional, but
adjust seasoning if not
using)
**½ tsp medium curry
powder**
¼ tsp cayenne pepper
1 tbsp mustard powder
1 tbsp baby capers
2 tbsp chives, finely
chopped
2 tbsp tarragon leaves,
finely chopped
1 tbsp parsley, finely
chopped
2 tsp thyme leaves
**110ml single or whipping
cream**
2 tsp lemon juice

A long time ago, in Paris, Ixta had a steak with Café de Paris sauce and thought she'd died and gone to butter heaven. This single memory, etched in her mind since childhood, formed the basis on which we relied when creating this dish, plus a bunch of conflicting versions published over the years that had a stab at cracking the secret recipe. Whether our version gets us anywhere near the original we will probably never know, but it certainly delivers in turning celeriac seriously meaty, only without the meat, and making it the perfect alternative to a Sunday roast (serve it along with the iceberg wedges with smoky aubergine cream, p. 38, and the oven chips, p. 89).

Don't worry about the sauce splitting; it's supposed to.

1. Put the first seven ingredients for the sauce and ¼ teaspoon of flaked salt into a small saucepan on a medium heat. Cook for about 6 minutes, swirling the pan until the shallots have softened and the butter has melted and become golden and caramelised. Add the capers, herbs and a very generous grind of pepper and continue to cook for 1 minute, then remove from the heat.

2. Turn the oven to its highest grill setting. Arrange the celeriac steaks, spaced apart, on a large, parchment-lined baking tray big enough to fit the slices in a single layer. The steaks should have been brushed with their cooking oil and celeriac caramel by this point, but if not, brush with some olive oil and a little maple syrup or honey (see p. 54). Make sure there is no overhanging parchment that could burn. Grill the steaks on the top shelf of the oven, until they are golden-brown on top, 6–8 minutes. Turn the oven off, keeping the tray warm in the oven until you're ready to serve.

3. Return the sauce to a medium heat and gently cook for a minute, then add the cream and lemon juice. Swirl for another 2 minutes or until warm, but don't mix it too much – you want the sauce to be split, not emulsified.

4. Pour the sauce on to a large platter with a lip and arrange the celeriac steaks on top (or plate individually with some sauce poured on top and the rest served alongside). Sprinkle the steaks with a little flaked salt and black pepper, and serve.

SPICED PLANTAIN WITH COCONUT, APPLE AND GINGER SALAD

SERVES FOUR

---

2 very ripe plantains, peeled, sliced in half widthways and lengthways (400g)

60ml olive oil

2 tsp soft light brown sugar

½ tsp fresh ginger, peeled and finely grated

¾ tsp ground cinnamon

¾ tsp ground cumin

½ tsp cayenne pepper

½ tsp ground nutmeg

½ small coconut, thinly sliced on a mandolin, if you have one, or by hand (90g)

2 limes: finely grate the zest to get 1 tsp and juice to get 2 tbsp, then cut the remainder into wedges to serve

1 green chilli, deseeded and julienned

1 Granny Smith apple, skin on, core removed and julienned (140g)

15g unsalted butter

10g picked coriander leaves

10g picked mint leaves

salt

Ixta's mother grew up in Brazil and Cuba eating plantains alongside pretty much every savoury meal, from feijoadas (the national Brazilian dish) to guisos (Cuban stews). It was a tradition that carried through to Ixta's childhood, where plantains featured at nearly every mealtime.

Plantains are larger, firmer and slightly less sweet than bananas. For this recipe, you need very ripe plantains: deep yellow, soft and covered in black spots. You should be able to find them in many greengrocers, and especially in West Indian supermarkets.

This is a special starter, or could be bulked up with some fried tofu or grilled prawns to make a meal. *Pictured overleaf.*

1. Place the plantains in a medium bowl with 3 tablespoons of oil, the sugar, ¼ teaspoon of ginger, ½ teaspoon of cinnamon, ½ teaspoon of cumin and all the cayenne and nutmeg. Mix to coat, then set aside to marinate for at least 30 minutes.

2. Meanwhile, prepare the salad. Place the coconut, lime zest and juice, chilli, apple, the remaining ginger, cinnamon and cumin and the remaining tablespoon of oil in a medium bowl with a pinch of salt. Mix well and set aside.

3. Preheat the oven to 180°C fan.

4. Put the butter into a large, ovenproof non-stick frying pan and place on a high heat. Once the butter has melted and is hot, add the plantain, spaced apart (if you don't have a big enough pan, you can fry the plantain in two batches). Reserve the oil and spices in the bowl in which you marinated the plantains – you need these later on for the salad. Reduce the heat to medium-high and fry the plantains for 3 minutes, turning them every so often until all sides are golden-brown and crisp. Transfer the pan to the oven and cook for another 3 minutes.

5. Add the coriander, mint and the salad to the bowl in which you marinated the plantain. Toss together, making sure to incorporate the oil and spice marinade left in the bowl.

6. Divide the plantain and salad between four plates and serve with the lime wedges alongside.

CURRY-CRUSTED SWEDE STEAKS

SERVES FOUR
As a main

2–3 swedes (1.8kg), peeled and cut widthways into 8 (total) 3cm-thick steaks
120g crème fraîche (or coconut yoghurt)
salt

FENUGREEK MARINADE
1½ tbsp fenugreek seeds
6 small garlic cloves, peeled and roughly chopped (25g)
1½ tsp cayenne pepper
1½ tsp ground turmeric
2 tsp caster sugar
2 tbsp lime juice
75ml olive oil

SALAD
3–4 ruby grapefruits (750g unpeeled weight)
1–2 banana shallots, finely sliced on a mandolin, if you have one, or by hand (70g)
2 red chillies, finely sliced into rounds
20g picked mint leaves
10g picked coriander leaves
2 tsp olive oil
2 limes: juice to get 1 tbsp, then cut into wedges, to serve

This vegetarian main course – easily veganised by using an alternative to the crème fraîche, such as coconut yoghurt – celebrates the natural bitterness of swede, complemented by a sweet, sharp and spicy marinade which permeates the flesh and coats it with a delicious crust. Due to the fenugreek, the general flavour of the dish is like a great Indian curry (in fact, this dish works perfectly as part of the korma feast, p. 303). Beware, though, the smell of this wondrous seed will linger in your kitchen for quite a while (we love this, but not everyone does).

The marinade will keep in the fridge in a sealed jar for up to 2 weeks, if you want to get ahead. Make double or triple, if you like, to use as a base for curries or for marinating vegetables or different meats. *Pictured overleaf.*

1. Preheat the oven to 180°C fan.

2. For the marinade, put all the ingredients into a spice grinder or the small bowl of a food processor with ¾ teaspoon of salt and blitz to a paste, scraping the sides as you go if necessary. Put 2 teaspoons of the marinade into a small serving bowl and set aside.

3. Put the remaining marinade into a large bowl with the swede steaks and mix well to coat all sides (this is easiest with gloved hands). Place the steaks, spaced apart, on a large, parchment-lined baking tray. Cover tightly with foil and roast for 1 hour and 20 minutes. Remove the foil, turn the oven to the grill setting, and grill for 3–4 minutes, until the swede is cooked through and the marinade has turned into a golden-brown crust.

4. When the swede is nearly cooked, prepare the salad. Cut the grapefruits into thin wedges by removing the skin and the white pith, then release the segments by cutting in between the white membrane, discarding any pips. Put the wedges into a large bowl, avoiding the juice (which can be kept for another use).

5. When you're ready to serve, add all the remaining salad ingredients to the bowl with a generous pinch of salt and gently mix together.

6. Arrange the steaks and any marinade left on the tray on a large platter with the salad (or plate individually). Swirl the crème fraîche into the remaining marinade and serve alongside the steaks, with the lime wedges squeezed on top.

SERVES FOUR

As a side dish or six as a dip

1–2 red chillies, finely sliced into rounds (deseeded for less heat)

1½ tbsp white wine vinegar

½ tsp caster sugar

800g carrots (that's roughly 8), peeled and roughly chopped into 2cm pieces

2 tbsp olive oil

1 tsp medium curry powder

¼ tsp ground cinnamon

30g unsalted butter (or 2 tbsp olive oil)

5g fresh ginger, peeled and julienned

½ tsp nigella seeds

½ tsp fennel seeds

½ tsp cumin seeds

½ tbsp lime juice

1 spring onion, trimmed and julienned (10g)

5g mint leaves, finely shredded

salt

CURRIED CARROT MASH WITH BROWN BUTTER

You'll be surprised how much delicious carrotiness you'll get from simply steamed carrots when they are matched with browned butter, sweet spices and chilli heat. You can then count on them to inject a whole meal with deep flavour, and serve them alongside some grilled tofu, haloumi, fish or chicken, or as part of a selection of vegetable dishes.

The mash and pickled chillies can be made the day before if you want to get ahead, but the butter should be made not long before serving, so the seeds stay crunchy. Use olive oil instead of butter if you want to keep this dairy-free.

1. Put the chillies, vinegar and sugar into a small bowl with ¼ teaspoon of salt, massage together and set aside to pickle for at least 30 minutes.

2. Put the carrots into a steaming basket or colander, place on a high heat, cover with a lid and steam for about 25 minutes, or until you can cut through them easily with a knife. Put the carrots into the bowl of a food processor with the oil, curry powder, cinnamon and 1 teaspoon of salt, and blitz for about a minute until you get a semi-smooth mash (it should still have some texture and not be completely smooth).

3. While the carrots are steaming, put the butter, ginger and nigella, fennel and cumin seeds, with a generous pinch of salt, into a small saucepan on a medium heat. Gently cook for 3–5 minutes, stirring occasionally until the butter begins to foam and turn light brown and the seeds become fragrant. Set aside until ready to serve. You may need to gently melt the butter again when you're plating, if it has set.

4. Spoon the mash on to a large plate, creating dips with the back of the spoon. Drizzle over the butter with the ginger and seeds, followed by the lime juice. Drain the pickled chillies well and scatter them over the mash. Finish with the spring onions and mint, and serve warm.

BARLEY, TOMATO AND WATERCRESS STEW

SERVES FOUR
As a main

4 small kohlrabi (1kg)

4 anchovy fillets in olive oil, drained and finely chopped (optional, but adjust seasoning if not using)

140ml olive oil, plus extra for drizzling

1 large head of garlic, top fifth cut off to expose the cloves, plus 4 extra cloves, crushed

300g sweet, ripe cherry tomatoes (such as Datterini)

300g pearl barley

2–3 banana shallots, finely sliced (120g)

2 tsp caraway seeds

2 lemons: finely shave the skin of 1 to get 5 strips and juice to get 2 tbsp, then cut the remainder into wedges to serve

1 red Scotch bonnet chilli (optional)

3 tbsp tomato paste

150ml dry white wine

100g watercress

60ml double cream (optional)

salt and black pepper

Mostly eaten raw, kohlrabi isn't the first vegetable you would think to roast. We'd love you try, though, because, in the process, it morphs into a gloriously caramelised golden-brown version of its former self. We use it here to spoon over a rich barley stew, resulting in a one-pot meal which is light enough for a summer's evening but also warming when the temperatures start to drop.

Vegans, vegetarians and those who don't like too much heat are welcome to make this stew without the anchovies (increase the salt if you do that) or cream, or with less or no chilli. There is still plenty going on to keep everyone jolly.

This dish is not at all complicated to make, as long as you are okay cooking three things simultaneously: roasting the vegetables that go on top of the barley, boiling the barley itself and preparing the aromatics that flavour the stew. They are all super easy and come together simply at the end. *Pictured overleaf.*

1. Preheat the oven to 190°C fan.

2. Trim and peel each kohlrabi, then cut lengthways into eight wedges. You want the wedges to be about 2½cm wide, so if the kohlrabi is particularly large, you may need to cut it into more wedges. Put the wedges into a large bowl and toss together with the anchovies (if using), 2 tablespoons of oil, half the crushed garlic, ½ teaspoon of salt and a good grind of pepper. Spread out on a large, parchment-lined baking tray. Drizzle the garlic bulb with a little oil and sprinkle with a little salt and pepper. Wrap the bulb tightly in foil, place in one corner of the kohlrabi tray and roast for 25 minutes. Turn the kohlrabi wedges, add the tomatoes to the tray around the kohlrabi, then return to the oven for another 15–20 minutes, or until the kohlrabi wedges are soft and a deep golden-brown and the tomatoes are blistered. Keep warm (or warm up when you serve).

3. When cool enough to handle, remove the foil from the garlic and squeeze the cloves out into a small bowl, discarding the papery skin.

4. While the vegetables are in the oven, put the barley into a medium saucepan, cover with plenty of cold water and place on a medium-high heat. Simmer for 20 minutes, until the barley is semi-cooked but still retains a good bite. Drain and set aside.

5. While the barley is simmering, place a large sauté pan, for which you have a lid, on a medium-high heat with 50ml of the oil, the cooked and remaining crushed garlic, the shallots, caraway seeds, lemon strips, Scotch bonnet (if using) and 2½ teaspoons of salt. Gently fry for 12 minutes, stirring often, until the shallots are soft and golden-brown. Turn the heat down to medium if the shallots are colouring too quickly. Add the tomato paste and continue to cook for 30 seconds before adding the wine, 500ml of water and plenty of pepper. Bring to a gentle simmer over a medium heat and cook for 7 minutes, then add the cooked barley and continue to cook for 10 minutes, until the barley has swollen a little and taken on the flavour of the sauce. Discard the Scotch bonnet and lemon strips.

6. In a spice grinder or the small bowl of a food processor, blitz half the watercress with the lemon juice, the remaining 60ml of oil and ¼ teaspoon of salt to get a smooth salsa.

7. Transfer to a large serving bowl or serve straight from the pan: drizzle the watercress salsa and cream (if using) over the barley and gently swirl them in. Top with the fresh watercress, the roasted kohlrabi and the roasted tomatoes. Serve hot, with the lemon wedges alongside.

As a side or as part of
a spread

4–5 banana shallots,
sliced 3mm thick on
a mandolin, if you have
one, or by hand (220g)
2 garlic cloves, crushed
2 tbsp olive oil
**1.4kg Yukon Gold
potatoes** (or another
baking potato that's
somewhere in between
floury and waxy), skin
on and sliced 3mm
thick on a mandolin,
if you have one, or by
hand (about 6 medium
potatoes)
100g coconut cream,
melted
3 limes: finely grate the
zest to get 1½ tsp, then
juice to get 60ml
**200ml vegetable or
chicken stock**
**salt, flaked sea salt and
black pepper**

CRISPY AROMATICS
150ml olive oil
2 red chillies, finely sliced
into rounds
3 garlic cloves, thinly
sliced
5g fresh ginger, peeled
and julienned
4 spring onions, finely
sliced at an angle (40g)

LIME AND COCONUT POTATO GRATIN

This gratin was part of a Christmas feast that we created for the *Guardian* which also included a roasted Szechuan lamb shoulder, steamed aubergines and a cucumber salad. You can easily stick to this spirit, even if you lose the lamb, and serve the gratin as part of a Chinese-ish vegetable feast with our cucumber salad à la Xi'an Impression (p. 113), steamed aubergines with charred chilli salsa (p. 45) and sweet and sour sprouts with chestnuts and grapes (p. 93).

Ideally, you want to cut the potatoes thinly using a mandolin or a food processor with the appropriate attachment. Don't worry if you have neither, though – cutting them by hand is also fine; you might just need to cook them a little longer if they are thicker than 3mm.

You can bake the gratin the day before and reheat it in a very hot oven just before serving if you want to get ahead. Top with the aromatics and zest just as you serve, and not before.

1. Preheat the oven to 180°C fan. Put the shallots, garlic, oil and ¼ teaspoon of salt into a 28cm ovenproof sauté pan on a medium heat. Fry for 8–10 minutes, stirring occasionally, until soft and deeply golden. Transfer to a large bowl and set the pan aside to be used again (no need to clean it).

2. Add the potatoes, coconut cream, lime juice, 2 teaspoons of salt and plenty of pepper to the bowl with the shallots and very gently mix everything together, taking care not to break the potato slices.

3. Add a quarter of the mixture to the sauté pan; any smaller or broken slices of potato are best used here, saving the larger, whole slices for the top. Spread out to create an even layer. Use the remaining three-quarters to create a spiral effect on top of this layer, so each slice is at an angle and overlapping the next. Pour over the stock, cover tightly with foil and bake for 40 minutes.

4. Meanwhile, make the crispy aromatics. Heat the oil in a medium pan on a medium heat, then gently fry the chillies, garlic and ginger for 5 minutes, stirring occasionally, until the garlic is a light golden-brown. Use a slotted spoon to transfer the aromatics to a plate. Add the spring onions to the oil and fry for 2 minutes, stirring to separate, until crisp. Add to the plate of garlic, spread everything out and sprinkle with some flaked sea salt. Remove the foil from the potatoes and drizzle 60ml of the aromatic oil (reserving any remaining oil for another use) evenly over the gratin, then return it to the oven uncovered and bake for another 50 minutes. Increase the heat to 200°C for the last 5 minutes, until the top is golden-brown and crispy.

5. Set aside to cool for 10 minutes, then top with the fried aromatics, the lime zest and a generous pinch of flaked sea salt.

SERVES FOUR
As a main

BKEILA, POTATO AND BUTT
BEAN STEW

80g coriander, plus 20g, roughly chopped, to serve

30g parsley

600g baby spinach

120ml olive oil, plus extra to serve

1 onion, finely chopped (150g)

5 garlic cloves, crushed

2 green chillies, finely chopped (deseeded for less heat)

1¼ tbsp ground cumin

1 tbsp ground coriander

¾ tsp ground cinnamon

1½ tsp caster sugar

2 lemons: juice to get 2 tbsp, then cut the remainder into wedges to serve

1 litre vegetable or chicken stock

500g waxy potatoes, peeled and cut into 3cm pieces

1 × 700g jar of good-quality cooked large butter beans, drained (500g) (we use Brindisa Navarrico large butter beans, but you can, of course, use tinned or cook your own)

salt

Tunisian Jews make a condiment called pkaila or bk
It is prepared by cooking down plenty of spinach for hours in a generous quantity of oil. The spinach – Swiss chard is often used as well – loses all its water, and very slowly fries in the oil, resulting in a small amount of greasy paste as black as crude oil, which is used to flavour all kinds of soups and stews. Our version here is modified and highly simplified but it still imparts an essence-of-spinach flavour in this rustic stew, which makes it rather special; the kind of dish you keep coming back to for sustenance and comfort.

If you have time to make the butter beans in smoked cascabel oil (p. 41), or indeed if you've cleverly made a stash already, they are a wonderful addition to this stew in place of the plain butter beans.

The stew will keep in the fridge for up to 3 days, or in the freezer for up to a month.

1. Put the herbs and spinach into a food processor in batches and pulse until finely chopped (or finely chop by hand). Set aside.

2. Put 75ml of oil into a large, heavy-based pot on a medium heat. Add the onion and gently fry for 8 minutes, stirring occasionally, until soft and golden. Add the garlic, chillies and spices, and continue to cook for 6 minutes, stirring often.

3. Increase the heat to high and add the chopped spinach and herbs to the pot along with the remaining 3 tablespoons of oil. Cook for 10 minutes, stirring occasionally, until the spinach turns a dark green, almost grey colour. You want the spinach to catch a bit at the bottom, but not to burn, so turn the heat down if necessary. Stir in the sugar, lemon juice, stock and 2 teaspoons of salt, scraping the bottom with a spatula as you go. Bring to a rapid simmer, then lower the heat to medium, add the potatoes and gently cook until they are soft all the way through, about 25 minutes. Add the butter beans and cook until warmed through, about 5 minutes.

4. Remove from the heat and stir in the remaining 20g of coriander. Divide between four bowls, drizzle with some oil and serve with the lemon wedges alongside.

350g cannellini beans, soaked overnight in plenty of cold water and **1 tsp bicarbonate of soda**
1 onion, peeled and cut into 8 wedges (150g)
10 garlic cloves, peeled
2 rosemary sprigs
3 thyme sprigs
1 green chilli, halved lengthways
200ml olive oil
1 tbsp Dijon mustard
2 anchovy fillets in olive oil, drained and roughly chopped (optional, but adjust seasoning if not using)
90ml lemon juice (from about 4 lemons)
10g dill, roughly chopped
½ tsp Aleppo chilli flakes (or ¼ tsp regular chilli flakes)
salt and black pepper

WHITE BEAN MASH WITH GARLIC AÏOLI

Garlic-infused olive oil is used three times here: first to flavour a basic bean mash, then to make a thick aïoli to go on top, and finally to dress a layer of whole cooked beans that add texture. The result is a happy symphony of beans, garlic and lemon, which can be served as part of a spread with bread and other dips (see p. 79 and 192). It can also be assembled on a heatproof dish and warmed in the oven, ready to double up as a side to a main.

Start a day ahead by soaking the beans in cold water and 1 teaspoon of bicarbonate of soda to ensure that they cook quickly and evenly. You can also use tinned or jarred beans, if you like, in which case you won't need the onion.

All elements of the dish can be made up to 3 days ahead and kept in the fridge, bringing back to room temperature and assembling when you're ready to serve.

1. Drain the beans and put them into a large saucepan with the onion. Cover with enough water to rise about 4cm above the beans. Place on a medium-high heat, bring to the boil, then lower the heat to medium and cook for about 50 minutes, or until the beans are completely soft and starting to break up; you may need to top with extra water as you go. Drain well.

2. While the beans are cooking, put the garlic, rosemary, thyme, green chilli and olive oil into a small saucepan, for which you have a lid. Place on a medium-low heat, covered, and cook for 25–30 minutes, or until the garlic has softened and is just beginning to colour. Leaving the lid on, remove from the heat and set aside for 10 minutes; the garlic will continue to cook in the heat of the oil. Strain through a sieve set over a bowl, reserving the oil. Pick out the garlic, herbs and chilli and set aside.

3. For the aïoli, put the cooked garlic into a food processor, with 100g of the cooked beans, the mustard, anchovies, 2 tablespoons of lemon juice, 75ml of the garlic oil, 1 tablespoon of water, ⅛ teaspoon of salt and a good grind of pepper. Blitz to a mayonnaise-like consistency and set aside.

4. For the dressed beans, combine 150g of cooked beans in a small bowl with 1½ tablespoons of lemon juice, 3 tablespoons of garlic oil, the dill, ¼ teaspoon of salt and a good grind of pepper. Set aside.

5. Once cool, put the remaining cooked beans and onion into a food processor with 2½ tablespoons of lemon juice, 3 tablespoons of garlic oil, ½ teaspoon of salt and a good grind of pepper. Blitz to a thick, smooth mash, then transfer to a shallow bowl and spread out to create a shallow well in the centre. Fill the well with the aïoli, then top with the dressed beans. Finish with the Aleppo chilli, reserved green chilli, rosemary and thyme.

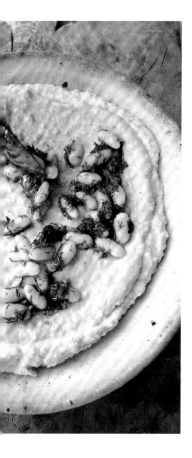

MAKES 600G

BASIC COOKED CHICKPEAS

250g dried chickpeas
1½ tsp bicarbonate of
  soda
salt

This recipe yields 600 grams of cooked chickpeas, enough to make both hummus recipes in the book (see below and p. 234).

1. Start the day before by soaking the chickpeas in plenty of cold water with 1 teaspoon of bicarbonate of soda. Drain and refresh, then put them into a large pot with 1.8 litres of water and ½ teaspoon of bicarbonate of soda. Bring to the boil on a medium-high heat, then lower the heat to medium, cover with a lid and cook for 35 minutes. Remove the lid, add 1 teaspoon of salt and continue to cook for 15 minutes, or until the chickpeas are very soft when squashed between your fingers (cook longer if you need to). Drain well.

SERVES FOUR
As part of a mezze spread

HUMMUS WITH LEMON, FRIED GARLIC AND CHILLI

HUMMUS
300g cooked chickpeas (see basic cooked chickpeas recipe above), or use good-quality jarred chickpeas
10g fresh ginger, peeled and finely grated
1 tbsp olive oil
1 tbsp tahini
1 small garlic clove, crushed
2 lemons: finely grate the zest to get 1 tbsp, then juice to get 3 tbsp
2 tbsp ice-cold water
flaked sea salt

FRIED AROMATICS
90ml olive oil
3 red chillies, deseeded and finely sliced
3 large garlic cloves, thinly sliced
15g fresh ginger, peeled and julienned
2 cinnamon sticks
15g coriander stalks, cut into 4cm lengths, plus 2 tbsp picked leaves to serve (optional)

This is great as part of a mezze spread. It's also lovely warm, with whole cooked chickpeas on top, or some shredded chicken or fried minced lamb.

The hummus can be made the day before and kept refrigerated if you want to get ahead. The aromatics should be fried on the day of serving, to ensure they stay crisp.

1. For the hummus, put all the ingredients and ¾ teaspoon of flaked salt into a food processor and blitz until smooth, scraping down the sides as you go if necessary.

2. For the fried aromatics, heat the oil in a large frying pan on a medium heat. Once hot, fry the chillies, garlic, ginger and cinnamon for 4–5 minutes, stirring every once in a while to separate the garlic slices, until the garlic is just starting to become golden. Add the coriander stalks and fry for one more minute, until the garlic is a light golden-brown and the chillies are aromatic. Transfer the aromatics to a plate with a slotted spoon (reserving the oil) and sprinkle them generously with flaked salt.

3. Spoon the hummus on to a large plate, creating a shallow well in the centre with the back of the spoon.

4. Spoon the aromatic oil inside the well. Top with the fried aromatics and the fresh coriander (if using) and serve with bread to mop up the oil.

As a starter or six as part
of a spread

MELON AND BUFFALO MOZZARELLA SALAD WITH KASHA AND CURRY LEAVES

1 large banana shallot,
finely sliced into rounds

2 lemons: finely grate the
zest to get ½ tsp, then
juice to get 3 tbsp

60ml olive oil

30 fresh curry leaves (if
you can't get any, use
20 basil leaves instead,
patted dry)

**1 tsp black mustard
seeds**

1 small watermelon,
skin on or off, halved
lengthways, then cut
into 2cm-thick triangles
(700g skin-on weight)

⅔ cantaloupe melon,
skin on or off, deseeded
and cut into 8 wedges
(600g skin-on weight)

**2–4 balls of buffalo
mozzarella,** roughly
broken into 10 pieces
(400g)

1 tbsp kasha (that's
toasted buckwheat
groats), roughly crushed
(optional)

flaked sea salt

This isn't the first time, and it's definitely not the last, that we combine fresh melons with young white cheeses, and every time something slightly different happens. On this occasion, it's not the saltiness of feta or the mild muskiness of goat's cheese or young pecorino that give the fruit a savoury edge, but rich mozzarella that adds a wonderful creaminess. The savoury flavours are achieved by a pool of olive oil infused with curry leaves and mustard seeds. A brilliant start to a summer's feast (see p. 304).

The salad tastes great once the flavours have had a chance to get to know each other, so dress the melons with the aromatic oil, shallots and lemon juice up to 1 hour before, if you want to get ahead, but hold off on topping with the lemon zest, mustard seeds, kasha and crispy curry leaves until you are ready to serve.

We love the look of the melons with their skin on, but you can, of course, remove the skin if you prefer.

This is a variation on a tomato salad by Peter Gordon. We thank him for the inspiration.

1. In a small bowl, combine the shallots with the lemon juice and a good pinch of flaked salt.

2. Put the oil into a small saucepan on a medium-high heat. Once hot, fry the curry (or basil) leaves and black mustard seeds for 30 seconds to 1 minute, swirling the pan, until crisp and fragrant. Strain through a sieve set over a small bowl, setting the oil and aromatics aside separately.

3. Arrange the watermelon, cantaloupe and mozzarella on a large platter and sprinkle with ½ teaspoon of flaked salt. Drizzle over the aromatic oil, then sprinkle over the shallots and lemon juice. Leave to sit for 10 minutes, or up to 1 hour, for the flavours to come together. Finish with the lemon zest, fried mustard seeds, kasha (if using) and crispy curry (or basil) leaves, and serve.

SERVES FOUR

CHILLED AVOCADO SOUP WITH CRUNCHY GARLIC OIL

60ml olive oil

½ tsp cumin seeds, lightly crushed

½ tsp coriander seeds, lightly crushed

2 garlic cloves, finely chopped

180g frozen peas, defrosted

2 large very ripe avocados, peeled and pitted (260g)

½ cucumber (160g), peeled and divided: 120g roughly cut into chunks and 40g finely diced

1 lemon: finely grate the zest to get 1½ tsp, then juice to get 1½ tbsp

1 small green chilli, deseeded and finely chopped

80g soured cream (optional)

1 tbsp dill fronds, finely chopped

salt

This soup is creamy from the avocado and refreshing from the cucumber all at once, so it's a great way to open a summery meal. It will keep in the fridge for 2 days without losing its bright green colour. The garlic oil can also be made ahead of time and will keep for up to 2 days in a sealed jar.

Make more of the aromatic olive oil, if you like. It's delicious drizzled over toast, salads or pasta.

1. Put 2 tablespoons of the oil into a small saucepan, along with the cumin and coriander seeds, garlic and a good pinch of salt. Place on a low heat and cook gently for 8 minutes, stirring often, until the garlic softens when mashed with the back of a spoon. Make sure not to heat the oil too much or the garlic will burn: if it does start to bubble, just remove it from the heat. Set aside to cool.

2. Put the peas into a blender and add the avocado, cucumber chunks, lemon zest, remaining 2 tablespoons of oil, ¾ teaspoon of salt and 400ml of cold water. Blitz to form a very smooth soup and put into the fridge to chill.

3. Put the diced cucumber into a small bowl along with the lemon juice, chilli and a pinch of salt.

4. To serve, divide the chilled soup between four bowls and top with a spoonful of the soured cream (if using), a spoonful of the cucumber salsa, a generous drizzle of the garlic oil and the dill.

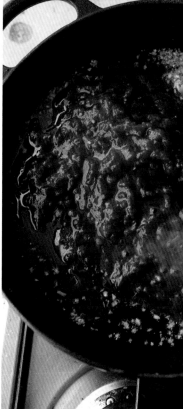

PAPPA AL POMODORO WITH LIME AND MUSTARD SEEDS

SERVES FOUR
As a side

SERVES FOUR
As a side

120ml olive oil
1–2 green chillies, finely sliced into rounds (15g)
1–2 red chillies, finely sliced into rounds (15g)
20 fresh curry leaves (if you can't get any, you can do without)
1½ tsp black mustard seeds
1 x 400g tin of peeled plum tomatoes
5 garlic cloves, finely chopped (not crushed)
6–8 ripe tomatoes, roughly chopped (600g)
2 bay leaves
10g basil leaves, roughly torn
1 tsp caster sugar
100g crustless sourdough bread, well toasted and roughly cut into 4cm pieces
1 lime: finely grate the zest to get ¼ tsp, then juice to get 1 tbsp
salt and black pepper

Pappa al pomodoro is a Tuscan peasant dish, typically prepared with overripe tomatoes that are too soft for a salad and stale bread that's too old for a sandwich. A delicious lesson in repurposing, this dish featured heavily in Ixta's childhood in Italy, most memorably at Podere il Poggiolo, a garden-to-table restaurant down the road from her childhood home, where the owner Serena makes pappa al pomodoro of dreams.

This version has been given a serious Ottolenghi twist with the addition of a mustard seed, chilli and curry-leaf-infused oil. It's an unlikely combination that really works, but you can also do without the fresh curry leaves if you can't get hold of them; the pappa will still have tons of flavour.

Make the pappa a few hours before, if you like – the flavours will only get better – but hold off on topping with the crispy aromatics, basil and lime zest until you're ready to serve.

This makes a wonderful starter to an Italian-inspired three-course meal (see p. 303).

1. Heat the oil in a large sauté pan on a medium-high heat. Once hot, add the chillies and gently fry for 3 minutes. Add the curry leaves (if using) and fry for 45 seconds, then add the mustard seeds for a final 15 seconds, swirling the pan as you go. Strain the oil through a sieve set over a heatproof bowl. Transfer the chillies, curry leaves and mustard seeds to a plate lined with kitchen paper and sprinkle generously with salt. Leave the oil to cool for 5 minutes.

2. In a medium bowl, roughly crush the tinned plum tomatoes with a fork until broken up, along with any liquid from the tin.

3. Return 3 tablespoons of the reserved oil to the same sauté pan and place on a medium heat with the garlic and ¼ teaspoon of salt. Gently fry for 4 minutes, stirring, until soft and fragrant (you don't want the garlic to brown, so turn the heat down if necessary). Add the tinned plum tomatoes, 400g of the fresh tomatoes, the bay leaves, two-thirds of the basil, the sugar, ½ teaspoon of salt and a generous grind of pepper, then increase the heat to medium-high and simmer for 8 minutes. Remove from the heat, stir in the bread and the remaining tomatoes, and leave to soak up the sauce for 5 minutes. Discard the bay leaves.

4. Spoon on to a large, lipped platter and drizzle over the lime juice and 3 tablespoons of the remaining aromatic oil (reserving the rest for another use). Leave to sit for at least 25 minutes, or up to a few hours, for the flavours to come together. Finish with the lime zest, the fried aromatics and the remaining basil and serve at room temperature.

SERVES FOUR
As a side

BLACK BEANS WITH COCONUT, CHILLI AND LIME

———————

2 **banana shallots,** finely chopped (120g)
2 **garlic cloves,** crushed
4 **fresh kaffir lime leaves**
1 **ancho chilli,** torn in half
350g **black turtle beans,** soaked overnight in plenty of cold water with
   1 **tsp bicarbonate of soda** (or 800g if starting with cooked beans)
3 **tbsp lime juice**
½ **small coconut,** finely shaved on a mandolin, if you have one, or roughly grated (50g)
salt

FRIED AROMATICS
90ml **olive oil**
2 **garlic cloves,** thinly sliced
2 **red chillies,** thinly sliced into rounds
10 **fresh kaffir lime leaves**
2 **tsp black mustard seeds**

Lime, chilli and garlic are the predominant flavours here, coming through both the infused oil and the crispy sprinkle at the end, and making these beans particularly delicious.

We suggest starting with dried beans, in which case you'll need to soak them a day in advance, but you can also opt for tinned or jarred beans: simply skip the stage where they get simmered – just add them to the cooked shallots, along with around 60ml of water, and cook until heated through.

1. Start with the fried aromatics. Heat the oil in a small saucepan on a medium-high heat. Once the oil is hot, reduce the heat to medium, add the garlic, chillies and lime leaves and fry for 2 minutes, stirring to separate the garlic slices, or until the garlic is beginning to turn golden. Add the mustard seeds and fry for another 30 seconds or so, until the garlic starts to turn a light golden-brown. Strain the aromatics through a sieve set over a bowl to collect the oil. Set the aromatics and oil aside separately.

2. For the beans, put 3 tablespoons of the reserved aromatic oil into a medium saucepan on a medium-high heat, then add the shallots, garlic, lime leaves, ancho chilli and 1¼ teaspoons of salt. Reduce the heat to medium and fry for 6 minutes, stirring often, until the shallots are soft and golden-brown. Rinse the beans well, then add them to the pan with 700ml of fresh water. Bring to a simmer, then lower the heat to medium and cook for 40 minutes, stirring occasionally, until the beans are cooked through but still hold their shape. Remove from the heat, cover with a lid and leave for 10 minutes.

3. To serve, transfer the beans to a lipped platter or a large, shallow bowl. Discard the lime leaves and ancho chilli. Drizzle over the lime juice and the remaining reserved aromatic oil. Top with the coconut, then the fried aromatics, and serve.

OVEN CHIPS WITH CURR' MAYONNAISE

1kg Maris Piper potatoes, skin on and cut into 1cm-thick chips
45ml sunflower oil
salt and flaked sea salt

CURRY LEAF MAYO
14 cardamom pods, pods discarded and seeds blitzed in a spice grinder (or crushed in a pestle and mortar)
30 fresh curry leaves, 20 blitzed in a spice grinder (or finely chopped) and the rest left whole
120ml sunflower oil
1 egg yolk
½ small garlic clove, crushed
4 limes: finely grate the zest to get 1½ tbsp and juice to get 20ml, then cut the remainder into wedges to serve

You won't regret putting a little extra effort into yᴏ promise! Taking our cue from Belgium and Holland, where ᴄ time ago that nothing beats mayonnaise as a chip sauce, we havᴄ mayo with curry and cardamom flavour. The chips themselves are also tosᴄ with lime salt, so you end up with a potato experience which is at once rich, warm, sharp and creamy.

Double the mayonnaise, if you like. It will keep in the fridge for up to 2 weeks and will transform your sandwich, burger and wrap repertoire. Or you can do as we do at our restaurant ROVI and serve it alongside freshly grilled prawns. The chips go exceptionally well with the celeriac steaks with Café de Paris sauce (see p. 60) or the Romano pepper schnitzels (see p. 146).

1. For the mayonnaise, put the cardamom and the blitzed curry leaves into a small saucepan on a high heat for 1 minute, until fragrant. Pour in the oil and heat for 30 seconds, or until gently bubbling, before adding the whole curry leaves and gently frying until they are crisp, about 30 seconds. Take the pan off the heat, remove the whole curry leaves with a slotted spoon and set them aside, to garnish. Leave the oil to infuse with the rest of the aromatics for half an hour, or until completely cool. Set aside ½ tablespoon of the oil (with some of the aromatics), to serve. Strain the remaining oil into a measuring jug, discarding the remaining aromatics.

2. Put the egg yolk, garlic, 1 tablespoon of the lime juice and ⅛ teaspoon of salt into the small bowl of a food processor and blitz to combine. With the motor running, start adding the cooled infused oil, very slowly and in a very thin stream, until it thickens to mayonnaise. Transfer to a small bowl and stir in the remaining teaspoon of lime juice to let the mayonnaise down a little. If it splits or gets too thick, whisk in a teaspoon of water until it's emulsified.

3. Preheat the oven to 200°C fan.

4. Spread the chips out on a large, parchment-lined tray. Add the oil and ¾ teaspoon of salt and gently toss to coat the chips. Immediately transfer to the oven and bake for 20 minutes, then turn the chips and bake for another 25 minutes, turning the chips again halfway, until crisp and golden-brown all over.

5. Mix the lime zest with ½ tablespoon of flaked sea salt, gently crushing it as you go. Add the lime salt to the chips and toss to coat. Transfer the chips to a large platter. Drizzle the mayonnaise with the reserved infused oil and top with the crispy curry leaves. Serve at once, with the lime wedges alongside.

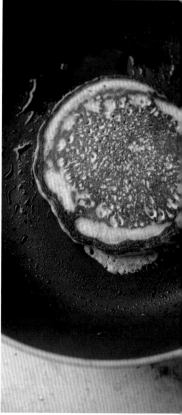

40ml olive oil
12 fresh curry leaves (if
    you can't get any, use
    mint leaves instead,
    patted dry)
2 tsp fresh ginger,
    peeled and finely
    minced
2 small garlic cloves,
    crushed
1 green chilli, finely
    chopped
2 spring onions, finely
    chopped
60ml sunflower oil,
    for frying
salt

BATTER
250g chickpea flour
50g cornflour
1 tsp baking powder
300ml sparkling water
60ml apple cider vinegar
1 tsp ground cumin
1½ tsp garam masala
    spice mix

MANGO PICKLE
YOGHURT
150g Greek-style
    yoghurt
½ mango, peeled and
    finely chopped (60g)
2 tbsp hot mango pickle,
    roughly chopped
1 lime: finely grate the
    zest to get 1 tsp, then
    cut the remainder into
    wedges to serve

CHICKPEA PANCAKES WI\`
PICKLE YOGHURT

These vegan pancakes, flavoured with ginge., ⌐
and soft all at once – sort of like savoury American-style pɑ.
eggs are a welcome addition, but feel free to leave out the egg and use ˻
yoghurt alternative if you want to keep things vegan.

These are great with a quick salad of spring onions, mint, coriander and
green chilli, dressed with lime juice. Or for a more substantial meal, serve the
pancakes with some roasted aubergines (p. 251), or our berbere ratatouille
(p. 209) or both! The pancakes tend to lose their puffy texture as they sit, so eat
them as soon as they've been fried.

1. Heat the olive oil in a small saucepan on a medium-high heat. Once the
oil is very hot, add the curry (or mint) leaves and fry until crisp and bright
green, 30 seconds to 1 minute. Use a slotted spoon to transfer the leaves to
a plate lined with kitchen paper, leaving the oil in the pan. Take the pan off
the heat for the oil to cool for a few minutes, then return it to a medium-low
heat with the ginger, garlic, chilli and spring onions. Gently fry for 6 minutes,
stirring often until soft and aromatic. Set aside to cool.

2. While the spring onion and ginger mixture is cooling, whisk all the batter
ingredients and 1 teaspoon of salt together in a large bowl until smooth. Stir
in the cooled spring onion mixture and leave for 15 minutes, for the flavours
to come together.

3. Put all the ingredients for the yoghurt into a small bowl with a good pinch
of salt, swirl to get streaks, and set aside.

4. Put ½ tablespoon of sunflower oil into a large, non-stick frying pan over
a medium-high heat and swirl to coat the bottom. Once hot, pour in about
80g (5–6 tbsp) of the pancake batter; don't swirl it too much – you want the
pancakes to be about 12cm in diameter. Fry for 1–1½ minutes on each side,
until puffed and golden-brown. Keep the pancakes warm while you continue
with the remaining batter, adding more oil as needed.

5. Divide the pancakes between four plates, spoon the yoghurt alongside and
top with the crispy curry (or mint) leaves. Serve at once with the salad and
eggs, if you've made them, and the lime wedges.

SERVES FOUR
As a side

SWEET AND SOUR SPROUTS WITH CHESTNUTS AND GRAPES

————

12 small shallots (240g), peeled and left whole (220g)
5 garlic cloves, peeled and crushed with the side of a knife
250g ready-cooked and peeled chestnuts
4 bay leaves
1 tbsp maple syrup
130ml olive oil
90ml Shaoxing rice wine (or pale dry sherry)
60ml soy sauce
180g red grapes
800g Brussels sprouts, trimmed and halved lengthways
2 green chillies, finely sliced into rounds
2 tbsp rice vinegar
1 tsp caster sugar
3 tbsp picked parsley leaves
salt

Something magical happens to the sprouts, chestnuts and grapes when they are left to soak with each other in a bath of Shaoxing, soy sauce and their own natural juices. A subtle sharp sweetness, with hints of bitterness, gradually emerges, giving the dish a real festive quality. It's Shaoxing rice wine that makes the greatest impact (see more on p. 20), with its complex sweetness and depth. This Chinese wine, fermented from rice, is available in most Asian supermarkets, but if you can't get hold of it, use pale dry sherry instead.

The sprouts and chestnuts make this dish an obvious candidate for a Christmas feast. Luckily, you can easily get ahead by cooking the shallots, garlic, chestnuts and grapes the day before and leaving them to sit in the liquids overnight (refrigerated). The Brussels sprouts should be roasted and added to the bath the day you plan to serve the dish. Hold off on adding the pickled chillies and parsley until you serve.

1. Preheat the oven to 160°C fan.

2. Put the first five ingredients into a large 34cm x 26cm high-sided roasting tin with 100ml of the oil, 75ml of the Shaoxing rice wine and 2 tablespoons of soy sauce. Cover tightly with foil and cook for 35 minutes, until the shallots are soft but still hold their shape. Stir in the grapes, cover again with foil and cook for another 10 minutes. Remove the roasting tin from the oven, take off the foil and set the tin aside while you prepare the sprouts. Increase the temperature to 220°C fan.

3. Mix the sprouts with the remaining 2 tablespoons of oil and ¼ teaspoon of salt, then spread out on two parchment-lined baking trays. Roast for 16 minutes, switching the trays halfway through, until the sprouts are browned. Add the sprouts to the tin of grapes and chestnuts, gently mix everything together and leave, uncovered, at room temperature for 1 hour, if you can, or at least 30 minutes, for the flavours to develop.

4. Meanwhile, in a small bowl mix the chillies with the rice vinegar, sugar and ⅛ teaspoon of salt and leave to pickle for at least 30 minutes.

5. Once the Brussels sprouts have sat for a while, stir in the remaining tablespoon of Shaoxing rice wine and the remaining 2 tablespoons of soy sauce. Stir through the parsley and transfer to a large, shallow serving bowl. Top with the pickled chillies and the pickling liquid and serve.

SWEDE GNOCCHI WITH MISO BUTTER

SERVES FOUR
As a main

1–2 Maris Piper potatoes, skin on (400g)

2–3 small swedes, peeled and cut into roughly 2cm cubes (600g)

70ml olive oil

1 egg yolk

150g '00' grade pasta flour

500ml vegetable or chicken stock

200g morning glory (or large-leaf spinach), roughly chopped into 8cm lengths

1 tbsp white miso paste

1 lime: finely grate the zest to get 1 tsp, then juice to get 2 tsp

5g fresh ginger, peeled and finely grated

50g unsalted butter, cut into 1½cm cubes

2 spring onions, thinly sliced (30g)

1 tsp white sesame seeds, toasted

salt

If you want to use shop-bought potato gnocchi instead of making your own, you are more than welcome to – the miso butter will transform them. If, however, you choose to make our swede and potato gnocchi, which have a seductive bitter-sweetness to them, we can make your life slightly easier. Instead of rolling and cutting the gnocchi, which can be messy, we spoon the mixture into a piping bag (you can use a Ziploc bag), snip off the end and squeeze them directly into simmering water. It's a nice trick that also makes the gnocchi lighter because you don't need the extra flour to roll them with.

Morning glory is an Asian leafy green; its hollow stalks make it the perfect vehicle for the sauce. It's available in most Asian supermarkets, but if you can't get hold of it, large-leaf spinach will also work well.

The gnocchi mixture can be made the day before and stored in a piping bag in the fridge until you are ready to cook. You can also boil the gnocchi the day before and keep them refrigerated, ready to be fried the next day. *Pictured overleaf.*

1. Preheat the oven to 220°C fan.

2. Wrap the potatoes individually in foil and bake for 1 hour or until cooked through. While still warm, peel the potatoes, discarding the skin, and mash them in a bowl using a potato ricer or masher to get about 230g of smooth mash.

3. Once the potatoes are in the oven, place the swede on a parchment-lined baking tray. Toss with ½ tablespoon of olive oil, cover with foil and bake for 30 minutes or until cooked through (you can roast the swede at the same time as the potatoes). Transfer to a food processor with 2 tablespoons of olive oil and blitz until smooth with no lumps – you may need to stop and scrape down the sides a few times. You should have about 320g of swede. Add to the bowl of mash along with the egg yolk and ¼ teaspoon of salt and mix well to combine, then fold in the flour until well combined with no lumps. Transfer the dough to a piping bag and refrigerate for an hour or until well chilled.

4. Snip the end off the piping bag to give you an opening about 2cm wide. Fill a medium pot with 1½ litres of water, add 2 teaspoons of salt and bring to the boil, then lower the heat to medium-high so the water is simmering gently. Cook the gnocchi (homemade or shop-bought – see the introduction) in about five batches so as not to overcrowd the pan. Pipe 3cm pieces of gnocchi into the water, using a small sharp knife to cut off each piece of dough. Cook for 2–3 minutes, or until the gnocchi float to the top. Lift out the cooked gnocchi with a slotted spoon and place them on a parchment-lined tray, spaced apart. Once all the gnocchi are cooked, drizzle them with 2 teaspoons of oil and refrigerate for 20 minutes until slightly chilled – this will help them to set and keep their shape when you fry them.

5. Pour the stock into a large sauté pan on a medium-high heat and cook for 12–14 minutes, or until reduced to 200ml. Add the morning glory (or spinach) and cook for 2 minutes until tender, then remove from the pan and set aside, leaving most of the liquid in the pan. Return the pan to a medium heat and whisk in the miso, lime juice, ginger and butter, then cook for 3 minutes, whisking until the butter melts and the sauce is smooth and slightly thickened. Take care not to let it boil, as it will split. Remove the pan from the heat and set aside.

6. Heat the remaining 1 ½ tablespoons of oil in a large frying pan on a medium-high heat. Once it's very hot, add half the gnocchi and fry for 1–2 minutes on each side, or until nicely browned all over. Transfer to a plate and continue with the other half. Add the cooked gnocchi and morning glory (or spinach) to the pan of sauce, return to a medium-high heat and gently heat through for a minute or two.

7. Divide between four plates, sprinkle with the lime zest, spring onions and sesame seeds, and serve at once.

**2–3 large baking
potatoes,** peeled and
cut into 4cm x ½cm
batons (380g)
1 small kohlrabi, peeled
and cut into 4cm x ½cm
batons (160g)
**1 tbsp gochujang chilli
paste** (adjust according
to the brand you are
using; see p. 18)
2 tsp white miso paste
2 small garlic cloves,
crushed
3 tbsp olive oil, plus extra
for greasing
8 eggs
1 lime, cut into wedges,
to serve
salt

SALSA
1 tbsp lime juice
**1 tsp gochujang chilli
paste** (adjust according
to the brand you are
using; see p. 18)
2 tbsp olive oil
2 tsp chives, finely
chopped
**2 tsp white or black
sesame seeds,**
preferably a mixture of
both, toasted

POTATO AND GOCHUJAN

Eggs are baked nestled inside a giant rösti with a cr
American breakfast of hash browns and eggs, all in
kohlrabi, feel free to use potato only, though we like
brings with it. Try to stick to ½cm batons for the vege
because you won't get the crispiness you're after whe   grated. You can
achieve this using a sharp knife or, more conveniently, with a mandolin or a food
processor with the appropriate attachment. Prep the vegetables just before you
cook them, so they don't get soggy.

Try to source good-quality gochujang, a Korean fermented chilli paste (see
more on p. 18), and not the generic supermarket brands. It makes all the
difference.

1. Preheat the oven to 200°C fan. Lightly grease a large 28cm non-stick sauté
pan, for which you have a lid, or a similar-sized round ovenproof dish, and
transfer it to the oven to heat for 5 minutes.

2. In a large bowl, combine the first six ingredients and ¼ teaspoon salt until
thoroughly coated (this is easiest with gloved hands). Remove the pan from
the oven, tip in the potato mixture and spread out evenly. Bake for 25 minutes,
uncovered, rotating the pan halfway through cooking until golden-brown and
crisp on top.

3. Make eight wells with the back of a spoon. Crack an egg into each hole,
then cover the pan with the lid and return it to the oven for 8–10 minutes, or
until the whites are cooked and the yolks are still runny. Use a small spoon to
carefully peel away the white film that has formed over the eggs, if you like,
to reveal the yolks beneath. Season them with a little salt.

4. Mix all the ingredients for the salsa together in a small bowl, drizzle over the
eggs and serve straight from the pan, with the lime wedges squeezed on top.

SERVES SIX TO EIGHT

THE ULTIMATE TRAYBAKE RAGÙ

3 **carrots,** peeled and
chopped into large
chunks (250g)

2 **onions,** peeled and
chopped into large
chunks (300g)

300g **oyster mushrooms,**
roughly chopped

60g **dried porcini,** roughly
blitzed

4 **garlic cloves,** crushed

3–4 **plum tomatoes,**
chopped into large
chunks (350g)

120ml **olive oil**

70g **white miso paste**

40g **rose harissa** (adjust
according to the brand
you are using; see p. 20)

4 tbsp **tomato paste**

90ml **soy sauce**

2 tsp **cumin seeds,**
crushed

180g **dried brown or
green lentils**

100g **pearl barley**

1 litre **vegetable or
chicken stock**

160g **coconut cream**

100ml **red wine**

salt and black pepper

Enough versions were made to sink a large ship in our mission to create the best meatless ragù (Ixta nearly lost her will to live, but that has happened once or twice before). There's no denying the list of ingredients is long, but these are all there to give the ragù its fantastic umaminess. The method, however, could not be simpler. If you have a food processor, the first six ingredients can all be pulsed in it until finely chopped, saving you lots of time and effort.

The ragù will keep in the fridge for up to 3 days, or in the freezer for a month, ready to be spooned over anything from pasta to polenta (try it with the fresh corn polenta on p. 140, minus the peppers and egg), or used as the base for lasagne or shepherd's pie. For the latter two, cook the ragù a bit less, as it will carry on cooking in the oven.

Thank you to Emily Moore and Josh Renaut, who tirelessly took home every single version of this ragù to give their thoughtful feedback as recent converts to veganism.

1. Preheat the oven to 190°C fan.

2. Working in batches, put the first six ingredients into a food processor and pulse until everything is very finely chopped (or very finely chop everything by hand if you don't have a food processor).

3. Put the chopped vegetables into a large, 36cm x 28cm non-stick high-sided baking tray with the oil, miso, harissa, tomato paste, soy sauce and cumin seeds and mix very well. Bake for 40 minutes, stirring halfway through, until browned around the edges and bubbling.

4. Reduce the heat to 180°C fan.

5. Add all the remaining ingredients to the tray, along with 150ml of water, 1/3 teaspoon of salt and a very generous grind of black pepper. Stir very well, scraping the crispy sides and bottom with a spatula. Cover tightly with foil and bake for another 40 minutes. Remove the foil and bake for a final 5 minutes. Set aside to rest for 15 minutes for the sauce to be absorbed a little before serving.

MAKES FOUR
PANCAKES
To serve two for brunch

ASPARAGUS AND GOCHUJANG PANCAKES

135g plain flour
60g rice flour (not Asian
   glutinous rice flour)
1 egg
325ml ice-cold water
**1½ tbsp gochujang chilli
paste** (adjust according
   to the brand you are
   using; see p. 18)
 5g coriander, roughly
   chopped, plus extra to
   serve
½ red chilli, deseeded
   and finely chopped (5g)
75ml sunflower oil
400g asparagus, woody
   ends trimmed and
   discarded and spears
   halved lengthways
   (280g)
120g spring onions
   (about 6–7), halved
   widthways and then
   again lengthways
salt

DIPPING SAUCE
50ml light soy sauce
1 tbsp runny honey
2 tsp sesame seeds,
   toasted
2 tsp rice vinegar
1 garlic clove, crushed
½ red chilli, deseeded
   and finely chopped (5g)

These pancakes are springy and less cakey than regular pancakes, which helps preserve the texture of the asparagus. They are only moderately spicy and are wonderful served at a weekend breakfast or as a light lunch or supper.

When it comes to gochujang, a Korean fermented chilli paste, you want to get your hands on the real deal. Korean brands of gochujang, such as O'Food, have a serious depth to them, compared to the often dull own-brands sold in supermarkets (see more on p. 18). If you still end up with a mild gochujang, serve some extra on the side alongside the dipping sauce.

Serve with an avocado salad and some grilled prawns, if you like.

1. For the dipping sauce, whisk together all the ingredients in a small bowl until well combined.

2. Put both flours into a large bowl along with ½ teaspoon of salt and mix well to combine. In a separate bowl, lightly whisk together the egg, water, gochujang, coriander and chilli. Make a well in the centre of the flour mixture, then slowly pour in the wet ingredients and whisk until just smooth; don't overmix.

3. Add just over a tablespoon of oil to a medium (18cm) non-stick pan on a medium-high heat. Once hot, add a quarter of the asparagus and a tiny pinch of salt, with the asparagus all pointing in the same direction, and cook for 1½ to 2 minutes, turning over a few times, or until beginning to soften and colour. Add a quarter of the spring onions and cook for 30 seconds more. Pour over 140g (about a quarter) of the pancake batter, spreading it to cover the bottom of the pan, and cook for 2½ minutes before flipping over and cooking for 2½ minutes more, or until crispy and golden. Transfer to a plate and continue in this way to make four pancakes in total. You will need to adjust the heat and timings a little as you go along.

4. Divide the pancakes between two plates, sprinkling over some chopped coriander, and serve the sauce alongside, or lightly drizzled on top.

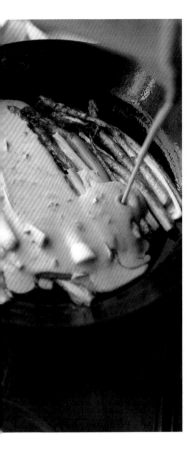

ZA'ATAR CACIO E PEPE

400g dried bucatini (or another long pasta, cooking time adjusted if necessary)
50g unsalted butter
10g za'atar, plus 1½ tsp to serve
2 tsp freshly cracked black pepper
130g Parmesan, very finely grated
30g Pecorino Romano, very finely grated
2½ tbsp olive oil
2 tsp picked marjoram leaves (optional)
salt

Messing with an Italian classic is not something that we do lightly, but adding za'atar really doesn't take anything away from the much-admired simplicity of this dish. All it does is add a layer of delicious herbiness that goes hand in hand with the pepper and the cheese.

The technique for getting your cacio e pepe right is not complicated, but it's essential that you follow it to a tee if you want to get a rich and smooth sauce, as Ixta would confirm after testing it about a thousand times. Using a wide pan and little water to cook the pasta is essential because it ensures there is a lot of starch in the water, which is the key to getting the sauce to emulsify. Grate the Parmesan and pecorino as finely as possible, and keep them separated to make sure they melt happily into the sauce. Finally, have everything measured out before you begin cooking; it all happens rather quickly after that.

1. Bring 1.3 litres of water to the boil in a wide pan on a medium-high heat, then season with ¾ teaspoon of salt. Add the bucatini and cook for 9 minutes (or per packet instructions) until al dente, stirring every now and then so they don't stick together or to the bottom of the pan, and to ensure they are submerged. Drain, reserving all the cooking water (you should have about 520ml – if not, top up with a little hot water).

2. Melt the butter in a large, high-sided, non-stick sauté pan on a high heat until bubbling, then add the za'atar and pepper and cook for another minute, stirring, until fragrant. Add the reserved cooking water, bring to a rapid boil and cook for 5 minutes, until silky and reduced a little. Add the pasta and stir vigorously into the sauce. Add the Parmesan in two batches, continuing to stir vigorously as you go and waiting until the first half has melted before adding the next. Once the Parmesan has all melted, add the pecorino, continuing to stir until it has also melted and the sauce is smooth and silky.

3. Transfer to a lipped platter and finish with the oil, the marjoram (if using), the remaining za'atar and a small pinch of salt. Serve at once.

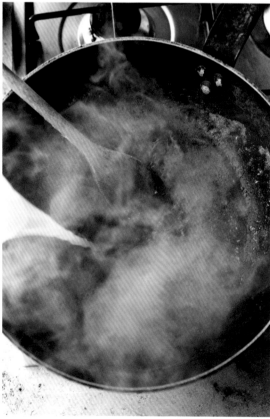

SPRING VEGETABLES IN PARMESAN BROTH WITH CHARRED LEMON SALSA

BROTH
2 tbsp olive oil
½ onion, finely chopped
2 garlic cloves, crushed
80g Nocellara olives
  (or another green
  olive), pitted and finely
  chopped (50g)
100g Parmesan, cut into
  3 chunks (the cut-off
  rind should be included
  in the weight here),
  plus extra, finely grated,
  to serve
1 tbsp lemon juice
5g parsley stalks
5g basil stalks
100g mangetout, finely
  sliced at an angle
100g fresh or frozen peas
  (defrosted if frozen)
400g sugar snap peas,
  halved lengthways at
  an angle
salt

**CHARRED LEMON
SALSA**
1 small lemon, cut into
  8 x ½cm-thick slices and
  deseeded (60g)
70g Nocellara olives
  (or another green
  olive), pitted and finely
  chopped (40g)
2 small garlic cloves,
  finely chopped
10g parsley leaves,
  finely chopped
10g basil leaves, finely
  chopped
75ml olive oil

You can do as much or as little as you like with the spring's bounty of peas and beans. Here we go for a maximalist approach, stirring them into a broth loaded with the intensity of lemon, olive, garlic and Parmesan.

There are three good takeaways from this recipe. First, never throw out your cheese rinds. They keep in the fridge or freezer for months, ready to be added to stocks, stews and broths for extra flavour. Second, the sautéed onion, garlic and olive base packs a heavy punch, adding serious depth to the broth. You could double or triple this part alone, blitz it to a paste and keep it refrigerated to use in soups and stews. Thirdly, the charred lemon salsa is a wonderful recipe in its own right. Double it, if you like, it will keep in a jar in the fridge for 2 days, ready to be spooned over grilled vegetables, fish or chicken, or to toss through salads.

If you want to get ahead, the broth and salsa can be made the day before and kept refrigerated, but don't cook the vegetables in the broth until you are ready to serve. Bring the broth back up to a simmer and the salsa to room temperature, if making ahead.

1. For the broth, put the oil, onion and ¾ teaspoon of salt into a large saucepan on a medium-high heat. Gently fry for 6 minutes, stirring every now and then, until soft and golden. Add the garlic and olives and continue to fry for 2 minutes until soft and fragrant. Add the Parmesan rind and chunks and fry for 30 seconds, then add the lemon juice, herb stalks, 1.8 litres of water and 1¼ teaspoons of salt. Bring to a simmer, then lower the heat to medium and cook for 20 minutes. Strain the broth, then return it to the saucepan to keep warm. Discard the left-behind vegetables and Parmesan.

2. To make the charred lemon salsa, heat a non-stick frying pan on a high heat and, once hot, char four of the lemon slices for about 3 minutes on each side, or until nicely charred but not completely burnt. Finely chop the charred slices, along with the fresh slices, and put into a small serving bowl. Stir in all the remaining ingredients for the salsa and ¼ teaspoon of salt, and set aside, to serve.

3. Once the broth has been strained, return it to a medium-high heat and bring to a simmer. Reduce the heat to the lowest setting, stir in all the vegetables and cook for 3 minutes, until they are just cooked and still crunchy.

4. Divide between four bowls and top each with a tablespoonful of the salsa. Finish with some grated Parmesan and serve with the rest of the salsa alongside.

SERVES FOUR
As a starter

GRILLED FIGS WITH SHAOXING DRESSING

8 ripe purple figs,
  halved (320g)
1 tbsp soy sauce
2½ tbsp maple syrup
2 tbsp Shaoxing rice wine
  (or pale dry sherry)
2½ tsp Chinkiang vinegar
  (or half the amount of
  balsamic vinegar)
60ml olive oil
2 red chillies, finely sliced
  into rounds (20g)
1 lemon: finely shave the
  skin to get 5 strips
60g rocket
140g ricotta

On paper it may not sound like it would work, but the combination of figs, Chinese rice wine and ricotta is a truly marvellous one. The dish is a fine balance of sweet and savoury, so it's important that your figs are ripe and sweet. If they aren't, increase the amount of maple syrup a little.

The infused oil and cooked figs need time to marinate, so make them a day ahead if you like. The figs, in fact, can be cooked up to 3 days before and kept in the fridge (just bring them back to room temperature before you assemble the salad). You can even leave them in the fridge for up to 3 weeks to ferment (or at least become a little funky); they make a great addition to a cheese board.

1. Preheat the oven to its highest grill setting.

2. Toss the figs in a medium bowl together with the soy sauce and 1½ tablespoons of maple syrup, then arrange, cut side up and spaced apart, on a medium, parchment-lined baking tray. Make sure there is no overhanging parchment that could burn under the grill. Roast for 12 minutes on the top shelf of the oven, until the figs are soft and caramelised, but still holding their shape. Return the figs and cooking juices to the same bowl, along with the Shaoxing rice wine, Chinkiang vinegar and the remaining tablespoon of maple syrup. Gently mix, then set aside for at least 1 hour (or overnight) for the flavours to come together.

3. Meanwhile, heat the oil in a small saucepan on a medium heat and, once hot, fry the chillies for 3 minutes, stirring to separate the slices. Add the lemon strips and fry for 30 seconds until fragrant, then immediately pour into a heatproof bowl and set aside to infuse for at least 30 minutes (or overnight).

4. Arrange the rocket on a platter and top with the figs and dressing. Dot with spoonfuls of the ricotta, finish with the infused oil, chillies and lemon strips, and serve.

SERVES FOUR
As a side

CUCUMBER SALAD À LA XI'AN IMPRESSION

SERVES FOUR
As a side

2–3 cucumbers, halved lengthways, watery centres scraped out and cut into 2cm pieces (700g)
2 garlic cloves, crushed
2 tsp rice vinegar
3 tbsp lime juice
3 tbsp sunflower oil
2 spring onions, finely sliced at an angle
½ tbsp black sesame seeds, lightly toasted
flaked sea salt

TAHINI AND
SOY DRESSING
60g tahini
2 tbsp soy sauce
1½ tbsp mirin (or maple syrup)
1½ tbsp rice vinegar

Xi'an Impression and Master Wei are sister restaurants in London serving the food of Xi'an, the capital of Shaanxi Province in central China. These restaurants, which also inspired the cabbage with ginger cream and numbing oil (p. 196), are tremendously popular with Ottolenghi chefs for their big flavours, based on a brazenly liberal use of chillies, vinegar, soy sauce and oil. A particular cucumber salad always appears first on the table and it is also a loose inspiration for this salad.

The dressing can be made up to a week ahead and kept refrigerated – just stir again to loosen it, adding a little water if necessary.

Serve with a few other vegetable dishes to make a meal, such as the asparagus and gochujang pancakes (p. 102) and the fusion caponata (p. 135).

1. Put the cucumber into a bowl with the garlic, vinegar, lime juice and 3 teaspoons of flaked sea salt. Mix to combine, using your hands to lightly crush the cucumber pieces. Gently heat the oil in a small saucepan until warm, about 2 minutes, then pour over the cucumber pieces. Set aside to marinate for 30 minutes or up to 2 hours.

2. Whisk all the ingredients for the dressing together with 1 tablespoon of water until you get a very smooth sauce (it will seize a bit at first, but will then become very smooth).

3. Pour the dressing on to a large plate with a lip, so that it naturally pools into a circle. Drain the cucumbers very well, discarding the liquid, and pile on top of the sauce. Finish with the sesame seeds and spring onions and serve at once.

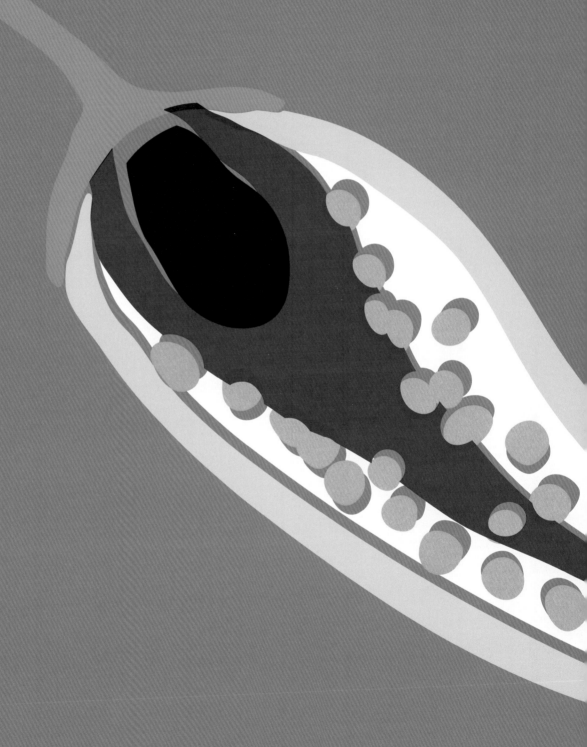

PAIRING

Flavour, as we'll see, can be dialled up by the pairings within a dish. It's not so much what you do to an ingredient ('process') or the ingredient itself ('produce'), but the combination of various ingredients with what we have identified to be the four most important 'pairings': sweetness, fat, acidity and chilli heat. These pairings play out, in big and small ways, in so many of the things we all love to eat.

Think of your favourite sandwich. Sandwiches are, arguably, *the* ultimate elevation of the most everyday of ingredients – bread – by virtue of what it's paired with. Spread the bread with butter and you've already hit first base: fat. Ask Ixta what her dream sandwich is and she'll say porchetta and apricot mustard. The combination is not, for obvious reasons, one found in this book but it does demonstrate the principle. The porchetta brings the fat to the equation and then the apricot mustard – which neatly ticks all the remaining sweet, chilli heat and acidity boxes – makes this an easy home run. Yotam's sandwich would be a mix of olive-oil-roasted vegetables and chillies, piled over toasted sourdough with some pecorino shavings or crumbled feta on top. Again: tick, tick, tick, tick. Not all sandwiches need to hit every note to make perfect sense – think of peanut butter and jam, or smashed avocado and chilli, prawn mayonnaise or a BLT. You'll see one or two or all of these pairings playing out. Let's look at sweetness, fat, acidity and chilli heat one at a time.

SWEETNESS

When we try to understand how sweetness works in a savoury setting, as opposed to the more apparent puddingy context (SEE P. 223–5), it is useful to pull back to the title of this book for a minute. *FLAVOUR* – what is it, actually? How does it relate to taste? What are the forces that shape this complex sensory experience of ours?

Taste is what we detect with the taste buds in our mouth. We have five tastes. Sweetness is one of them. The others are sour, bitter, salt and savoury (umami). Flavour, on the other hand, is picked up by the olfactory cells inside our noses. These cells respond to airborne compounds, many of which are released as we chew our food. Flavour is taste plus aroma. The sweet taste of a peach will be happily detected by our little taste buds when we take our first bite. Flavour, though, can't be realised without the additional smell, the aroma, the *fragrance* of that perfectly ripe fruit.

Appreciating the complexity of flavour is essential to shedding light on how sweetness plays its role in a savoury dish. Just as flavour is made up of taste and aroma, the different tastes also never work in isolation. In a savoury context, something is not simply 'sweet', nor is it simply 'sour' or 'bitter' or 'salty'. Rather, it is a combination of one or two or all of these things. Take some of

SATISFACTION IS ABOUT THE COMBINATION, THE LAYERING, THE CONTRAST OF TASTES

our favourite sweet ingredients in the recipes here. White miso or mirin, for example, pink grapefruit, tomatoes, oranges, maple syrup. The experience of eating these is not that they form a neat queue along the taste buds which say 'sweetness'. Rather, they charge an assault on all the senses!

Not only are all ingredients a combination of more than one 'thing' – sweet *and* salty, sweet *and* savoury – these tastes all need and rely on each other in order to shine. What would bitter cocoa powder be, after all, without its very opposite, sweet sugar? Satisfaction is about the combination, the layering, the contrast of tastes. With sweetness this is particularly pertinent because, without the complexity, you're running the risk of turning your dish into a dessert. Whatever the pairing – whether it's about layering together two of the same tastes or contrasting one against another – it's always about the *balance*. Let's look at some of our recipes to see this playing out.

First, layering. This is where one sweet ingredient pairs with one or two others. The effect is to bring complexity – another dimension – to a straightforwardly sweet taste. This is where wedges of sweet pumpkin, for example, are roasted together with a sweet spice like cinnamon, as we do in our GIANT COUSCOUS AND PUMPKIN WITH TOMATO AND STAR

ANISE SAUCE (P. 137). Or where a tablespoon or two of rich maple syrup and sweet-savoury white miso are added to a tray of butternut squash, as we do with ESME'S ROUGH SQUASH MASH (P. 136), before the whole thing gets roasted.

A WHOLE GENERATION OF KIDS PREFERRING 'SWEET' CARROTS TO 'BITTER' BRUSSELS SPROUTS IS NOT JUST A GREAT BIG CONSPIRACY AGAINST THEIR PARENTS

All these combinations of sweetness upon sweetness need to be kept in check, though. It's one thing layering so as to introduce depth of flavour, but sweetness can tip into cloying. Anyone who has tried the dish sometimes served at a Thanksgiving meal, which combines sweet potato, sweet cinnamon, marshmallows and maple syrup, will know what we mean. Roasting a sweet potato alone shows how much long and slow cooking sweetens this starchy vegetable. This is thanks to the action of an enzyme that attacks the starch and breaks it down to maltose, a sugar made up of two glucose molecules that's about a third as sweet as table sugar. And that's all before the maple syrup and marshmallows have been added to the equation. As well as giving us a little lesson in starch conversion, this particular dish is also basically a controlled experiment in the need for a salty slice of ham or rasher of bacon at the Thanksgiving table. In the absence of either in *FLAVOUR*, other ingredients do as well.

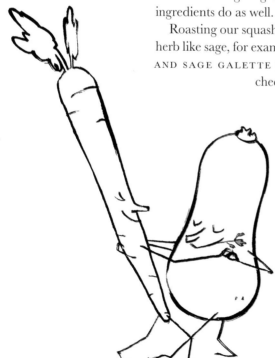

Roasting our squash and carrots with a woody spice like caraway or a hard herb like sage, for example, is something we do in our BUTTERNUT, ORANGE AND SAGE GALETTE (P. 132). Doing this keeps the vegetable's sweetness in check (rather than drawing it out, as a sweet spice like cinnamon would). Sprigs of thyme do this for the CHARRED PEPPERS on P. 140. Spreading the base of the galette with a layer of mascarpone also works. At other times it's a squeeze of lime or lemon juice or the use of a sharp vinegar that does the work to balance the sweetness.

It can, on the other hand, be the addition of something acidic or hot which is the thing that keeps (or even heightens) the desired sweetness in an ingredient in the first place. Think of a slice of pineapple. Take a bite and the dominant taste is sweet. Sprinkle it with a little salt and chilli and try it again. The addition of salt and chilli, counter-intuitively, serves to actually amplify the fruit's sweetness.

We often talk about the 'experience' of tasting sweetness rather than the taste of sweetness being an absolute. This is because everyone's experience of sweetness is different. Furthermore, taste buds change and develop over time. What we experience as bitter or sweet changes as we grow up. A whole generation of kids preferring 'sweet' carrots to 'bitter' Brussels sprouts is not just a great big conspiracy against their parents. Infants have around 30,000 taste buds, only about a third of which survive into adulthood. Their sensitivity towards extremes of bitter or sweet really *is* heightened.

Separate from what an ingredient is paired with, there can, as well, be a huge range of sweetness within an ingredient itself. Compare an aged balsamic vinegar with a younger version, for example, and you'll be reaching for words far beyond simple 'sweetness'. Ditto premium-grade maple syrup or Shaoxing rice wine. Think about those chunks of pumpkin and squash as another example, the many varieties of which could fill a whole book. Pumpkin is just one variety of squash. There are, in addition, all the Asian and African varieties: the cucumbers and gherkins, for example, the melons, watermelons and gourds. Then there are the North and South American varieties. These are divided into winter squashes (firm and sweet) and summer squashes (soft and only mildly sweet). A deep dive to end on, but it's all to say that discussions about whether we have four or five tastes slightly miss the point: we have about thirty-five different kinds of 'sweetness' for squash, for starters! And we haven't even got to pudding! Forget about what to call things, perhaps. Focus instead on the taste, the aroma – the combination of which makes the flavour – of our sweetness-showcasing recipes instead.

FAT

Twice already we've drawn attention to the unscientific nature of our system for understanding flavour through what an ingredient is paired with. It's not that we're not interested in the science per se; it's just not the *real* reason we reach for things in the kitchen. When it comes to analysing our cooking experiences – how they work and what happens if they don't – the option to get technical is absolutely there.

Olive oil and how it works so well as a cooking medium is a good place to start. Olive oil belongs to a large chemical family called lipids, and lipids are chemically unlike water. One of their differences is that they have a much higher boiling point. This allows for a much higher cooking temperature, which, in turn, gives the surface of whatever is being cooked time to dry out and for the texture to become really crispy. With the water removed, the flavour then becomes more concentrated and intense. As we saw when looking at browning in the first chapter (p. 28–30), vegetables boiled in water are only ever going to taste like hot versions of themselves. Switch the water for oil, though – oil being a 'liquid fat' – and the conditions for the production of intense browning-reaction flavours (the Maillard reaction) are set up. Fat is what makes our KIMCHI FRITTERS (P. 166) crispy when fried. It's what makes our slices of aubergine lightly browned when roasted for the CURRY AND COCONUT DAL (P. 152). All the wonderful, intense, interesting flavour and texture is, in short, thanks to the use – or pairing – of fat with the ingredient being cooked from the outset.

At the other end of the proceedings, the science can also tell us why fat is such a great way to finish off or complete a dish (rather than to cook with at the outset). Take a simple salad – tomato and basil, for example – and it's one thing. It's refreshing and sweet and lovely. That's three things, we know, but

VEGETABLES BOILED IN WATER ARE ONLY EVER GOING TO TASTE LIKE HOT VERSIONS OF THEMSELVES

you get the picture. Add some slices of mozzarella, though, or some chunks of tangy feta, and it becomes something entirely different. It's no longer just the picture; it's the entire summer holiday. The tangy taste of a sea-salt holiday, to be specific. Add another layer of fat in the form of the requisite olive oil and the dish is complete.

The reason the flavour of a good cheese seems to really *fill* the mouth is due to the enzymes from the milk and the rennet and the microbes. These break down the concentrated protein and fat in the cheese into a wide range of flavour compounds. The more diverse the cast of ripening enzymes, the more complex the resulting collection and the richer the flavour will be. The reason barrel-aged feta has a richer and more complex flavour than standard feta is because the enzymes have had longer to ripen (they need six months to be called 'aged', rather than the requisite two) and are, thanks to the beech barrels in which their ageing takes place, more diverse.

What the science *doesn't* tell us, though, is the instinctive reason *we* – both in the Ottolenghi test kitchen and in our homes – find ourselves so often reaching for a bottle of olive oil when we are starting or finishing a meal. We reach for it whether we're chopping an onion at the outset or finishing off a dish before serving. We do this for the unashamedly unscientific reason that we just love it. We love the grassy, peppery taste of the oil. We love the green and shiny look of it. To us, a bottle of good-quality olive oil is the Mediterranean sun made liquid.

So, with a little nod to the science and a slightly bigger wink to our appetites, we can have a quick look at the other fats in our recipes and what they are bringing to the dishes they're in.

If olive oil is in the first category of fats – liquid fats – then sunflower oil and butter, once melted and clarified, are part of the same group. You have to match the fat you choose with the dish you are cooking. Butter and olive oil are well suited to the rich Italian polenta, for example (P. 163), but when frying KIMCHI FRITTERS, on the other hand (P. 166), you want all of the benefits that cooking in oil can bring (a crispy outside, in the case of the fritters) without what's being cooked taking on any of the flavour from the oil. Here, it's oils such as sunflower (or groundnut or another mild-flavoured variety) that work best.

As well as these 'liquid fats', we have used all sorts of dairy products in our recipes, all with a very high fat content. Cheddar cheese has 33 grams of fat per 100 grams, for example, closely followed by Gruyère, Parmesan, feta and then mozzarella at 17 grams of fat per 100 grams. We hope that putting a figure on the fat does not make anyone baulk. Fat is flavour and fat is, in our line of work, good. When reaching for something which is 'fat free' or 'low in fat', just remember that if something has come out then it needs to be replaced by something else going in. In the case of a lot of low-fat yoghurts, for example, this something is often going to be sugar. Give us a spoonful of full-fat, Greek-style plain yoghurt any day of the week.

Many is the Otttolenghi recipe, over the years, which has come with the recommendation to serve 'with a spoonful of yoghurt alongside'. In the case of our TOMATO SALAD WITH LIME AND CARDAMOM YOGHURT (P. 164), up the spoonful to a ladleful so that the yoghurt can form the basis of a rich, creamy dressing. Up the ladleful to a whole pot, no less, if the dressing is to become an entire sauce, served warm with the MAFALDA pasta (P. 151). Here, the yoghurt, with its natural acidity, has the ability to make a pasta sauce which is rich and creamy without any of the 'cloying' or 'unctuousness' of a cream-based sauce.

Our last category of fats, in these recipes, is vegetable fats such as coconut and avocado. Here, the contribution they bring is to do with both flavour and texture. Cooking the dal for our STUFFED AUBERGINES in coconut milk (with at least 70% coconut extract) (P. 152), again, brings a richness, smoothness and also sweetness that water alone or a vegetable stock could

TO US, A BOTTLE OF GOOD-QUALITY OLIVE OIL IS THE MEDITERRANEAN SUN MADE LIQUID

not have done. An avocado is grassy and nutty and rich and buttery to taste, yes, but it also brings an incredible fatty smoothness, like butter, to all that it is paired with. Set it against any or all of the CHEESE TAMALES accompaniments (P. 158) – the pickled onions, the spicy salsa roja or chilli oil – and the science of pairing fat with sweetness, chilli heat and acidity speaks for itself.

ACIDITY

Acidity. On the one hand it's really simple. It's a squeeze of lemon, a wedge of lime; it's the vinegar in pickles, the tang of feta. Squeeze that certainty, though, and there's a fair bit of give. Is tanginess quite the same thing as acidity, for example? And while the juice of a lemon is acidic, isn't the zest more floral or citrusy? And might bitter be a better word for describing the fruit's pith? Or what about astringent? Or sharp? Or sour? Or tart?

We love acidity. We love acidity so much that few of our recipes don't have a pronounced acidic element to them. If Yotam brings lemons to the test kitchen party, then Ixta walks in with jars full of vinegary quick-pickles under both arms. Noor Murad, our test kitchen colleague, is also there, blitzing up her favourite dried black Omani limes to flavour TOFU (P. 176), for example, or piercing them to add to some BRAISED GREENS WITH YOGHURT (P. 175).

ACID HOUSE PARTY, OTTOLENGHI-STYLE!

Tomatoes are at the party too, with their sweet and earthy acidity, bopping along with tamarind pulp, with all the sweet-savoury tartness and complexity it brings to proceedings. Many of the dishes being served at this party would have Greek-style yoghurt added to them, and a party is not an Ottolenghi party, as we all know, without sumac and pomegranate molasses. Acid house party, Ottolenghi-style!

So, with our party players assembled, everyone can take a seat and listen to the speeches. First, then: what actually *is* acidity? Once we've established what it is then we can look at what it *does*. Then we can get back to the party.

Scientifically defined, acids are substances which dissolve in water to release hydrogen ions (i.e. charged atoms). They tend to remove oxygen from other substances and combine it with the hydrogen to form water. If oxygen generally causes food to spoil, then acids act as a preservative. This little controlled experiment will be understood by anyone who's ever made a pot of jam or a jar of ferments or pickles. Any bit of the fruit or vegetable exposed to the air – the top layer of the jam, for example – will develop a layer of mould. Everything below the surface – unexposed to oxygen and preserved by the acetic acid in the vinegar, which inhibits the growth of many microbes – will, meanwhile, be absolutely fine.

Acids are classed as either strong or weak depending on their pH level. The 'p' stands for 'potential' and the 'H' stands for hydrogen. The pH level depends, therefore, on the quantity of hydrogen ions something can release. Lemon juice is, speaking generally, about 2.1, wine vinegar is about 2.5. Ketchup is about 3.9 and yoghurt is about 4.0. Milk is about 6.7. Distilled water, which is neutral, sits at pH7. Anything above that is alkaline (and would taste soapy to eat).

As ever, our priority is a bit more in-your-face: a bit more 'What do we get from this and how does it make our food taste great?' Knowing what acidity is might be all well and good, but what does it *do* for us in the kitchen?

The first thing is to do with colour, the second is to do with texture and the third, of course, it to do with flavour.

First: colour. As a preservative, adding an acidic substance to certain vegetables and fruit once they're peeled prevents them from losing their colour and turning grey. These are the fruit and veg which are prone to oxidation: bananas and apples, for example, artichokes and avocados. Left exposed, they'll discolour. Rub them with a little bit of lemon juice, though, or submerge them in water which has a squeeze of lemon or a cap full of vinegar in it, and they'll stay the colour you want them to be.

On the other hand, adding acid too soon to certain vegetables will be the precise thing that *causes* them to lose their colour and turn grey. Very often, in our recipes, the addition of a dressing to a salad is followed by the slightly unrelaxed instruction to 'serve at once'. The day won't actually implode if you don't bolt straight to the table and shout at everyone to start eating NOW, but, still, the vibrancy of your ASPARAGUS SALAD (P. 171), for example, will diminish fairly quickly once the tamarind and lime dressing is spooned over. Make the dressing in advance, by all means, and just keep it separate. Everything else can be ready and waiting.

The second great 'use' of acidity in the kitchen is to do with texture. The addition of acidic substances to fruit, vegetables and legumes often causes them to cook much more slowly and, also, to toughen up. The reason we always soak a batch of dried chickpeas, for example, in a teaspoon or so of bicarbonate of soda is the very *opposite*. As bicarbonate of soda is an alkaline substance, it softens up the chickpeas and so speeds up the cooking time. Adding an acidic substance to one's cooking is totally fine (and often very welcome), but this needs to be done after the onions are softened and sweated down in the pan, for example, or after the beans have been cooked.

When you don't cook them, however, adding something acidic like vinegar to onions will actually start to break down their cell structure rather than harden it. As well as softening onion slices, for example, there is an exchange of flavour the other way – from the onion to the vinegar – which, in turn, can take the harsh edge off the vinegar before it, too, is used in the dish. A mutual mellowing, if you like, as seen in things like the pickled onions served on top of NOOR'S BLACK LIME TOFU, for example (P. 176).

The third – and most exciting – point of acidity in the kitchen is to do with flavour, where the main role it plays is that of balance. Think back to those favourite sandwiches we talked about at the beginning of this chapter. None of these fully makes sense or hits the spot without the acidic element. Together, they offer a great example of how versatile acidity is when it comes to balance, counteracting *fat* (vinegary mustard in Ixta's porchetta sandwich), *sweetness* and *chilli heat* (tangy feta in Yotam's roasted vegetable and chilli

TASTING YOUR INGREDIENTS THROUGHOUT THE COOKING PROCESS WILL ALWAYS BE YOUR BEST PARTY TRICK

sandwich). This is seen playing out in so many of our recipes: the sumac and lime juice dressing balancing the sweetness of the maple-syrup-roasted carrots in the ROASTED CARROT SALAD (P. 187), for example. The dried black lime or lime juice working to balance the richness of the yoghurt in the both the BRAISED GREENS (P. 175) and the CHAAT MASALA POTATOES (P. 193).

The balance works both ways, with the impact of an ingredient's acidity depending very much on what it is paired with. The more maple syrup added to the tray of carrots roasting, for example, the sweeter the dish is going to taste. The pH level of the lime juice or the sumac is not going to change – they will be as inherently acidic as they would be by themselves – but their impact on the dish as a whole will be reduced. It's a balancing act, and you can only set the scales to where you want them to be if you know what you're working with from the outset. It's not just apples and oranges you can't compare when it comes to acidity: you can't really even compare oranges and oranges. Or tomatoes and tomatoes. Or shop-bought tamarind paste with making your own from pulp (SEE P. 20). It's why tasting your ingredients throughout the cooking process – before, during and just before serving – will always be your best party trick.

CHILLI HEAT

Every time we publish a book, it feels like the Ottolenghi pantry needs a new shelf. A place to house our latest discoveries and obsessions. For *OTTOLENGHI FLAVOUR*, this new shelf would be full of chillies. Fresh chillies, dried chillies, chilli flakes, chilli pastes, chilli oils, chilli butters, chilli spice mixes, pickled chillies. If Ixta had her way – thanks, Mexico! – we'd have to find a whole new cupboard. We didn't find a cupboard, however, so the kitchen got pretty crowded. It got so crowded because the question of 'What's needed?' in a dish was, so often, answered with 'chilli heat'. If we *had* had such a cupboard, though, this is what it might have looked like.

On one shelf we'd have bowls of fresh chillies. These would be the Fresno or serenade varieties – those often sold in supermarkets as just regular 'chillies' – in both red and green. The difference between the two is one of ripeness. As with bell peppers (a member of the chilli family, albeit one without the 'heat'), green chillies are unripe and not as sweet as those which are ripe and red.

The Scoville scale, devised in 1912, assesses how hot a chilli is. It counts the number of times that extracts of chilli dissolved in alcohol can be diluted with sugar water before the capsaicin (the compound which makes them hot) is no longer discernible to the palate. The more heat units it scores, the more fiery the chilli. Sweet chillies (aka peppers, capsicums, bell peppers) score zero. Our

THE QUESTION OF 'WHAT'S NEEDED?' IN A DISH WAS, SO OFTEN, ANSWERED WITH 'CHILLI HEAT'

'regular' Fresno or serenade chillies score between 2,500 and 8,000. There's always quite a range because the amount of capsaicin in individual chillies of the same type can vary dramatically. Between types, the range is obviously dramatically wider: jalapeño and cayenne score around 3,000 on the scale, tabasco peppers around 60,000 and habaneros from 100,000 to 300,000.

As we said above, chillies are hot because they contain capsaicin. Capsaicin is a flavourless, odourless compound found in the chilli flesh. It's concentrated particularly in the white ribs inside the chilli where the seeds are (this is why we are asked to deseed a chilli to moderate its heat; as you shave away the seeds, which aren't actually hot, you also remove the hot white ribs). It's this, the capsaicin, which binds to pain receptors on the tongue and creates a sensation of burning. This increases as the green chillies ripen but then loses its fire the riper, redder and sweeter they become. If you want the hottest fresh chillies, choose those which are at the turning point from green to red.

The flavour of a fresh chilli can be dialled right up through being charred, as we do with the fresh chillies in our SPICY BERBERE RATATOUILLE (P. 209). Charring, as we saw on P. 25–7, concentrates flavour. It imparts complexity, bitterness and sweetness. It's what gives many a sauce or salsa that extra depth of flavour, the thing that takes them to 'the next level'. Another way of dialling up the flavour of fresh chillies is to pickle them, as we do for the SAFFRON TAGLIATELLE (P. 199), where they're spooned over before serving as a wake-up garnish. If charring intensifies flavour, then pickling softens the kick, allowing the chillies to bring their 'stand-to-attention' freshness to all the other elements in a dish.

So that's the fresh chilli shelf: chillies as they are, chillies heading off to be charred and fresh chillies, in jars, quickly pickled. The next shelf (or three) would be for the dried chillies. This is where we'd have to be disciplined about how much space we'd allow and how much of the globe we'd be allowed to trot over in our search for chillies (a very tiny fraction, it turns out). There would be jars full of whole dried chillies, ready to be crumbled

THERE ARE VERY FEW THINGS NOT IMPROVED BY THE ADDITION OF FAT AND HEAT COMBINED

or steeped into a slowly cooked dish. Smoky chipotle chillies would be there, the dried and mild version of the jalapeño chilli. Round and red cascabels, as well, from central Mexico, which are sweet and nutty and woody. Their name means 'little bell', in Spanish, on account of the sound the loose seeds make inside the pod when they're shaken. Mexican ancho chillies would also be in permanent residence. These are the dried and wide ('wide' being what 'ancho' means in Spanish) version of the poblano chilli. They're fruity and sweet and mild in their heat.

Then we'd have little jars full of dried chillies that have been blitzed up to become chilli flakes. We might have to colour-code these, just for fun. Bright red bell pepper flakes would be at one end, imparting their vibrant colour into infusions. Next to these would be the vibrant, burgundy Aleppo chilli flakes. Like the bell pepper flakes, these are as much about the colour and sweet aroma they bring to a sauce such as our ORANGE NAM JIM (P. 202) as they are about their heat, which is mild. Next to these would be the chipotle chilli flakes and then, alongside and far darker in colour, would be the small pots of crimson – almost black – Turkish Urfa chilli flakes.

It's these top shelves that we'd be reaching for to infuse the numbing oil for our CABBAGE WITH GINGER CREAM (P. 196), for example, or for making chilli butter to smear over our roasted CAULIFLOWER (P. 205). In terms of pairing, in fact, there are very few things not improved by the addition of fat (butter) and heat (chilli) combined. Eggs, chicken, tofu, all vegetables, fish, rice: the CHILLI BUTTER on P. 205 can be sitting for two weeks on the shelf (in the fridge, this time), ready to be used as a rub or melted to become a marinade or final garnish.

These top shelves are where we'd also be reaching to make our own chilli pastes were it not for the fact that great-quality chilli pastes are so easy and available to buy. As such, for the purposes of our imaginary chilli-filled cupboard, we'd have shelves given over to all corners of the world. North African rose harissa, bringing its rose-softened kick to our SUPER-SOFT COURGETTES (P. 204), for example, along with Korean gochujang fermented chilli paste. Argentinian chimichurri, Tripolitan Jewish chraimeh sauce, Louisianan hot sauce, Mexican Luchito smoked chilli paste, Thai nam prik, African piri piri, Malaysian sambal, Thai sriracha, Middle Eastern zhoug and shatta: there would be few days and few simple suppers not pepped up with a spoonful or two or one of these.

Any or all of these chillies and pastes and oils and powders are just so useful to have around because, when thinking about food pairing, they can shoot in virtually any direction, even puddings, as in our TANGERINE AND ANCHO CHILLI FLAN (P. 278). Chillies' great gift, for us, is their ability to somehow marry together a range of flavours – or even to wake up the palate to the existence of these other flavours – and, in so doing, to create a singular harmony. We just need to find a big enough cupboard now to keep everything in.

SWEET POTATO IN TOMATO, LIME AND CARDAMOM SAUCE

SERVES FOUR
As a main

4–5 medium sweet potatoes, skin on and cut widthways into 2½cm-thick rounds (1kg)
2 tbsp olive oil
1½ tbsp maple syrup
½ tsp ground cardamom
½ tsp ground cumin
salt and black pepper

TOMATO, LIME AND CARDAMOM SAUCE
75ml olive oil
6 garlic cloves, finely chopped (not crushed)
2 green chillies, finely chopped (deseeded for less heat)
2 small banana shallots, finely chopped (100g)
1 x 400g tin of plum tomatoes, blitzed in a food processor or blender until smooth
1 tbsp tomato paste
1½ tsp caster sugar
1½ tsp ground cardamom
1 tsp ground cumin
2 limes: finely grate the zest to get 1 tsp and juice to get 1 tbsp, then cut the remainder into wedges to serve
2 tsp dill, finely chopped, to serve

This dish has had countless incarnations. It started its life as mackerel kofte in a sauce made with tomato, lime and cardamom that we both fell in love with. It then went through a range of vegan dumplings served in the same sauce. In the end, after an embarrassing number of attempts and every member of the crew giving it a go, we figured that simply roasted sweet potato works best. It is a brilliant combination, but the sauce would also be delicious with chickpeas, tofu, fish or chicken. In any case, serve rice or couscous alongside.

1. Preheat the oven to 240°C fan.

2. In a large bowl, mix the sweet potato with the olive oil, maple syrup, cardamom, cumin, ½ teaspoon of salt and a good grind of pepper. Spread out on a large, parchment-lined baking tray, cover tightly with foil, and bake for 25 minutes. Remove the foil and return to the oven for 10–12 minutes, or until the rounds are cooked through and the undersides are very nicely browned (this might take longer if your sweet potato rounds are particularly large, or indeed less time if they are smaller, so do keep an eye on them).

3. Meanwhile, make the sauce. Put the oil, garlic, chilli and ⅛ teaspoon of salt into a large sauté pan, for which you have a lid, and place on a medium heat. Fry very gently for 8–10 minutes, stirring every now and then, until the garlic is soft and fragrant (you don't want the garlic to brown or become crisp, so turn the heat down if necessary). Transfer half the oil, chilli and garlic to a small bowl, leaving the rest in the pan. Add the shallots to the same pan on a medium heat and cook for 5 minutes, stirring often, until soft and translucent. Add the blitzed tinned tomatoes, tomato paste, sugar, cardamom, cumin, lime zest and 1 teaspoon of salt, and cook for 5 minutes, stirring a few times. Add 250ml of water and bring to a gentle simmer, then cook for 5 minutes.

4. Transfer the sweet potatoes, browned side up, to the pan of sauce (not all of them will fit in the sauce, but that's fine, just pile them up haphazardly). Turn the heat to low, cover with the lid and continue to cook for 10 minutes.

5. Mix the dill and lime juice with the reserved chilli and garlic oil and drizzle over the sweet potatoes. Serve from the pan, with the lime wedges alongside.

SERVES FOUR

BUTTERNUT, ORANGE AND SAGE GALETTE

1 small butternut
squash, skin on,
deseeded and sliced
into 1cm-thick half-
moons (680g)

2 carrots, peeled and cut
into 1cm rounds (180g)

2 tbsp olive oil, plus extra
for drizzling

2 tbsp finely chopped
sage leaves, plus extra
whole leaves, to serve

2 tsp caraway seeds,
toasted and roughly
crushed

1 head of garlic, top fifth
cut off to expose the
cloves

1 large banana shallot,
skin left on and top
trimmed to expose the
shallot (160g)

2–3 oranges: finely grate
the zest to get 1½ tsp,
then juice to get 160ml

50ml maple syrup

125g mascarpone

1 small egg, beaten

salt, flaked sea salt and
black pepper

PASTRY

100g plain flour, plus
extra for dusting

30g wholemeal flour

20g quick-cook polenta

1½ tsp caster sugar

¾ tsp flaked sea salt

1 tbsp sage leaves, finely
chopped (about 6
leaves)

¼ tsp freshly ground
black pepper

20ml olive oil

80g unsalted butter,
fridge cold and cut into
1½cm cubes

60ml ice-cold water

The hyper-flaky pastry, which is rich from the butter and crunchy from the polenta, is the star here. Double it and keep half in the freezer, ready to use in all sorts of savoury bakes.

1. Preheat the oven to 220°C fan. For the pastry, mix the first eight ingredients together in a large bowl. Add the butter and incorporate into the flour by lightly squashing each cube between your fingers. Don't over-work the butter, you want chunks throughout the dough. Add the water, using your hands to gather the dough together – it will be quite sticky. Transfer to a very well-floured work surface and roll into a 28cm x 18cm rectangle, flouring the rolling pin, surface and pastry as you go. Fold the longer ends in towards each other so that they meet at the centre and roll out once. Fold in the shorter ends in the same way, roll out once, then fold in half to make a square. Use your hands to form the dough into a 14cm-wide circle, wrap tightly with cling film and refrigerate for 30 minutes.

2. Meanwhile, toss the butternut squash and carrots with the oil, 1 tablespoon of chopped sage leaves, the caraway seeds, 1 teaspoon of flaked salt and plenty of pepper. Spread out on two large, parchment-lined trays. Drizzle the garlic bulb and shallot with a little oil, wrap individually in foil and add to the trays. Roast the squash and carrots for 25 minutes, or until golden-brown, and remove from the oven. Continue to roast the garlic and shallot for another 15 minutes, then set aside. When cool enough, squeeze the garlic and shallot out of their papery skins, and finely chop them. Reduce the oven to 200°C fan.

3. Transfer the dough back to a well-floured surface and roll out into a 30cm-wide circle, dusting your rolling pin as you go. Gently lift the dough on to a parchment-lined tray and refrigerate for another 30 minutes.

4. Put the orange juice and maple syrup into a small saucepan on a medium-high heat and cook for about 10 minutes, or until the liquid reduces to the consistency of a thickened, sticky maple syrup.

5. Put the mascarpone into a bowl with the chopped garlic and shallot, orange zest and the remaining chopped sage. Season with a pinch of salt and plenty of pepper and stir everything together well.

6. Remove the dough from the fridge and spread with the mascarpone mixture, leaving a 4cm rim around the edge. Cover the mascarpone with the squash and carrot, then evenly drizzle over the orange caramel. Fold the edges of the pastry up and over the squash. Brush the exposed pastry with the egg, then bake for 30 minutes, until golden-brown. Leave to cool for 20 minutes, then scatter with the remaining sage leaves and serve.

SERVES FOUR
As a main or six as a
starter

2 medium aubergines,
cut into 1½cm chunks
(550g)
120ml sunflower oil
1 small celery stick,
chopped into ½cm
cubes (65g)
20g pine nuts, very well
toasted
**80g sweet ripe cherry
tomatoes,** roughly
chopped
20g fresh ginger, peeled
and julienned
5–6 spring onions, finely
sliced (60g)
**1¼ tbsp mixed black and
white sesame seeds,**
toasted
40g raisins
60ml soy sauce
100ml Shaoxing rice wine
(or pale dry sherry)
3½ tbsp rice vinegar
2½ tbsp maple syrup
3 large, mild red chillies,
2 left whole and one
deseeded and finely
sliced to serve
**2 x 300g blocks of silken
tofu,** each block cut
into 8 x 1½cm-thick
slices (600g)
salt and flaked sea salt

FUSION CAPONATA WITH SILKEN TOFU

The word 'fusion' is greeted with suspicion these days. For cooking to be described as fusion is almost to say, without saying, that it is confused and lacks focus. This is odd, really, since ideas travel across the world at the speed it takes to refresh a mobile phone screen, and many chefs and home cooks seem perfectly happy to dabble in plenty of mixing and matching. When done considerately, cross-cultural hybrids can be both eye-opening and delicious. In fact, every kitchen classic was probably considered as fusion at some point in time. Here, caponata (a sweet and sour Sicilian aubergine dish) meets mapo tofu (a spicy and aromatic Szechuan tofu dish) in a union so wrong it's right.

Serve as an elegant starter, or as a main with some sticky rice and sautéed greens. The caponata will keep in a sealed container in the fridge for up to a week and the flavour only gets better with time. Try it in a cheese toastie in place of pickles.

1. Preheat the oven to 210°C fan.

2. Toss the aubergines with 75ml of sunflower oil and ⅓ teaspoon of salt and spread out on a large, 40cm x 30cm parchment-lined baking tray. Roast for 15 minutes, stir well, then add the celery and continue to roast for 15 minutes, until the aubergine chunks are a dark, golden-brown. Set aside to cool, then transfer to a large bowl with the pine nuts, tomatoes and three quarters each of the ginger, spring onions and sesame seeds.

3. Heat the raisins, soy sauce, Shaoxing rice wine, vinegar and maple syrup in a small saucepan on a medium-high heat until bubbling. Set aside to soak for 10 minutes, then add to the bowl of aubergines.

4. Place a small frying pan on a high heat and, once very hot, add the whole chillies and cook for about 9 minutes, turning them a few times until well charred on all sides. Set aside to cool for 5 minutes, then roughly chop them, removing the seeds if you prefer less heat. Add to the bowl of aubergines.

5. Heat the remaining 3 tablespoons of oil in a small saucepan until bubbling, then pour over the aubergine mixture. Add 1 tablespoon of water, gently mix everything together and leave to marinate for at least 2 hours, or overnight.

6. Divide the silken tofu slices between four shallow bowls for a main, or six bowls for a starter, and sprinkle generously with flaked sea salt. Spoon the caponata next to the tofu, drizzling about a tablespoon of the liquid over the whole dish. Top with the remaining ginger, spring onions, sesame seeds and chillies and serve at room temperature.

ESME'S ROUGH SQUASH MASH

SERVES FOUR
As a side or six as a
warm dip

**2 small butternut
squash,** peeled,
deseeded and cut into
3–4cm chunks (1.2kg)
50ml olive oil, plus 2 tbsp
to serve
1½ tbsp maple syrup
2 tbsp white miso paste
2 jalapeños, halved
lengthways
½ tsp ground cinnamon
½ tsp ground cumin
4 garlic cloves, peeled
and crushed with the
side of a knife
2 limes: finely grate the
zest to get 1½ tsp, then
cut into wedges
1 spring onion, finely
sliced into 4cm-long
strips
salt

Esme Howarth, a friend, an ex-test kitchen colleague and a chef of great talent, has a particular knack for creating flavour-packed one-pan dishes with minimal effort. This mash is an incredibly easy and delicious case in point. It can double up both as a warm side dish and as a dip, at room temperature, served with plenty of bread and olive oil. Other varieties of squash, such as Kabocha or Crown Prince, would work equally well here.

The mash can be made the day before and gently heated, or served at room temperature, if you want to get ahead.

1. Preheat the oven to 220°C fan.

2. Put the first eight ingredients, 2 tablespoons of water and ½ teaspoon of salt into a high-sided baking dish so that everything fits snugly. Mix well, cover with foil, then roast for 40 minutes, until beginning to soften. Remove the foil, then continue to roast for 35–40 minutes, or until very soft and browned on top. Remove the jalapeños, finely slice them and set aside.

3. Roughly mash the squash with a fork or potato masher, then drizzle over the remaining oil and squeeze over half the lime wedges. Finish with the lime zest, spring onions and jalapeño slices and serve with the remaining lime wedges alongside.

GIANT COUSCOUS AND PUMPKIN WITH TOMATO AND STAR ANISE SAUCE

SERVES FOUR
As a main

½ **Crown Prince pumpkin** (750g), skin on, deseeded, cut into 2cm wedges and then halved widthways if large (butternut squash can be used instead)

3 **tsp ground cinnamon**

8 **garlic cloves,** crushed

105ml **olive oil**

2 **large onions** (360g), 1 cut into 1 cm-thick rounds and the other finely chopped

2½ **tsp caster sugar**

4 **whole star anise**

⅓ **tsp chilli flakes**

750g **plum tomatoes** (that's 6–7), coarsely grated and skins discarded (600g)

1 **tbsp tomato paste**

250g **giant couscous**

250g **baby spinach**

15g **coriander,** roughly chopped

salt and black pepper

Crown Prince is a sweet and buttery pumpkin. Its tough skin is hard to cut through when raw, so you'll need a big knife and a strong arm, or alternatively you can use other squashes such as butternut.

If you are lucky, you will get a crisp, caramelised layer of couscous at the bottom of the pan. It doesn't happen every time, but it will still be totally delicious without it.

1. Preheat the oven to 230°C fan. Toss the pumpkin with 1 teaspoon of cinnamon, a quarter of the garlic, 2 tablespoons of oil, ¾ teaspoon of salt and a good grind of pepper. Spread out on a parchment-lined baking tray and bake for 30 minutes, until cooked through and nicely browned.

2. Place the onion rounds, keeping them intact, on a separate parchment-lined tray and drizzle with 1 ½ teaspoons of oil. Sprinkle with ½ teaspoon of sugar and a pinch of salt and pepper. Bake for 18 minutes, flipping them halfway, or until softened and deeply charred. Remove and keep warm.

3. While the vegetables are roasting, make the sauce. Put 3 tablespoons of oil into a large sauté pan, for which you have a lid, on a medium-high heat. Add the chopped onion and star anise and cook, stirring occasionally, for 8 minutes or until softened and browned. Add the remaining garlic and the remaining 2 teaspoons of ground cinnamon and cook for 30 seconds more, or until fragrant. Add the chilli, tomatoes, tomato paste, the remaining 2 teaspoons of sugar, 1 ½ teaspoons of salt and a good grind of black pepper. Cook for 8 minutes, stirring often, until thickened, then pour in 500ml of water and bring to the boil. Reduce the heat to medium and simmer for 30 minutes, or until the sauce is thick and rich. Measure out 400ml of sauce, leaving the star anise in the pan, into a separate saucepan and keep warm.

4. Meanwhile, add the couscous to the original pan containing the remaining sauce and mix well to combine. Add 375ml of water and ¼ teaspoon of salt and bring to the boil. Cover with the lid, reduce the heat to medium and leave to cook for 30 minutes, or until all the liquid is absorbed and the edges of the couscous have crisped up.

5. Put 1 tablespoon of oil into a large frying pan on a medium-high heat. Add the spinach, ⅛ teaspoon of salt and a good grind of black pepper, and cook until barely wilted, about 2 minutes. Stir in the coriander and set aside.

6. To serve, top the couscous with the reserved sauce, pumpkin and spinach, layering as you go, and finish with the onion rounds. Drizzle with the remaining 1 ½ teaspoons of oil and serve warm.

SERVES FOUR
As a main

50ml olive oil, plus 2 tbsp
to serve

6 garlic cloves, crushed

1 x 400g tin of
chickpeas, drained well
and patted dry (240g)
(reserve the chickpea
water to make the
coconut ice cream on
p. 286)

2 tsp hot smoked
paprika

2 tsp ground cumin

¾ tbsp tomato paste

40g parsley, roughly
chopped

2 tsp lemon zest

3 tbsp baby capers

125g Nocellara olives (or
another green olive),
pitted and roughly
chopped in half (80g)

250g small, sweet cherry
tomatoes

2 tsp caster sugar

½ tbsp caraway seeds,
lightly toasted and
crushed

250g dried orecchiette

500ml vegetable or
chicken stock

salt and black pepper

ONE-PAN ORECCHIETTE PUTTANESCA

This is a sweetened version of puttanesca – the famous pasta sauce from Naples 'in the style of the prostitute' – minus the anchovies, plus chickpeas and spices. It's quick and super practical to make because the pasta actually cooks in the sauce. Try it, and you may not feel the need to boil pasta ever again.

1. Put the first six ingredients and ½ teaspoon of salt into a large sauté pan, for which you have a lid, and place on a medium-high heat. Fry for 12 minutes, stirring every now and then, until the chickpeas are slightly crisp – you may need to turn the heat down a little if they start to colour too much. Remove one-third of the chickpeas and set aside to use as a garnish.

2. In a small bowl, combine the parsley, lemon zest, capers and olives. Add two-thirds of the parsley mixture to the sauté pan, along with the cherry tomatoes, sugar and caraway seeds, and cook for 2 minutes on a medium-high heat, stirring often. Add the pasta, stock, ¾ teaspoon of salt and 200ml of water, and bring to a simmer. Reduce the heat to medium, cover with the lid and cook for 12–14 minutes, or until the pasta is al dente.

3. Stir in the remaining parsley mixture, drizzle with the remaining 2 tablespoons of oil and garnish with the fried chickpeas and a good grind of pepper.

CHARRED PEPPERS AND FRESH CORN POLENTA WITH SOY-CURED YOLK

70ml soy sauce
4 good-quality, rich-yolk eggs
12 small mixed red, orange and yellow Romano peppers, stalks left on (1.1kg)
1 head of garlic, top fifth cut off to expose the cloves, plus 2 extra cloves, skin left on and crushed with the side of a knife
1 tbsp maple syrup
1 tsp apple cider vinegar
10g thyme sprigs
1 lemon: finely grate the zest to get ½ tsp, then finely shave the remaining skin to get 5 strips
60ml olive oil, plus extra to serve
5g basil, finely shredded
salt and black pepper

POLENTA
4–6 small fresh corn on the cob, kernels shaved off (500g), or 500g frozen corn kernels, defrosted
40g unsalted butter
180g Greek-style yoghurt
40g Parmesan, finely grated, plus extra to serve
100g quick-cook polenta

Curing yolks in soy, as we do here, adds creaminess, complexity and a hit of umami to this polenta. It's a nifty technique to add to your repertoire and the process couldn't be simpler. You can use these to top any grain-based dishes, such as pasta or rice, or to top thick soups. Good-quality eggs, preferably organic with rich yolks, are best here, as they will be eaten raw.

Roast and marinate the peppers up to 3 days before, if you like. The polenta will set quite quickly, so it is best made just before serving.

1. Put the soy sauce into a medium bowl. Separate the eggs, carefully adding the yolks to the bowl of soy sauce. Reserve the whites for another recipe. Leave the yolks to cure for a minimum of 1 hour, and up to 2 hours, very gently turning them halfway with a spoon. Don't cure the yolks for any longer – you want them to be soft and oozy.

2. Preheat the oven to 220°C fan.

3. Place the peppers on a large, parchment-lined baking tray, spread out as much as possible. Sprinkle the whole garlic bulb with a little salt and pepper and wrap it tightly in foil. Place on the tray with the peppers and roast for 20 minutes, then carefully turn the peppers over and roast the peppers and garlic for another 10 minutes, until the peppers are cooked through and blackened in places. We like the skin, but if you prefer to peel the peppers, do this now. Place the peppers in a large bowl with the crushed raw garlic, maple syrup, vinegar, thyme, lemon strips, oil, ¼ teaspoon of salt and a good grind of pepper. Once cool enough to handle, unwrap the cooked garlic and squeeze the cloves out into the bowl with the peppers, discarding the papery skin. Gently mix the peppers, keeping the stalks intact, then cover with a large plate and leave to marinate for at least an hour, or overnight.

4. For the polenta, put the corn into a food processor and blitz to a wet paste. Transfer to a large sauté pan on a medium heat with the butter, yoghurt, Parmesan, 1¾ teaspoons of salt and 600ml of water. Cook for 7 minutes, then turn the heat down as low as it will go and sprinkle in the polenta, stirring continuously to avoid lumps for another 5 minutes, until cooked.

5. Divide the polenta between four bowls, then top with three peppers each, drizzling some of the marinade over, but avoiding the aromatics. Carefully lift a yolk out of the soy sauce and place on the polenta, next to the peppers. Finish with a good drizzle of oil, along with the basil, lemon zest, a sprinkle of salt, a good grind of pepper and some freshly grated Parmesan.

To serve two to four

COCONUT AND TURMERIC
OMELETTE FEAST

_____

These are much thinner than your average omelette, more like crêpes or pancakes, in fact, but without the flour. They are meant to be eaten like bánh xèo (Vietnamese pancakes), stuffing the herb salad into the omelettes and dipping the whole thing into the sauce. It's a messy business, but that's half the fun.

Use a coconut milk with a high percentage of coconut extract, 70% or more, if possible (the ingredient list on the tin should specify the percentage).

You can make the batter the day before, if you want to get ahead. The omelettes themselves can be fried up to 2 hours before serving, carefully laying them on a parchment-lined tray as you finish cooking them, ready to be reheated for a few minutes in a very hot oven (220°C fan) when you're ready to serve.

OMELETTES
90ml sunflower oil
3 garlic cloves, crushed
2 green chillies, finely chopped (deseeded for less heat)
3 banana shallots, finely chopped
5g fresh ginger, peeled and finely chopped
¾ tsp ground turmeric
1 lime: finely grate the zest to get 1 tsp, then cut into wedges, to serve
6 eggs
1 x 400ml tin of coconut milk (at least 70% coconut extract)
salt

GRAPEFRUIT DIPPING SAUCE
120ml pink grapefruit juice, including the bits (1–2 grapefruits)
2 tbsp rice vinegar
2 tbsp mirin
1 tbsp lime juice
2 red chillies, finely chopped (deseeded for less heat)

SALAD
3 spring onions, julienned (50g)
15g mint leaves
15g coriander leaves
70g beansprouts
70g breakfast or rainbow radishes, finely sliced

1. For the omelettes, put 2 tablespoons of oil into a large, non-stick frying pan, for which you have a lid, on a medium-high heat. Add the garlic, chillies, shallots, ginger and ½ teaspoon of salt and gently fry for 8–10 minutes, stirring often, until soft and golden. Set aside to cool for 5 minutes.

2. In a large bowl, whisk the turmeric, lime zest, eggs, coconut milk and ½ teaspoon of salt until smooth and combined, then stir in the cooled shallot mixture. Transfer to a measuring jug.

3. Mix all the ingredients for the grapefruit dipping sauce, including the reserved pulp, together with ⅛ teaspoon of salt.

4. Toss all the salad ingredients together.

5. Wipe the pan clean and return it to a high heat. Once very hot, add 1½ teaspoons of oil. Pour in about 100g of batter and swirl to coat most of the pan. Fry for 1½ minutes, until the bottom is golden brown, then cover with the lid and continue to cook for another 20–30 seconds, or until the top is set. Transfer to a parchment-lined baking tray and keep warm in a very low oven. Continue with the remaining oil and batter in the same way until you have eight omelettes.

6. Carefully arrange the omelettes on a large platter, golden-brown side up. They are very delicate, so they might naturally fold or tear, which is fine. Serve hot, with the salad, dipping sauce and lime wedges alongside.

ROMANO PEPPER SCHNITZELS

SERVES FOUR
As a starter

8 red Romano peppers (850g)

100g plain flour

4 eggs, beaten

100g panko breadcrumbs

60g white or black sesame seeds, or a mixture of both

16 fresh kaffir lime leaves, stalks discarded and leaves finely chopped

1 tbsp nori sprinkles (or finely blitz a sheet of nori in a spice grinder and use 1 tbsp)

600ml sunflower oil, for deep-frying

2 limes: finely grate the zest to get 2 tsp, then cut into wedges to serve

salt, flaked sea salt and black pepper

MARIE ROSE SAUCE (OPTIONAL)

1 whole head of garlic, top fifth cut off to expose the cloves

180g cherry tomatoes

4 large red chillies (75g)

1 tbsp maple syrup

2 tsp Worcestershire sauce

½ tsp chipotle flakes

60g mayonnaise

In 2016, the German minister for agriculture called for a ban on vegetable-based foods being named after their meat-based counterparts, claiming terms like 'vegetarian schnitzel' were unsettling and misleading. Ours aren't vegetarian schnitzels, they are vegetable schnitzels, which is a semantic difference but quite a big one. In any case, we hope that our choice of title does not offend, but if you do have any doubts about whether these can live up to the original, we're confident they'll be dispelled once you try them.

The sauce is a take on the classic Marie Rose but turbocharged, with heavily charred chillies and tomatoes and a whole head of garlic. Double the recipe, if you like; it's great in sandwiches and will keep in the fridge for up to a week. The fried peppers work perfectly well without the sauce, and just a squeeze of lime, if you'd rather not make it.

Make a decadent meal out of these peppers and serve with the oven chips (p. 89) and the cucumber, za'atar and chopped lemon salad (p. 191). *Pictured overleaf.*

1. Preheat the oven to 230°C fan.

2. Start with the Marie Rose sauce, if you are making it. Sprinkle the garlic bulb with some salt and pepper, then wrap tightly in foil and place on a parchment-lined baking tray with the tomatoes and chillies. Roast for 30 minutes, until the tomatoes and chillies begin to blacken and blister. Remove from the oven and, when cool, squeeze the garlic into the small bowl of a food processor, discarding the skins. Add the chillies (deseeded for less heat), tomatoes, maple syrup, Worcestershire sauce, chipotle flakes and ¼ teaspoon of salt and blitz to a coarse paste. Leave to cool completely, then mix in the mayonnaise and refrigerate until you're ready to serve.

3. Meanwhile, cut a 5cm slit vertically in the base of each pepper, then place them on a large parchment-lined baking tray (you can roast the peppers on a separate tray at the same time as the garlic and tomatoes, towards the bottom of the oven). Roast for 16 minutes, turning the peppers over halfway, until cooked through and beginning to blacken a little. Transfer to a sieve cut side down, to drain any liquid, taking care to keep the stalks intact. Once cool enough to handle, carefully peel away as much of the skin as possible without puncturing the flesh, then sprinkle each pepper with a good pinch of salt and set aside.

4. Prepare three shallow containers long enough to fit the length of the peppers. Mix the flour with 1 teaspoon of flaked salt and plenty of black pepper in the first container. Put the eggs into the second container. In the last container, mix the panko breadcrumbs, sesame seeds, lime leaves, nori, 2 teaspoons of flaked salt and a generous grind of pepper.

5. Set a large metal rack over a tray (on which to place the panko-coated peppers). Prepare a separate tray lined with plenty of kitchen paper (on which to place the fried peppers). Dip each pepper first into the flour, then into the egg and finally into the panko mixture, shaking any excess off as you go, and lay it on the rack while you repeat with the rest of the peppers.

6. Pour the oil into a large, high-sided sauté pan or wok and place on a medium-high heat. Once very hot (180°C if you have a temperature probe), fry the peppers two at a time so you don't overcrowd the pan. Lower each pepper carefully into the oil and fry for 1½–2 minutes on each side, until golden-brown and crisp. Transfer to the kitchen paper-lined tray as you go.

7. Serve the peppers straight away, with the lime zest and some flaked salt sprinkled on top and the lime wedges and Marie Rose sauce (if you made it) alongside.

MAFALDA AND ROASTED BUTTERNUT IN WARM YOGHURT SAUCE

---

1 butternut squash (1kg), peeled, deseeded and cut into roughly 2½cm cubes (850g)

1 onion, peeled and cut into 6 wedges (150g)

90ml olive oil

6 garlic cloves, thinly sliced

200g short mafalda (or another dried pasta, cooking time adjusted if necessary)

500g Greek-style yoghurt, at room temperature

1¼ tsp ground cumin

2 egg yolks

1½ tsp cornflour

5g parsley leaves, roughly chopped, plus extra to garnish

salt and black pepper

QUICK CHILLI SAUCE

1 plum tomato, roughly chopped (90g)

3 red chillies, deseeded and roughly chopped (45g)

1½ tbsp cider vinegar

2 tbsp olive oil

Yoghurt, as opposed to cream, has a natural acidity, so it makes creamy pasta sauces which are rich but not in any way cloying or unctuous. These are found all over the Middle East, but aren't quite as popular elsewhere. Try this version, where a tomato and chilli sauce helps cut the fattiness even further. Yoghurt can split when heated, so egg yolks and flour are often used to stabilise it, as they do here. Cooking the sauce slowly will give you the smoothest result, so don't try to speed up the process by increasing the heat.

The quick chilli sauce is excellent to have on hand. Yotam's fridge is never without a jar or two of the stuff. Double or triple the quantities, if you like – it will keep in the fridge for up to 2 weeks, ready to be used as a condiment in sandwiches and wraps, or alongside grilled meats, tofu or fish.

1. Preheat the oven to 230°C fan.

2. Put the squash, onion, 3 tablespoons of oil, ¾ teaspoon of salt and a good grind of pepper into a medium bowl and mix well to combine. Transfer on to a parchment-lined baking tray and roast for about 30 minutes, stirring once or twice, until softened and charred. Keep warm until ready to use.

3. Meanwhile, put the sliced garlic and 2 tablespoons of oil into a small frying pan and place on a medium heat. Cook gently until the garlic becomes deeply golden and crispy, stirring occasionally, about 12 minutes. Reserving the oil, use a slotted spoon to transfer the garlic to a plate lined with kitchen paper.

4. For the quick chilli sauce, put the tomato, chillies and ¼ teaspoon of salt into the small bowl of a food processor and blitz until finely minced, scraping down the sides of the bowl. Add the vinegar and olive oil and pulse for a few seconds more. Transfer to a small bowl and set aside.

5. Cook the pasta in plenty of salted boiling water until almost al dente, about 7 minutes. Reserving 200ml of cooking liquid, drain the pasta well.

6. Put the yoghurt, the remaining tablespoon of oil, the cumin, egg yolks, cornflour and ⅓ teaspoon of salt into a blender and blitz until smooth, about a minute. Pour the mixture into a large sauté pan on a medium heat. Cook, stirring continuously, until thickened and just beginning to bubble, about 15 minutes. Add the pasta, reserved pasta water, parsley and half the squash mixture and cook for another 4 minutes, or until just heated through. Transfer to a large serving platter and top with the remaining squash mixture. Drizzle with a third of the chilli sauce, serving the remainder alongside, and top with the fried garlic, parsley and reserved garlic oil.

STUFFED AUBERGINE IN CURRY AND COCONUT DAL

SERVES FOUR
As a main

3 large aubergines, stalks removed, each aubergine cut lengthways into 6 x ½cm-thick slices (750g)

3 tbsp olive oil

220g paneer (or extra-firm tofu), roughly grated

2 limes: finely grate the zest to get 1 tsp, then juice to get 2 tbsp

45g hot mango pickle, roughly chopped, plus extra to serve

5g coriander, roughly chopped, plus extra to serve

100g large (not baby) spinach leaves, stems removed (60g)

salt and black pepper

COCONUT DAL

3 tbsp olive oil

5 banana shallots, peeled and finely chopped (250g)

45g fresh ginger, peeled and finely chopped

2 red chillies, finely chopped

30 fresh curry leaves (if you can't get any, you can also do without)

1 tsp black mustard seeds

1 tsp ground cumin

1 tsp ground coriander

½ tsp ground turmeric

2 tsp medium curry powder

2 tsp tomato paste

100g dried red lentils

1 x 400ml tin of coconut milk (at least 70% coconut extract)

Only two ingredients – lemon and milk – are what it takes to make paneer at home. It's an experiment worth trying (it certainly feels like conducting a chemistry experiment), both for a sense of achievement and for unrivalled freshness. Yotam has published a recipe in the *Guardian*, but many others are also available online. If you buy your paneer – which makes the most satisfying filling for the grilled aubergines here, as it soaks up the coconut sauce – try to find a soft variety, which has a texture like compressed ricotta. Other varieties, which are harder and slightly rubbery, are more suitable for making vegetarian tikka kebabs, but they will also do if that's what you've got. For a vegan option, use extra-firm tofu. Try to get a good-quality, chunky Indian mango pickle for this.

Both the aubergine slices and the lentil sauce can be prepared the day before, if you want to get ahead. In fact, you can make the whole dish a day ahead, up until before it goes into the oven, chill in the fridge and then just bring to room temperature before warming up.

The coconut dal is a great recipe in its own right. Double it, if you like, and serve with our curry-crusted swede steaks (see p. 63), and some rice. *Pictured overleaf.*

1. Heat the oven to 220°C fan.

2. In a large bowl, toss the aubergines together with the oil, ¾ teaspoon of salt and a good grind of black pepper. Spread out on two parchment-lined baking trays and bake for 25 minutes, flipping halfway, until softened and lightly browned. Set aside to cool.

3. For the coconut dal, put 2 tablespoons of the oil into a large sauté pan on a medium-high heat. Once hot, add the shallots and fry for 8 minutes, until golden. Add the ginger, half the chilli and half the curry leaves (if using), cook for 2 minutes, then add the spices, tomato paste and lentils. Stir for a minute, then add the coconut milk, 600ml of water and ¾ teaspoon of salt. Bring to the boil, then reduce the heat to medium and leave to simmer for 20 minutes, stirring once in a while, until the lentils are soft and the sauce is thick. Pour into a medium baking dish, around 28cm x 18cm, if making the aubergine rolls, and set aside.

4. In a small bowl, toss together the paneer, lime zest, mango pickle, 1 tablespoon of lime juice, the coriander and ⅛ teaspoon of salt.

5. Place one spinach leaf on top of each slice of aubergine. Put a heaped teaspoon of the paneer mixture in the middle, then roll up the aubergine, from the thinner end at the top down to the thicker bottom end, so the filling is encased. Put the aubergine roll seam side down in the lentil sauce, and repeat with the remaining aubergine slices, spinach and paneer. You should end up with about 18 rolls, all sitting snugly in the sauce. Press the rolls gently into the sauce, but not so far that they are submerged, and bake for 15–20 minutes, until the aubergine is golden-brown on top and the sauce is bubbling. Remove from the oven and leave to rest for 5 minutes.

6. Heat the remaining tablespoon of oil in a small pan on a medium-high heat. Add the remaining chilli and curry leaves and fry for a minute, until the curry leaves are crisp and fragrant. Spoon over the aubergine rolls, drizzle over the lime juice and serve with the coriander sprinkled on top.

AUBERGINE DUMPLINGS ALLA PARMIGIANA

90g fresh breadcrumbs, preferably sourdough (that's 2–3 slices)

4 aubergines, roughly cut into 2½cm cubes (1kg)

150ml olive oil, plus extra for shaping

100g ricotta

75g Parmesan, finely grated, plus extra to serve

10g parsley, finely chopped

1 egg, plus 1 yolk

1½ tbsp plain flour

6 garlic cloves, crushed

15g basil leaves, roughly chopped

1½ x 400g tins of peeled plum tomatoes, blitzed until smooth (600g)

1½ tsp tomato paste

1½ tsp caster sugar

¼ tsp chilli flakes

¾ tsp paprika

2 tsp fresh oregano leaves, finely chopped

45g pitted Kalamata olives, roughly torn in half

salt and black pepper

If you like melanzane alla parmigiana, these taste like the Italian classic but in dumpling form. The dumplings are gloriously rich and cheesy and yet somehow incredibly light.

Make the sauce ahead and keep it in the fridge for up to 3 days, or in the freezer for a month. The dumpling mix can be made up to a few hours in advance and chilled, ready to roll into balls and sear. Serve with spaghetti, rice or some sautéed greens.

1. Preheat the oven to 160°C fan. Spread the breadcrumbs out on a baking tray and bake for 12 minutes, until lightly browned and dried out. Set aside to cool and turn the oven temperature up to 220°C fan.

2. On a large, parchment-lined tray, toss the aubergines with 75ml of oil, ½ teaspoon of salt and a good grind of black pepper. Spread out as much as possible and bake for 30 minutes, tossing halfway through, until golden-brown.

3. Roughly chop the aubergines into a chunky mash, then transfer to a large bowl and refrigerate for 20 minutes, or until cool. Once cool, add the ricotta, Parmesan, parsley, egg, yolk, flour, breadcrumbs, a third of the garlic, 10g of basil, ¼ teaspoon of salt and a good grind of black pepper. Mix well, then with lightly oiled hands, shape the mixture into 16 golf-ball-sized dumplings, about 55g each, compressing them as you go so they hold together.

4. Put 2 tablespoons of oil into a large non-stick frying pan on a medium-high heat. In two batches, fry the dumplings for 3–4 minutes, turning them until golden-brown all over. Adjust the heat if they're browning too much. Add another 1 tablespoon of oil and fry the remaining dumplings in the same way. Transfer to a plate and set aside.

5. Preheat the oven to 180°C fan. Put the remaining 2 tablespoons of oil into a large sauté pan on a medium-high heat. Add the remaining garlic and cook for 1 minute until fragrant, then add the tinned tomatoes, tomato paste, sugar, chilli flakes, paprika, oregano, 1 teaspoon of salt and a good grind of black pepper and cook for 8 minutes or until thickened slightly, stirring occasionally. Pour in 400ml of water, bring to a simmer, then lower the heat to medium and simmer for another 10 minutes.

6. Pour the sauce into a medium baking dish, top with the dumplings and bake for 20 minutes, until bubbling. Remove from the oven, scatter over the olives, the remaining basil and a grating of Parmesan, and serve.

To serve six as a starter
or three as a main

TAMALES
4–6 small fresh corn on the cob, kernels shaved off (500g), or 500g frozen corn kernels, defrosted
15g unsalted butter
100ml double cream
2 tsp cumin seeds, toasted and finely crushed
110g masa harina
½ tbsp olive oil, plus extra for shaping
1 tsp baking powder
1 egg, whisked
60g mature Cheddar, grated
60g block of mozzarella, grated
salt

HIBISCUS PICKLED ONIONS (OPTIONAL)
120ml white wine vinegar
2 tsp caster sugar
2 hibiscus tea bags, or 5g dried hibiscus flowers
finely shaved skin of 1 lime
1 garlic clove, skin on, roughly crushed with the flat side of a knife
1 red onion, finely sliced on a mandolin, if you have one, or by hand

CHEESE TAMALES WITH ALL (OR SOME OF) THE TRIMMINGS

These are inspired by the street corners of Mexico City, where at rickety food stalls Ixta has eaten some of the best meals of her life. Business at taco stalls is pretty constant; with no real need to advertise their wares, vendors chat away to their customers, who sit on sticky plastic chairs, sipping on warm coca-colas. Tamale vendors, on the other hand, are *extremely* vocal, and it's not unusual to hear calls of 'TAMAAAAALES' from streets away, which is very handy as you know in which direction to run to get your hands on them.

We would love to be more taco than tamale vendors here and simply play it cool, but we can't possibly do that. Our tamales are just so good, we simply won't allow you to just walk by! In fact, we are so uncoolly keen that you make them, that we have made all the delicious accompaniments completely optional. Simply serve your tamales hot, with some lime wedges alongside, and watch the world go by.

If you do choose to make the accompaniments, or at least some of them, you will not regret it. Each brings an extra personality to the meal, with heat, acidity, richness and depth. You can also make the accompaniments without the tamales, and pile them on top of warm tortilla chips for a very special nacho experience.

You'll make more salsa roja than you need, but it will keep in the fridge for 3 days, or in the freezer for a month, if you want to get ahead. *Pictured overleaf.*

1. For the hibiscus pickled onions, combine all the ingredients in a medium bowl with ½ teaspoon of salt and leave to pickle for at least 2 hours, or overnight.

2. For the salsa roja, put the oil, garlic and onion into a large saucepan on a medium heat and gently fry for 7–9 minutes, until soft. Add all the remaining ingredients, along with 400ml of hot water and ¾ teaspoon of salt, and simmer for 25 minutes, or until the tomatoes have softened completely.

3. Discard the habanero chilli (if using) then transfer to a blender or food processor and blitz to a smooth sauce. Keep warm.

4. For the chilli oil, lightly toast the chipotle and pepper flakes in a small frying pan on a medium-high heat for 1 minute, until very fragrant, then add the oil and ¼ teaspoon of salt. Heat for about 30 seconds, or until the oil bubbles gently, then remove from the heat and set aside.

5. For the tamales, blitz the corn in a food processor until you get a wet mash. Put a large sauté pan on a medium-high heat and add the butter. Once melted, add the corn, cream, 1 teaspoon of cumin and 1 teaspoon of salt. Cook for 3 minutes, stirring a few times, until the corn is cooked

SALSA ROJA (OPTIONAL)

2 tbsp olive oil
2 garlic cloves, crushed
½ red onion, finely chopped
1½ tsp cumin seeds, toasted and crushed
3 plum tomatoes, quartered
½ tsp dried oregano
1 tbsp red bell pepper flakes
1 dried ancho chilli, stalks and seeds removed (or half, if you prefer less heat)
½ dried habanero chilli, stalks and seeds removed (leave this out if you prefer less heat)
2 tsp tomato paste
1½ tsp caster sugar

CHILLI OIL (OPTIONAL)

2 tsp chipotle flakes
2 tsp red bell pepper flakes
60ml sunflower oil

AVOCADO SALAD (OPTIONAL)

2 avocados, peeled, pitted and thinly sliced
6 spring onions, finely sliced at an angle (90g)
20g coriander leaves
4 jalapeños, finely sliced into rounds (deseeded for less heat)
90ml lime juice (from 5 limes)
20ml olive oil

through and has the consistency of porridge. Remove from the heat and leave to cool for 5 minutes, then stir in the masa harina, oil, baking powder and egg until well incorporated – it should have the consistency of playdough.

6. Cut six rectangles of baking parchment, roughly 25cm x 16cm each. With lightly oiled hands, take about 110g of the dough and shape into a smooth ball. Place in the middle of one of the rectangles of parchment and flatten to make a 15cm x 9cm rectangle. Combine the cheeses in a small bowl with the remaining teaspoon of cumin, then place 20g of the cheese mixture along the centre of the dough. Use your hands to mould the dough over to enclose the cheese on all sides, pinching and smoothing it with your fingers so there are no cracks, to get a 12cm x 6cm rectangle. Fold the parchment on all sides to enclose the tamale, using the paper to help you shape it, then place the parcel seam side down on a tray while you make the remaining five tamales.

7. Put a large saucepan, for which you have a fitted steaming basket and lid, on a high heat with plenty of water. Once boiling, place the tamales, seam side down, in the steaming basket (you may have to pile some on top of each other, which is fine). Cover with the lid, then reduce the heat to medium and steam for 30 minutes. Leave to cool for a few minutes before unwrapping.

8. Meanwhile, mix all the ingredients for the salad together with a good pinch of salt.

9. Serve the tamales on a large platter, with the chilli oil drizzled on top and the salad, hibiscus pickled onions (discarding the tea bags) and a bowl of the warm salsa alongside.

SERVES FOUR TO SIX
For brunch or as a light
lunch

POLENTA WITH FRESH CORN AND BRAISED EGGS

250g fresh or frozen corn kernels, defrosted if frozen
200g baby spinach, roughly shredded
10g parsley, roughly chopped
10g dill, roughly chopped
20g coriander, roughly chopped, plus an extra tbsp
4 spring onions, finely sliced (60g), plus an extra 2 tbsp
4 garlic cloves, crushed
150g coarse polenta (cornmeal), not the quick-cook variety
50g Parmesan, finely grated
520ml whole milk
450ml vegetable or chicken stock
40g unsalted butter, cut into 2cm cubes
150g feta, roughly crumbled
8 eggs
2 tbsp olive oil
½ tsp chilli flakes
salt and black pepper

For Yotam's father, who was born in Italy, there was only one way to cook polenta. He would put everything into a pot and then stand by it watchfully and continuously for a good hour, stirring the polenta with great patience, making sure it turned out perfectly and didn't stick to the bottom of the pan. For a *New York Times* column in which we turned classical dishes on their heads and cooked them in the oven in one single pan, our test kitchen colleague Noor Murad didn't only bust Yotam's childhood myth about the only way to cook polenta, she also did away with the sauce it was normally served with and simply added whole eggs to braise inside the polenta. The result is a rather 'bumpy' type of polenta, full of textures and surprises. It's still marvellously delicious, and means you can read a few pages of your favourite book while the polenta essentially cooks itself.

Try to find coarse cornmeal polenta here rather than the quick-cooking kind, as it simply won't yield the result that you're looking for. This is a great brunch dish, but will work equally well for lunch or a light dinner with a crunchy green salad. The polenta hardens as it sits, so eat this soon after it comes out of the oven.

1. Preheat the oven to 180°C fan.

2. Put the corn into a food processor and pulse once or twice, until just roughly chopped, then transfer to a large bowl. Add the spinach, herbs, spring onions, garlic, coarse polenta, Parmesan, 1½ teaspoons of salt and a good grind of pepper, stirring to combine. Put this mixture into a large, high-sided ovenproof sauté pan, then add the milk, stock and butter, stirring to mix through. Bake for 20 minutes, then remove from the oven and give everything a good whisk before returning it to the oven for another 20 minutes, or until the cornmeal is cooked through and the mixture has thickened. Give the polenta a good whisk – it should be smooth and not completely set – then stir in half the feta. Increase the oven temperature to 200°C fan.

3. Make eight wells in the polenta, cracking an egg into each and sprinkling lightly with salt and pepper. Sprinkle over the remaining feta and return to the oven for 12–14 minutes, or until the whites are cooked and the yolks are still runny.

4. Meanwhile, combine the extra coriander and spring onion in a bowl with the oil. Spoon this mixture all over the polenta once ready to serve, followed by a sprinkling of the chilli. Serve at once.

TOMATO SALAD WITH LIME AND CARDAMOM YOGHURT

SERVES FOUR

70g Greek-style yoghurt

50g soft, rindless goat's cheese

½ small garlic clove, crushed

1–2 limes: finely grate the zest to get 1 tsp, then juice to get 1½ tbsp

15 cardamom pods, skin discarded and seeds finely crushed (¾ tsp)

1 large green chilli, finely chopped (deseeded for less heat)

500g ripe, sweet cherry tomatoes, halved (or any other great, sweet tomato you can get)

1 large banana shallot, finely sliced (60g)

60ml olive oil

10g mint leaves, roughly torn

salt

This recipe has some useful takeaways. First, the timeless combination of tomatoes and finely sliced shallots, which is the base for an infinite number of summery salads, the simplest of which involves only a drizzle of oil and a splash of vinegar. Then there's the dressing made by mixing together yoghurt, soft goat's cheese and garlic; it's great for potato or cucumber salad, for example (just add lemon juice and some olive oil). Finally, tomato, lime and cardamom might not be a familiar combination but we absolutely adore it, either in a salad like this one or when cooked together, as in the sweet potato in tomato, lime and cardamom sauce (see p. 131). We urge you to try it. Serve with bread to soak up the tomato juices.

1. Mix the yoghurt, goat's cheese, garlic and a pinch of salt in a large bowl until smooth. Add half the lime zest, half the crushed cardamom and half the chilli and stir to combine.

2. In a separate bowl, mix together the tomatoes, shallot, lime juice, 2 tablespoons of oil and ½ teaspoon of salt with the remaining lime zest, cardamom and chilli, then add the yoghurt mixture and the mint. Gently mix everything together but not completely: you want to see the red of the tomatoes and the green of the mint in places. Transfer to a platter, drizzle with the remaining 2 tablespoons of oil, and serve.

KIMCHI AND GRUYÈRE RICE FRITTERS

3 tbsp olive oil
½ onion, finely chopped
3 garlic cloves, crushed
200ml whole milk
1 x 250g packet of
   cooked brown basmati
   and wild rice mix (or
   any other combination
   of cooked rice)
2 eggs, yolks and whites
   separated
500g good-quality
   classic kimchi (we like
   the Cultured Collective
   brand)
80g green beans,
   trimmed and finely
   chopped
1½ tbsp coriander, finely
   chopped
80g Gruyère, cut into
   1½cm cubes (you can
   use another mature
   cheese instead)
2 tbsp mixed black and
   white sesame seeds,
   toasted, plus an extra
   1½ tsp to serve
90g plain flour
800ml sunflower oil, for
   deep-frying
2 lemons: juice to get
   2 tbsp, then cut the
   remainder into wedges
   to serve
salt and flaked sea salt

These were conceived to make use of leftover rice, an open jar of kimchi and some scraps of cheese we had knocking about in the test kitchen fridge. While the contents of your fridge is likely to be different, we're pretty positive you will sometimes find leftover rice there and some cheese. For these (and other happy) occasions, these fritters are perfect.

If you don't happen to have leftover rice, though, you can easily make the fritters with ready-cooked rice or by cooking rice from scratch and letting it cool down. (Most rice will triple in volume and weight when cooked, so start with about 85g uncooked.) Any combination of white, brown or mixed rice will work, although we like the nuttiness of brown and wild.

The kimchi we use tends to have a lot of liquid, which we repurpose into a dipping sauce here, with the addition of lemon juice. Don't worry if your kimchi doesn't yield much liquid with which to make a sauce; the fritters are still absolutely delicious with just a simple squeeze of lemon or some hot sauce, if you have some to hand.

The fritters, which are great as a snack but also as part of a meal, can be fried up to 3 hours ahead. Simply heat up in the oven at 180°C fan for about 5 minutes, or until warmed through. *Pictured overleaf.*

1. Put the oil, onion and ¾ teaspoon of salt into a medium saucepan on a medium-high heat and gently fry for 6 minutes, stirring every now and then, until soft and golden. Add the garlic and continue to fry, stirring, for 30 seconds to 1 minute, until fragrant. Add the milk, lower the heat to medium and simmer gently for 5 minutes, until thickened and reduced a little. Remove from the heat and leave to cool for 5 minutes, then stir in the rice, egg yolks and ⅛ teaspoon of salt. Refrigerate for 30 minutes, or until completely cool.

2. Meanwhile, set 160g of the kimchi aside, to serve. Squeeze the rest of the kimchi through a sieve, collecting 3 tablespoons of the liquid in a small serving bowl (set this aside until later), and transferring the drained kimchi to a chopping board (you should have about 250g). Roughly chop the kimchi and add to the pan with the cooled rice mixture, along with the green beans, coriander, Gruyère, sesame seeds and flour. Stir until fully combined.

3. Whip the egg whites with a small pinch of salt, either by hand or with an electric whisk, until you get medium-stiff peaks. Gently fold the egg whites through the rice mixture until combined, taking care not to overmix.

4. Heat the oil in a large high-sided saucepan on
it reaches about 180°C. Test the oil is hot enough
of batter; it should sizzle but shouldn't turn golden
the fritters in batches of three, to avoid lowering th⸺⸺⸺⸺ oil
too much. Using a large serving spoon, carefully drop around 90g of batter
per fritter into the oil and fry for 4–5 minutes, turning a few times until
crisp and golden-brown all over. You may need to turn the heat down if the
fritters are browning too quickly. Transfer the fritters to a tray lined with
kitchen paper and continue in the same way with the remaining batter.

5. Add the lemon juice to the bowl of kimchi liquid. Transfer the fritters to
a large platter, sprinkling over the remaining sesame seeds and some flaked
salt. Serve hot with the kimchi sauce, the lemon wedges and with the reserved
kimchi alongside.

ASPARAGUS SALAD WITH TAMARIND AND LIME

SERVES FOUR
As a side

400g thick-stemmed **asparagus,** woody ends trimmed

1½ tbsp olive oil

1 tbsp lime juice

15g mint leaves, roughly shredded

30g pistachios, very lightly toasted and roughly chopped

salt

TAMARIND AND LIME DRESSING

35g picked mint leaves

15g parsley, roughly chopped

1 tbsp white wine vinegar

1 tbsp runny honey

2 tsp shop-bought tamarind paste, or double if you're extracting it yourself from pulp (see p. 20)

1 anchovy fillet in olive oil, drained (optional, but adjust seasoning if not using)

½ tsp ground cardamom

½ tsp ground black lime (optional; see p. 18)

2 green chillies, deseeded and finely chopped

1 small garlic clove, crushed

1 tsp Dijon mustard

1 tsp lime zest

2 tbsp olive oil

We surprised ourselves twice with this salad: first, by how good raw asparagus can taste and feel in the mouth when sliced super thin; and, second, by how well it holds its own and actually benefits when being matched with intensely sharp ingredients such as tamarind and lime. Try it next time you get your hands on a bunch of extra-fresh, but not too thin (these will be hard to slice) asparagus spears.

You'll make more dressing than you need here, but it will keep in a sealed jar in the fridge for up to 3 days, ready to be tossed through salads or drizzled on roasted vegetables. It will discolour a little, but will still be fine to eat.

Slice the asparagus and mix the salad just before serving, to keep the thin asparagus slices as crunchy as possible.

Serve with fried tofu, roast chicken or alongside the potato and gochujang braised eggs (p. 99) for a light lunch or dinner.

1. Blitz all the ingredients for the dressing together with 2 tablespoons of water and ¼ teaspoon of salt, either in a food processor or a spice grinder (for a smoother sauce), until you have a thick paste. Spoon into a clean jar and refrigerate for up to 3 days.

2. Using a vegetable peeler, or a mandolin if you have one, finely slice the asparagus into long strips and mix with half the oil, half the lime juice, half the mint, half the pistachios and ⅛ teaspoon of salt. Transfer to a serving platter or bowl and set aside.

3. In a small bowl, stir together 2 tablespoons of the dressing with the remaining oil and lime juice and ⅛ teaspoon of salt. Spoon the dressing over the asparagus, finish with the remaining mint and pistachios and serve at once.

CARDAMOM TOFU WITH LIME GREENS

SERVES FOUR
As a main

100g plain flour
100g cornflour
1½ tbsp ground cardamom
900ml sunflower oil, for deep-frying, plus 2½ tbsp
700g firm silken tofu, cut into 2½cm squares
6 garlic cloves, thinly sliced
2 red chillies, finely sliced into rounds
600g choi sum, base trimmed and leaves and stalks separated and cut into 5cm lengths (500g)
2 tbsp sriracha hot sauce
3 tbsp soy sauce
2 limes: juice to get 2 tsp, then cut the remainder into wedges to serve
salt and black pepper

Aptly named, silken tofu genuinely delivers on the promise of super-smooth, light and creamy texture. Frying it, as we do here, creates a crisp crust which highlights this texture even more and, as frying does, makes it irresistible. It's definitely the one you want to serve your tofu-sceptic friends if you need them to 'see the light', as we heard from our recipe tester, Claudine Boulstridge.

This dish is great on its own for a light supper but you can also bulk it up with some rice, with extra soy sauce. Morning glory or large spinach will also work well here if you can't get hold of choi sum.

1. Place the plain flour, cornflour, cardamom, 2½ teaspoons salt and plenty of pepper in a medium bowl. Mix together and set aside.

2. Put 900ml of oil into a large, high-sided sauté pan or wok on a medium heat. Once the oil is hot (just under 180°C if you have a temperature probe), toss the tofu in the flour. In batches, carefully lower the cubes of tofu into the hot oil and fry for 3–4 minutes, turning halfway, until crisp and golden-brown. Use a slotted spoon to transfer the tofu to a plate lined with kitchen paper. Keep warm while you continue with the remaining batches. For the next step, you can use the same pan by transferring the oil to a heatproof container to be discarded once it has cooled (or you can use another large sauté pan or wok).

3. If using the same pan, wipe it clean, then dry well. Return the pan to a high heat with the remaining 2½ tablespoons of oil. Once hot, add the garlic and chillies and fry for 1–2 minutes, until the garlic is a light golden-brown. Add the choi sum stalks and stir-fry for 4 minutes, then add the leaves and fry, continuing to stir, until they are wilted, about 2 minutes.

4. Add the sriracha, soy sauce, lime juice and 1 tablespoon of water and stir through for a minute, until the liquid is bubbling. Divide between four plates and top with the crispy tofu. Serve at once, with the lime wedges squeezed on top.

BRAISED GREENS WITH YOGH

SERVES FOUR
As a side or as part of a
spread

1 **dried black lime** (see p.
   18), pierced a few times
   with a small sharp knife
60ml **olive oil**
1 **onion,** thinly sliced (150g)
3 **garlic cloves,** crushed
1 tsp **ground cinnamon**
35g **dill,** roughly chopped
35g **coriander,** roughly
   chopped
35g **parsley,** roughly
   chopped
4 **spring onions,** thinly
   sliced (60g)
300g **cavolo nero,** woody
   stems discarded and
   leaves roughly shredded
   (180g)
300g **Greek-style
   yoghurt**
1 tsp **dried mint**
salt and **black pepper**

Mixing extraordinary quantities of chopped herbs with lim
soups, stews or braises is such a genius way of using herbs
do anything else with them. This is the base for many popular dishes in Iran and
across the Gulf countries, and it is one we adopt whenever we can (see herb
and burnt aubergine soup, p. 42). We use black lime here for an intense hit of
earthy acidity (see p. 18 for more on black limes). If you can't get your hands
on dried limes, black or otherwise, substitute with half a regular fresh lime (no
need to soak), pips removed and flesh and rind finely chopped, adding 120ml of
water when the reserved soaking liquid is called for.

   Make the greens up to a few hours in advance, and warm up to serve, if you
want to get ahead.

   These greens are best served with saffron (or plain, if you prefer) rice.

1. Place the lime in a small bowl with 150ml of boiling water and top with
a smaller plate or saucer to fully submerge. Leave for 20 minutes to soften
slightly. Remove the lime, setting it aside until needed and reserving the water.

2. Put 3 tablespoons of oil into a large sauté pan on a medium heat. Once
hot, add the onion and the soaked black lime and cook, stirring occasionally,
until the onions are softened and lightly caramelised, about 20 minutes. Add
the garlic and cinnamon and cook for 2 minutes more, then remove the lime
and set aside. Add 30g of each of the herbs and all the spring onions and
cook for 15 minutes, stirring often, until fragrant and deeply green (you may
need to turn the heat down if they start to catch).

3. Meanwhile, finely chop the black lime and return it to the pan as the
herbs cook. Stir in the cavolo nero, reserved black lime water, 1 teaspoon
of salt and a good grind of black pepper, then increase the heat to medium-
high and cook for 10 minutes more, until the liquid has been absorbed
and the cavolo nero has softened. Remove from the heat and stir in the
remaining herbs. Keep warm until needed.

4. Put the yoghurt, mint and ¼ teaspoon of salt into a bowl and mix well
to combine. Spread the yoghurt over the base of a serving platter, creating
a slight well in the centre. Spoon the greens into the centre and drizzle with
the remaining tablespoon of olive oil.

1 tbsp apple cider
  vinegar
2 tsp caster sugar
1 small red onion, thinly
  sliced into rounds on a
  mandolin, if you have
  one, or by hand (60g)
600ml sunflower oil, for
  deep-frying
2 blocks of extra-firm
  tofu (560g), patted dry
  and cut into 2cm cubes
2 tbsp cornflour
2 onions (300g), roughly
  chopped
6 garlic cloves, roughly
  chopped
60ml olive oil
2 tsp cumin seeds,
  roughly crushed in a
  pestle and mortar
2–3 dried black limes
  (see p. 18), blitzed in
  a spice grinder to get
  2 tbsp (10g – use a food
  processor if you don't
  have a grinder, and
  pass through a sieve)
  (if you can't get any
  black limes, substitute
  with 1 tbsp lime juice
  and 1 tbsp lime zest)
2 tbsp tomato paste
20g parsley, roughly
  chopped
250g baby spinach
salt and black pepper

NOOR'S BLACK LIME TOFU

Dried limes have been a constant in the Ottolenghi pantry for years. Recently, though, we have been using them with extra vigour thanks to Noor Murad, our test kitchen colleague who grew up in Bahrain, where they consume dried limes intravenously (well, not literally). There the limes go by different names and come in different colours. Go for the black variety, if you can, though paler limes are also fine (see p. 18 for more on black limes).

We like to serve this dish with steamed rice or warm flatbreads.

1. Put the vinegar, 1 teaspoon of sugar, the red onion and $\frac{1}{8}$ teaspoon of salt into a small bowl and mix well to combine. Set aside to pickle while you continue with the rest.

2. Heat the sunflower oil in a medium high-sided sauté pan on a medium-high heat. Toss the tofu in a bowl with the cornflour until well coated. Once hot, fry the tofu (in two batches) until crispy and lightly browned, about 6 minutes per batch, then transfer to a plate lined with kitchen paper and set aside.

3. While the tofu is frying, prepare the sauce. Put the onions and garlic into a food processor and pulse a few times until very finely minced but not puréed. Put the olive oil into a large sauté pan on a medium-high heat. Add the onion mixture and cook, stirring occasionally, until softened and lightly browned, about 10 minutes. Add the cumin, black limes (or regular lime zest and juice) and tomato paste and cook for 1 minute more. Add 400ml of water, the remaining 1 teaspoon of sugar, 1 ¼ teaspoons of salt and a generous grind of pepper. Bring to a simmer and cook for 6 minutes, stirring occasionally, until thick and rich. Add the crispy tofu, parsley and another grind of pepper and stir to coat. Add the spinach in increments, stirring until just wilted, about 3 minutes.

4. To serve, transfer the mixture to a shallow serving platter and top with the pickled red onion (or serve straight from the pan).

SERVES FOUR
As a main

STICKY RICE BALLS IN TAMARIND RASAM BROTH

——————

TAMARIND RASAM
50g block of tamarind pulp
30g fresh ginger, skin on and thinly sliced
15g fresh turmeric, skin on and thinly sliced
1 large green chilli, roughly sliced (20g)
250g cherry tomatoes
2½ tbsp sunflower oil
½ lemon, halved again lengthways, then cut into ¼cm-thick half-moons (pips removed)
1½ tsp cumin seeds, finely crushed
1 tsp black mustard seeds
2 whole dried red chillies
20 fresh curry leaves (if you can't get any, you can also do without)
3 garlic cloves, crushed
3–4 plum tomatoes (300g), coarsely grated and skins discarded (250g)
2 tsp caster sugar
salt

RICE BALLS
200g Thai sticky rice, soaked for 1 hour in plenty of cold water, then drained well
2 tbsp sunflower oil, plus extra for shaping
1 onion, finely chopped (150g)
2 garlic cloves, crushed
15g fresh ginger, peeled and finely grated
10g coriander, roughly chopped, plus extra picked leaves and their stalks to garnish
2 spring onions, thinly sliced (30g)

Our version of rasam, a South Indian broth, is sharp, complex and rich from the spices and the charring of tomatoes and lemons. We urge you to try it, despite the longish ingredient list, if only to discover a whole range of new flavours.

Use tamarind pulp here, not paste. The pulp, available in any Indian supermarket, is more complex in flavour and provides the sweet–acid kick that you're after here (see more about tamarind on p. 20).

You'll need to soak the rice for an hour in water. The balls can be formed a day ahead and kept refrigerated in a sealed container. Just bring them back up to room temperature before pouring over the hot broth.

1. For the rasam, add the first four ingredients, 1.2 litres of water and 1 teaspoon of salt to a medium saucepan on a medium-high heat. Bring to the boil, then lower the heat to medium and simmer gently for 20 minutes, stirring to break apart the tamarind pulp. Strain through a sieve into a bowl, pushing down to extract as much flavour as possible. Discard the aromatics.

2. Meanwhile, put the rice into a medium saucepan, for which you have a lid, along with 220ml of water and ¾ teaspoon of salt. Bring to the boil on a medium-high heat, then lower the heat to medium-low and cover loosely with the lid, leaving a small gap for some steam to escape. Cook for 20 minutes, then remove from the heat and let sit, uncovered, until cool.

3. Toss the tomatoes in 1½ teaspoons of oil. Place a large sauté pan on a high heat. Once smoking, add the tomatoes and cook, tossing occasionally, until charred and blistered, about 4 minutes. Set aside. Add the lemons and cook until charred, 30–50 seconds per side, then set aside. Turn the heat down to medium-high, add the remaining 2 tablespoons of oil, the cumin and mustard seeds, dried chillies, curry leaves (if using) and garlic and cook for 90 seconds, until fragrant. Add the grated tomatoes and cook for 5 minutes more, then add the sugar, tamarind liquid, charred tomatoes and ½ teaspoon of salt. Bring back up to the boil and simmer for 8 minutes. Set aside while you prepare the rice balls.

4. For the rice balls, put the oil into a sauté pan on a medium-high heat. Add the onion and cook for 7 minutes, until softened and browned. Add the garlic and ginger and cook for 90 seconds. Remove from the heat and transfer to a bowl with the cooked rice, coriander and spring onion. Mix well. With lightly oiled hands, form into twelve balls, weighing 30–35g each.

5. To serve, return the pan of rasam to a medium-high heat to heat through, then add the charred lemon slices and the sticky rice balls. Top with the picked coriander and serve.

SERVES FOUR
As a side

RAINBOW CHARD WITH TOMATOES AND GREEN OLIVES

_____

400g rainbow chard, bases trimmed, leaves and stalks separated and each cut into 6cm lengths
125ml olive oil
5 garlic cloves, finely sliced
1 small onion, finely chopped (110g)
1 lemon: finely shave the skin to get 2 strips, then juice to get 1 tbsp
2–3 oregano sprigs (10g)
2–3 ripe plum tomatoes, cut into 1cm dice (300g)
120g Nocellara olives (or another green olive), pitted and halved or quartered if large (70g)
5g basil leaves, roughly torn
salt and black pepper

This summery side dish will really benefit from using the best-quality, ripe tomatoes. Rainbow chard looks beautiful but, for flavour, Swiss chard will do an equally good job here. Swiss chard stalks tend to be wider, though, so you may need to cut them three times lengthways, as well as widthways.

This dish is great served warm soon after it's made, but the flavours actually get better with time. Make it a few hours ahead, if you like, or even the day before, and serve it at room temperature, or gently warmed through. There's quite a lot of aromatic oil, so grab some crusty bread to mop it up with.

Serve alongside the za'atar cacio e pepe (p. 104) for a quick midweek dinner.

1. Cut any wider chard stalks in half lengthways (or into three if they are particularly wide). Place a large sauté pan on a medium-high heat with 1 teaspoon of oil. Add the chard stalks and sauté for 4 minutes, then add the leaves and sauté for another 3 minutes, until the leaves are just cooked. Transfer to a large bowl, cover with a plate and leave to soften in the residual heat for another 3 minutes, then remove the plate.

2. Wipe the pan clean and return to a medium heat with 90ml of the oil. Add the garlic, onion, lemon strips and oregano and gently fry for 12 minutes, stirring often, until the onion is soft and golden. Add the tomatoes, ½ teaspoon of salt and a good grind of pepper and continue to cook until the tomatoes are just beginning to soften (about 2 minutes if they are ripe, or a couple of minutes longer if they are not). Stir in the cooked chard and the olives, then remove from the heat and leave to sit for 5 minutes, for the flavours to come together.

3. Discard the oregano sprigs and lemon strips and transfer to a lipped platter. Drizzle over the lemon juice and the remaining 2 tablespoons of oil. Finish with the basil leaves and a good grind of pepper, and serve.

TEMPURA STEMS, LEAVES AND HERBS

SERVES SIX
As a snack or a little starter

70g beetroot stems and leaves, stems cut into 8cm lengths, washed and patted dry

20g dill, patted dry and separated into 8cm fronds

10g mint, patted dry, leaves picked

½ tbsp Szechuan peppercorns, crushed in a pestle and mortar

flaked sea salt

TANGERINE DIPPING SAUCE

50ml tangerine juice, with bits (from 2–3 tangerines)

3 tbsp lime juice

1½ tsp maple syrup

½ small garlic clove, finely chopped

4 fresh kaffir lime leaves, stalks discarded and leaves finely chopped

½ red chilli, deseeded and finely chopped

BATTER

80g self-raising flour

80g cornflour, plus an extra 50g for dipping

210ml ice-cold sparkling water (small bits of ice welcome)

1½ tbsp black sesame seeds

700ml sunflower oil, for deep-frying

Huge quantities of beets are roasted across the Ottolenghi restaurants, so we're always on the lookout for clever ways of using the stems and leaves. In ROVI in particular, where an imposing Spanish grill is both the restaurant's pièce de resistance and the place where many a root goes to get cooked and receive its smoky bouquet, we end up with big piles of tops and trimmings.

This dish might be the 'solution' to ROVI's highly popular hasselback beetroots (see p. 50), but it's totally brilliant in its own right (the two go very well together as part of the ROVI spread; see p. 303), with a super-crisp crust and a sweet and sour dipping sauce to counteract the oil. If you don't have beetroot stems and leaves, though, fear not – many different combinations of herbs, stems and leaves will work here. Try it with basil, parsley, sage or chard, for example. Just make sure the leaves are not limp and wet or, conversely, hard and dry. The batter will be enough for 100g of leaves and herbs of your choosing.

Organisation is key whenever you're frying, and especially with tempura. Make sure your prep is done well before the oil gets too hot, and that you have a slotted spoon and a rack lined with kitchen paper at the ready. Tempura doesn't sit too well, so try to eat it as soon as it's all been fried.

1. In a small serving bowl, stir together all the ingredients for the dipping sauce with ⅛ teaspoon of flaked salt and set aside.

2. Put the flour, the 80g of cornflour, the sparkling water, black sesame seeds and 1 teaspoon of flaked salt into a large bowl and whisk gently, not vigorously, until the mixture just comes together.

3. Pour the oil into a medium high-sided sauté pan and place on a high heat. Once very hot (just under 180°C if you have a temperature probe), reduce the heat to medium and test the heat by dropping in a little batter; it should sizzle but shouldn't brown straight away. In batches, toss the stems, leaves and herbs in the 50g of cornflour, shake to remove any excess, then dip in the batter. Lift, shake the excess batter over the bowl, then place in the oil as many pieces as can comfortably fit without touching. Fry for 30–60 seconds on each side, until crisp and pale golden, then transfer to a rack lined with kitchen paper, using a slotted spoon. Continue in the same way with the rest, then sprinkle the lot with the Szechuan pepper and a generous amount of flaked salt. Transfer to a platter and serve hot with the dipping sauce alongside.

BROCCOLI TWO WAYS WITH CHILLI AND CUMIN

SERVES FOUR
As a side

700g broccoli (that's about 2 heads), cut into bite-size florets, stems reserved
3 tbsp apple cider vinegar
½ red chilli, thinly sliced into rounds (5g)
35ml light soy sauce
2 tsp caster sugar
500ml sunflower oil, for deep-frying
5g basil leaves, roughly torn
⅓ tsp cumin seeds, toasted and roughly crushed in a pestle and mortar
salt

Unlike its cousins, cauliflower and cabbage, broccoli isn't very comfortable being cooked for a long while. All our past attempts at being clever and creating equivalents of cauliflower cheese, for example, only with broccoli at the centre, were total fiascos. The creamy sauce simply couldn't hold its own against the dominant broccoli, which went grey and soggy and miserable-looking. To keep things bright green and the broccoli generally happy, we recommend high-impact cooking, like frying, as we do here, grilling (see broccoli with mushroom ketchup and nori, p. 227) or charring.

The fried broccoli florets, tossed in sweetened soy, may remind you of similar Chinese dishes you had out of takeaway boxes. Here, they are combined with broccoli stems, which have been quickly pickled, so the richness is balanced with light acidity. Double the recipe to turn it into a main course, and serve with some sticky rice alongside.

Get ahead by pickling the broccoli stems up to 3 hours before, if you like, but not for any longer, or they'll lose their crunch. *Pictured overleaf.*

1. Trim each broccoli stem into a rough rectangle (they don't need to be perfectly rectangular). Use a mandolin to shave each stem lengthways into thin strips, or finely slice by hand. Stacking a few pieces on top of each other at a time, slice them into fine julienne strips. Place in a bowl along with ½ teaspoon of salt and toss well to combine. Leave to sit for 1 hour, then use your hands to gently squeeze out some of the salty liquid. Place in a clean bowl along with 2 tablespoons of vinegar and the chilli and mix well to combine. Set aside to pickle while you continue with the rest, or for up to 3 hours.

2. Put the soy sauce, sugar and remaining tablespoon of vinegar into a small saucepan on a medium-high heat. Bring to the boil, simmer for 2 minutes, then remove from the heat and set aside to cool. It will thicken as it sits.

3. Put the sunflower oil into a medium high-sided saucepan on a high heat. Once very hot (the broccoli should sizzle and begin to colour as soon as it touches the oil), fry the broccoli florets, a handful at a time, until softened and golden in places, about 45 seconds per batch (about six batches in total). You want the oil to be quite hot, so allow it to come back up to temperature if it cools down too much. Transfer to a tray lined with kitchen paper and continue with the rest. In a large bowl, toss the fried broccoli with the soy sauce mixture until well coated.

4. To serve, spread half the pickled broccoli mixture on a round plate, followed by the fried broccoli. Top with the remaining pickled broccoli mixture, and the basil and crushed cumin.

ROASTED CARROT SALAD W
CHAMOY

_____

1kg carrots, peeled and
cut at an angle into
8cm x 1cm batons
3 tbsp olive oil, plus
1½ tbsp to serve
1½ tbsp maple syrup
10g mint leaves
5g dill, roughly chopped
8 dried apricots, finely
sliced (70g)
**30g ready-roasted
and salted almonds,**
roughly chopped
salt and black pepper

CHAMOY
40g dried apricots
1 tsp maple syrup
2 tsp sumac
45ml lime juice, plus
2 tsp to serve
**1½ tsp Aleppo chilli
flakes** (or ¾ tsp regular
chilli flakes)
1 small garlic clove
2 tbsp olive oil

If you need to capture Ixta in a single foodstuff, look
It's made of pickled fruit (tick for pickle), lime juice (tick) and chilli (tick) and it
hails from Mexico (one big massive tick). It is sweet, salty, sour and spicy – all at
once – and it has a dramatic effect on any ingredient you pair it with: meat, fish,
vegetables and even fresh fruit. Traditional versions can range from liquid to
a paste-like consistency. Our (very) untraditional take on chamoy uses sumac
and Aleppo chilli, and dried instead of pickled apricots. It's a combination that
works well, but feel free to experiment with other dried or fresh chillies.

Double the chamoy recipe, if you like, and keep half in the fridge for up to a
week, ready to use as a marinade or condiment for roasted vegetables, chicken
or pork. The carrots can be roasted and dressed the day before, if you want to
get ahead, and finished with the herbs, extra apricots and nuts when you're
ready to serve.

This is great as part of a vegetarian spread (see p. 304), and also alongside
fatty cuts of meat, such as pork belly or duck breast. *Pictured overleaf.*

1. Preheat the oven to 240°C fan.

2. In a large bowl, mix the carrots with the oil, maple syrup, 1 ¼ teaspoons
of salt and a good grind of pepper. Spread them out as much as possible
over two large, 40cm x 30cm, parchment-lined baking trays and roast for 18
minutes, tossing the carrots and swapping the trays halfway through, until
the carrots are nicely browned but still retain a bite.

3. While the carrots are roasting, blitz all the ingredients for the chamoy with
¼ teaspoon of salt in a spice grinder (or the small bowl of a food processor)
to get a smooth paste.

4. As soon as the carrots are cooked, transfer them to a large bowl with the
chamoy, mix well and leave for 20 minutes for the flavours to come together.

5. Mix the carrots with the herbs and sliced apricots and transfer to a
serving platter. Finish with the almonds and the remaining oil and lime
juice, and serve.

SERVES FOUR
As a side

CUCUMBER, ZA'ATAR AND CHOPPED LEMON SALAD

————

3 lemons
4½ tbsp olive oil
1¼ tsp dried mint
1½ tsp za'atar
1 banana shallot, halved lengthways and finely sliced (40g)
1½ green chillies, finely sliced into strips (deseeded for less heat)
1 large cucumber, halved lengthways, watery centre scooped out, cut at an angle into ½cm-thick slices (450g)
60g lamb's lettuce
10g dill, roughly chopped
10g basil leaves
5g mint leaves
salt

This salad makes a seriously crisp and refreshing impact, thanks to all the lemon that goes into it: juice, flesh and skin. It will sit happily alongside virtually any dish in the book. The za'atar gives it a little extra edge, but leave it out if there's already a lot going on in any other dishes you're making.

1. Squeeze 1–2 lemons to get 2½ tablespoons of juice and put it into a large serving bowl. Cut seven thin slices from the remaining lemon, saving any extra for another recipe. Discard any pips, then pile the slices on top of each other. Remove and discard half the rind, then finely chop the slices, including the remaining rind, and add to the bowl along with the oil, dried mint, za'atar, shallots, green chillies, cucumber and 1 teaspoon of salt. Mix well, then add the lamb's lettuce and all the herbs, toss gently and serve at once.

MASHED SWEET POTATOES WITH YOGHURT AND LIME

2–3 purple (or regular orange) sweet potatoes, peeled and cut into 2cm pieces (550g)

40ml olive oil

2 limes: finely grate the zest to get 1½ tsp, then cut into wedges to serve

200g Greek-style yoghurt

½ small garlic clove, crushed

1½ tsp pomegranate molasses

2 tsp coriander leaves, finely sliced

½ large red chilli, deseeded and finely chopped

1½ tsp sesame seeds, toasted

salt

If you, or your taste buds, are feeling a bit sleepy, this mash will definitely shake things up for you. It's got an inbuilt tension between deep sweetness and extreme sharpness and it will sit amazingly well in the middle of a jolly mezze selection.

The mash can be made with purple sweet potatoes or with the more familiar orange or golden varieties. The purple potatoes are slightly more savoury, with a complex flavour that is smoky, almost bacon-like. They also look striking (be ready for an electric-violet psychedelic surprise in your cooking water).

Purple sweet potatoes tend to be drier than their orange cousins, so if you're using them, be sure to keep the cooking water once they've been boiled – you may need to use it to help loosen the mash.

The mash can be prepared the day before and kept refrigerated if you want to get ahead, assembling when you're ready to serve.

Serve as part of a dip spread (see p. 304), along with some grilled flatbreads.

1. Put the sweet potato and ¾ teaspoon of salt into a small saucepan. Pour over enough boiling water so that it rises just above the potatoes, put on a medium-high heat and cook for 10–12 minutes, until soft enough to mash. Drain the potatoes well (reserving the cooking water – you may need some to loosen the mash). Add 2 tablespoons of oil, then mash until smooth. Allow to cool slightly, then stir in half the lime zest and 2 tablespoons of the yoghurt until combined. Spoon on to a serving plate, creating dips with the back of the spoon.

2. Combine the remaining yoghurt with the garlic and spoon evenly over the mash. Drizzle over the pomegranate molasses and the remaining 2 teaspoons of oil, followed by the coriander, chilli, sesame seeds and the remaining lime zest. Season with a pinch of salt and serve with the lime wedges alongside.

CHAAT MASALA POTATOES WITH YOGHURT AND TAMARIND

750g baby new potatoes, cut lengthways into 1cm-thick slices
2 tbsp olive oil
1 tsp chaat masala
½ tsp ground turmeric
250g Greek-style yoghurt
½ small red onion, peeled and thinly sliced into rounds on a mandolin, if you have one, or by hand (45g)
1 green chilli, thinly sliced into rounds (10g)
1½ tsp coriander seeds, toasted
1½ tsp nigella seeds, toasted
salt

CORIANDER CHUTNEY
30g fresh coriander
1 green chilli, deseeded and roughly chopped (10g)
1 tbsp lime juice
60ml olive oil

SWEET TAMARIND DRESSING
1½ tbsp shop-bought tamarind paste, or double if you're extracting it yourself from pulp (see p. 20)
1½ tsp caster sugar
¼ tsp chaat masala

This dish is inspired by aloo chaat, an Indian street food that has many regional variations, all of which are not for the faint-hearted because they are loaded with sweet and sour and a fair bit of crunch. This is a slightly tamer version, though still pretty 'noisy', both in flavour and in looks. It's absolutely perfect for a weekend lunch, alongside other vegetables, such as the aubergine with herbs and crispy garlic (p. 251), or the radish and cucumber salad with chipotle peanuts (p. 263). You can also serve it as a side with roasted lamb or chicken.

Chaat masala is the slightly tangy spice mix that gives this dish its distinctive flavour. It gets its sharpness from amchoor, dried mango powder, which is used widely in Indian cooking as a souring agent. You'd recognise the flavour from samosas and pakoras, where it is often used.

Both the coriander chutney and the tamarind sauce are great condiments to have on hand to brighten up sandwiches and wraps, to spoon over eggs, or to serve alongside tofu or fish. Double or triple them, if you like – the coriander chutney will keep in the fridge for up to a week and the tamarind sauce for up to 2 weeks. *Pictured overleaf.*

1. Preheat the oven to 220°C fan.

2. Put the potatoes and 2 teaspoons of salt into a medium saucepan and top with enough cold water to cover by about 4cm. Place on a medium-high heat, bring to the boil, then simmer for 6 minutes, or until they're almost cooked through but still retain a bite. Drain through a sieve and pat dry, then transfer to a large parchment-lined baking tray and toss with the oil, chaat masala, turmeric, ⅓ teaspoon of salt and a good grind of pepper. Roast, stirring once or twice, for 35 minutes, or until deeply golden.

3. Meanwhile, make the coriander chutney. Put all the ingredients and ¼ teaspoon of salt into the small bowl of a food processor and blitz until smooth. Set aside until needed.

4. For the tamarind dressing, whisk together all the ingredients in a small bowl with 1 ½ teaspoons of water and set aside.

5. Spread the yoghurt out on a large round serving platter. Top with the coriander chutney, swirling it through without completely incorporating. Drizzle with half the tamarind dressing, and top with the potatoes, onion and chilli. Drizzle over the remaining tamarind, then sprinkle over the seeds and serve.

CABBAGE WITH GINGER CREAM AND NUMBING OIL

SERVES FOUR
As a side

50g fresh ginger, peeled and finely grated
220g cream cheese
¼ garlic clove, crushed
1 tbsp lime juice
1 pointed cabbage, ends trimmed, halved lengthways and leaves separated (820g)
1½ tbsp soy sauce
salt

NUMBING OIL
150ml sunflower oil
1 banana shallot, finely chopped (60g)
2 garlic cloves, finely chopped
10g fresh ginger, peeled and finely grated
½ red chilli, finely chopped
1 whole star anise
1 tbsp red bell pepper flakes
1 tsp chilli flakes
1½ tsp Szechuan peppercorns, roughly crushed
1½ tsp tomato paste
1 tsp black sesame seeds
1 tsp white sesame seeds

Yotam and Ixta share a love for the unassuming (but downright brilliant) Xi'an Impression restaurant in north London. Highlights there include cold noodles, cold poached chicken and smacked cucumbers (which inspired our cucumber salad à la Xi'an Impression, p. 113). These are all unique, but they are also unified by a wondrous aromatic oil that they are absolutely swimming in. Since we couldn't figure out how to make this oil, we came up with our own version.

Serve this cabbage with fried tofu, for example (see cardamom tofu with lime greens, p. 172), soy-roasted chicken or fried fish. Alternatively, have it with a host of aromatic dishes, such as the kohlrabi 'noodle' salad (p. 260), the tomato and plum salad with nori and sesame (p. 267) and the cucumber salad we mentioned (p. 113), along with a big bowl of rice.

You'll make more oil than you need, but you can store it in the fridge for up to 2 weeks, ready to serve alongside fried tofu, meat or fish, or to spoon over rice or noodles.

1. For the numbing oil, heat 2 tablespoons of sunflower oil in a small saucepan on a medium-high heat. Add the next eight ingredients and ¼ teaspoon of salt. Turn the heat down to medium and fry very gently for 5 minutes, stirring often, until the shallot is soft. Add the tomato paste and all the sesame seeds and cook for another 2 minutes. Stir in the remaining 120ml of oil, then reduce the heat to low and simmer very gently for 10 minutes. If the oil starts to bubble at all, just take it off the heat for a minute. Leave to cool and infuse for at least an hour.

2. Meanwhile, press the 50g of grated ginger through a fine-mesh sieve into a medium bowl to get 2 tablespoons of ginger juice. Discard the pulp. Add the cream cheese, garlic, lime juice and a good pinch of salt and whisk until smooth.

3. Bring a large pot of well-salted water to the boil. Blanch the cabbage leaves for 2 minutes, until just cooked. Drain through a sieve, then pat the leaves dry with kitchen paper – they shouldn't be wet. Leave to cool.

4. Combine the soy sauce with 3 tablespoons of the numbing oil and 1 tablespoon of the aromatics at the bottom of the oil. Spread the ginger cream on a platter, pile the cabbage leaves on top, then drizzle the oil and soy mixture evenly over and serve at once.

SAFFRON TAGLIATELLE

——————

¼ tsp saffron threads, soaked in 2½ tbsp boiling water for at least 20 minutes

225g '00' grade pasta flour, plus extra for dusting

70g fine semolina

2 eggs, plus 2 yolks

This pasta first came about because of the saffron tagliatelle with ricotta and crispy chipotle shallots recipe (see opposite). It is also delicious with our ultimate traybake ragù (see p. 101), the mushroom ragù from the spicy mushroom lasagne (see p. 228), or just with a plain tomato sauce, Parmesan and some olive oil. You will need a pasta machine to roll out the pasta. *Pictured overleaf.*

1. For the pasta, place all the ingredients (including the saffron soaking water) in the large bowl of a food processor and pulse for around 30 seconds to get the texture of sticky breadcrumbs. Tip the dough on to a lightly floured surface and knead vigorously for 7 minutes, until the dough becomes smooth and pliable. Shape it into a circle, wrap with cling film and leave to rest at room temperature for half an hour.

2. Secure the pasta machine to your work surface. Divide the dough into four pieces and keep them well covered. Removing one piece at a time, shape the dough into a rectangle, then roll it through the widest setting of the machine twice, dusting it with a little flour as you go. Fold the ragged sides to meet in the middle like a French door, then turn the sheet and roll it back through the machine twice, dusting as you go, so all sides are straight. Click the machine to the next setting and roll the pasta through twice, dusting as you go. Continue in the same way, rolling the pasta through each setting twice until you get to the fifth setting (or the one before the last; you don't want the pasta to be too thin).

3. Fold up the long pasta sheet four times along its length, sprinkling flour between the layers so they don't stick together. Use a sharp knife to cut the pasta at 2cm intervals, to make wide tagliatelle. Hang them on the back of a chair to dry while you continue with the rest. Arrange the tagliatelle into nests, flouring as you go, and place them on a floured tray. If you are making the saffron tagliatelle with ricotta and crispy chipotle shallots opposite, set your uncooked pasta aside now, covered, ready to be cooked when needed.

4. If you are not making the recipe opposite, cook the tagliatelle by bringing a large pot of salted water to the boil (the pot needs to be large so the pasta doesn't clump). Add the pasta and cook for 1 minute, stirring with a fork to separate the strands. Drain, toss together with your chosen sauce and serve.

SAFFRON TAGLIATELLE WITH RICOTTA AND CRISPY CHIPOTLE SHALLOTS

_____

50ml olive oil
3 garlic cloves, crushed
400g shop-bought fresh tagliatelle (or 1 quantity of saffron tagliatelle; see opposite)
¼ tsp saffron threads, soaked in 2½ tbsp boiling water for at least 20 minutes (double the saffron if using shop-bought pasta rather than the homemade saffron tagliatelle)
10g parsley, finely chopped, plus an extra ½ tbsp to serve
60g Parmesan, finely grated
120g ricotta
salt and black pepper

CRISPY CHIPOTLE SHALLOTS
2 tbsp olive oil
3–4 shallots, thinly sliced on a mandolin if you have one, or by hand, and rings pulled apart (150g)
2 tbsp maple syrup
¾ tsp coriander seeds
¾ tsp cumin seeds
½ tsp chipotle flakes

PICKLED GREEN CHILLIES
2 large green chillies, finely sliced into rounds (30g)
2 tbsp rice vinegar
½ tsp caster sugar

You can use shop-bought fresh or dried pasta here, or make your own saffron tagliatelle (see opposite). Either way, there is so much going on – from the Parmesan sauce to the pickled chillies to the crispy chipotle shallots – that you are sure to both surprise and delight the lucky recipients of this dish.

If you're making fresh pasta, have all your prep done before you boil the pasta because it only takes a minute or so to cook. *Pictured overleaf.*

1. For the shallots, heat the oil in a large, non-stick frying pan on a high heat. Once hot, add the shallots, maple syrup, coriander and cumin seeds, chipotle flakes and ¼ teaspoon of salt. Fry for 7 minutes, using a spatula to separate the shallots and stop them clumping so they crisp up evenly. Reduce the heat to medium-low and continue to cook for 6 minutes until they are caramelised and a deep, golden-brown. Transfer to a plate lined with kitchen paper and use two forks to spread the shallots out – they will be sticky but will crisp up a little as they cool.

2. Put the green chillies into a small bowl with the vinegar, sugar and ¼ teaspoon of salt, stir to mix and set aside.

3. For the pasta sauce, put the 50ml of oil, the garlic and ¼ teaspoon of salt into a large sauté pan on a medium-high heat. Gently fry for 2 minutes, then set aside.

4. Bring a very large pot of salted water to the boil (the pot needs to be large so the pasta doesn't clump). If you've made fresh saffron tagliatelle, cook for 1 minute, stirring with a fork to separate the strands. If using shop-bought, cook as per packet instructions, until al dente. Drain the pasta, reserving 140ml of the cooking water.

5. Add the cooked pasta to the sauté pan of garlic and return to a medium-high heat. Add the pasta water, the saffron and its soaking water, the parsley and a generous amount of pepper and toss everything together. Add the Parmesan slowly, tossing the pasta as you go and continuing to add more Parmesan as it melts into the sauce; this should take 2–3 minutes.

6. Transfer the pasta to a platter with a lip and dot the ricotta haphazardly over. Top with the crispy shallots, the pickled chillies along with ½ tablespoon of their pickling liquid, the remaining ½ tablespoon of parsley and a good grind of pepper. Serve at once.

UDON NOODLES WITH FRIED TOFU AND ORANGE NAM JIM

SERVES FOUR
As a main

600g pre-cooked udon noodles
10g Thai basil leaves
3 spring onions, julienned (50g)
10g coriander leaves, finely sliced
2 red chillies, julienned (40g)
1 tbsp white or black sesame seeds, or a mixture of both, toasted
salt

FRIED TOFU
1 small garlic clove, crushed
2 tbsp soy sauce
1 tbsp maple syrup
2½ tbsp sunflower oil
350g firm tofu, pressed to remove any water, very well patted dry and cut into 3cm x 1½cm rectangles

BLOOD ORANGE NAM JIM
½ tbsp basmati rice
¾ tbsp Aleppo chilli flakes (or ⅓ tsp regular chilli flakes)
4–5 blood (or regular) oranges: 160ml juice and the remainder cut into wedges to serve
20g shop-bought tamarind paste, or double if you're extracting it yourself from pulp (see p. 20)
2½ tbsp fish sauce (or light soy sauce)
2 tbsp maple syrup
2 tbsp soy sauce
½ small banana shallot, finely diced (40g)
5g coriander, finely chopped

In our take on Thai nam jim sauce – which wonderfully combines sweet, sour, spicy and salty – we use blood oranges to give a particular kind of sweet acidity. Their season is short, though, so use regular oranges instead if you need to, with a touch of lime juice for extra acidity.

To save time, we use pre-cooked noodles that you can just add to the pan. If you're starting with dried noodles, cook them as instructed on the packet and drain well before tossing them with the sauce. The noodles are good hot but they are best served at room temperature, having sat in, and soaked up, the sauce. The accompanying tofu is best hot and freshly fried.

Double the nam jim, if you like – it will keep in a jar in the fridge for up to a week and is great with anything from salads, noodles and rice to grilled meats and fish.

1. First marinate the tofu. Combine the garlic, soy sauce, maple syrup, 1 tablespoon of oil and ¼ teaspoon of salt in a container big enough to fit the pieces in a single layer. Add the tofu, gently toss to coat each piece and leave for 30 minutes to 1 hour, turning the pieces halfway through.

2. Meanwhile, make the nam jim. Put the rice into a small saucepan on a medium-high heat and toast for 2½ minutes, then add the Aleppo chilli flakes and toast for another 30 seconds, until both are fragrant. Transfer to a spice grinder or a pestle and mortar and blitz or pound to a coarse powder. Transfer the ground rice and chilli to a medium bowl and add the orange juice, tamarind, fish sauce, maple syrup, soy sauce, shallot and coriander. Mix well, then pour into a large sauté pan on a medium-high heat and gently cook for 2 minutes, until warm. Add the noodles and cook for another 3 minutes, stirring to separate the strands. Remove from the pan and set aside while you fry the tofu, or until cooled to room temperature.

3. Heat the remaining 1½ tablespoons of oil in a large non-stick pan on a medium-high heat until very hot, then add half the tofu to the pan, spaced apart. Fry for 1½–2 minutes on each side until crisp and golden-brown, taking care as it may spit. Set the cooked tofu aside while you fry the remaining tofu, adding a bit more oil if necessary and lowering the heat if the tofu is colouring too quickly. Stir any remaining tofu marinade into the noodles.

4. Toss the basil, spring onions, coriander leaves and chillies with the noodles, then transfer to a serving platter with a lip. Finish with the sesame seeds and the hot tofu and serve with the orange wedges alongside.

85ml olive oil

6 garlic cloves, finely sliced

1 tbsp rose harissa (adjust according to the brand you are using; see p. 20)

1 red chilli, finely chopped

½ preserved lemon, finely chopped, discarding any pips (10g)

1½ tbsp lemon juice

1kg courgettes, finely sliced

10g basil leaves, roughly torn

salt

SUPER-SOFT COURGETTES WITH HARISSA AND LEMON

Courgettes aren't strictly speaking controversial, but they do tend to get a pretty lukewarm reaction from many, including, regrettably, two of our test kitchen colleagues. The reason for this is probably courgettes' high water content, which tends to make them, well, watery. There are plenty of ways to combat this – frying and grilling are two examples – but we actually use it to our advantage here, cooking the courgettes slowly in their own juices, making them fantastically soft and enhancing their flavour by a long soak with fried garlic. (And in the process, we also managed to win over our two courgette-iffy colleagues, we're happy to announce.)

The courgettes are very good hot, but are even better after 15 minutes or so, or even at room temperature, once the flavours have had a chance to get to know each other. Make them a day in advance, if you want to get ahead; just hold off on adding the basil until you're ready to serve. *Pictured overleaf.*

1. Place a large, non-stick sauté pan on a medium-high heat with the oil and garlic. Gently fry for 4 minutes, stirring often, until soft, golden and aromatic. You don't want the garlic to become at all browned or crispy, so turn the heat down if necessary. Remove 3 tablespoons of oil, along with half the garlic, and transfer to a small bowl with the harissa, chilli, preserved lemon and lemon juice. Stir together and set aside.

2. Return the pan to a high heat and add the courgettes and 1¼ teaspoons of salt. Cook for 18 minutes, stirring often, until the courgettes are very soft, but are still mostly holding their shape (you don't want the courgettes to brown, so turn the heat down if necessary). Stir through half the basil and transfer to a platter. Spoon the harissa mixture over the courgettes. Leave to sit for 15 minutes, then sprinkle with a pinch of salt and finish with the remaining basil.

CAULIFLOWER ROASTED IN CHILLI BUTTER

SERVES FOUR

2 large whole
  cauliflowers, with
  leaves (1.9kg)
2 onions, peeled and cut
  into eighths
8 red chillies, whole, with
  a vertical slit cut into
  them
1 lemon, cut into wedges,
  to serve
salt

CHILLI BUTTER
120g unsalted butter,
  melted (or 120ml olive
  oil if you want to keep
  it vegan)
110ml olive oil
1¼ tbsp red bell pepper
  flakes
2½ tsp tomato paste
1¼ tsp Urfa chilli flakes
90g rose harissa (adjust
  according to the brand
  you are using; see p. 20)
¾ tsp Aleppo chilli flakes
  (or ⅓ tsp regular chilli
  flakes)
3 garlic cloves, crushed
1½ tsp caster sugar

Normally, when we give a vegetable centre stage on the dinner table, in the same way that meat or large fish are often served, our tendency is not to do much to it and to let it bask in its own simplicity. In this book, though, we often do the opposite and actually amp up the flavour dial for our whole vegetables (see also celeriac with Café de Paris sauce, p. 60, and curry-crusted swede steaks, p. 63). Through the combination of grilled chillies and onions, lots of browned butter and a long cooking process, the cauliflower here turns ridiculously rich in flavour, almost meaty.

The chilli butter can be made up to 2 weeks before and kept in the fridge in a sealed container if you want to get ahead. We'd urge you to make double, in fact; it's seriously special and wonderful melted over eggs, or used as a marinade for vegetables or a killer roast chicken.

Serve as a main, with some bread and a couple of simple salads, or as part of a festive spread (see p. 304). *Pictured overleaf.*

1. Trim the leaves at the top of each cauliflower, so that about 5cm of the actual cauliflower is exposed. Cut both cauliflowers into quarters lengthways, making sure the leaves remain attached at the base.

2. Fill a very large pan (large enough to fit all the cauliflower quarters) with well-salted water and bring to the boil. Once boiling, blanch the cauliflower quarters for 2 minutes, weighing them down with a lid a little smaller than the pan to ensure they stay submerged. Transfer to a colander to drain well. Preheat the oven to 180°C fan.

3. Mix all the ingredients for the chilli butter together in a small bowl with 1 teaspoon of salt. Place the cauliflower quarters, onions and chillies on a very large, parchment-lined baking tray and pour over the chilli butter. Carefully mix to make sure everything is very well coated (gloved hands are best for this). Arrange the cauliflower quarters so they are spaced apart as much as possible; one of the cut sides of each quarter should face down, so the leaves are exposed. Roast for 30 minutes, baste well, then turn the heat down to 170°C fan and continue to roast for another 35–40 minutes, basting twice, until the cauliflower is very well browned and the leaves are crispy.

4. Transfer everything to a platter, spooning over all the remaining chilli butter and browned aromatics from the baking tray. Serve at once, with the lemon wedges alongside.

SPICY BERBERE RATATOUILLE WITH COCONUT SALSA

RATATOUILLE

4 medium aubergines, cut into 2½cm squares (1.1kg)

4 mixed red and yellow Romano peppers, deseeded and cut into 3cm pieces (420g)

2 kohlrabi, peeled and cut into 1½cm squares (460g)

2 tbsp berbere spice mix (we use Bart's brand)

200ml olive oil

10g fresh ginger, peeled and finely chopped

3 small garlic cloves, crushed

3 tbsp soy sauce

2½ tbsp maple syrup

300g sweet, ripe cherry tomatoes, roughly chopped

2 tsp nigella seeds

3 mild or medium-hot chillies, red, green or a mix

salt

COCONUT AND CUCUMBER SALSA

1 cucumber, coarsely grated (300g)

15g coriander, finely chopped

25g fresh ginger, peeled and finely chopped

200g coconut cream

2 tbsp lime juice

If you can get hold of injera (a fermented flatbread used in Ethiopia and Eritrea to scoop up food) do serve it alongside the ratatouille. Alternatively, serve it with any other shop-bought or homemade flatbread, like our olive oil flatbreads with three-garlic butter (see p. 246), or even with rice or couscous.

The ratatouille can be made a few days in advance and kept refrigerated; the flavours will improve with time. The salsa, which really helps balance the spiciness of the dish, should be made within a few hours of serving, as it tends to split if left to sit for too long.

The coconut cream you use for the salsa should be thick, not liquid. You can test the consistency by shaking the can or carton; if it's thick enough, you shouldn't be able to hear it sloshing around inside.

1. Preheat the oven to 210°C fan.

2. Combine the first five ingredients for the ratatouille and ¾ teaspoon of salt in a large bowl, then spread out over two large, 40cm x 30cm parchment-lined baking trays. Roast for 40 minutes, stirring the vegetables and swapping the trays round halfway, until the vegetables are cooked and a deep golden-brown. Place in a large bowl with the ginger, garlic, soy sauce, maple syrup, cherry tomatoes and nigella seeds.

3. While the vegetables are roasting, place a frying pan on a high heat and, once very hot, cook the chillies for 12 minutes, turning them a few times until well charred all over. Finely chop the chillies (deseeding them if you prefer less heat) and stir into the bowl with the vegetables. Set aside for half an hour for the flavours to come together. This can be made up to 3 days ahead and gently warmed through before serving.

4. For the salsa, place the cucumber in a clean tea towel and squeeze to get rid of as much water as possible. You should be left with 180g of drained cucumber. Place in a large bowl and stir in all the remaining ingredients and ⅓ teaspoon of salt. Refrigerate until ready to serve.

5. Serve the ratatouille with the coconut salsa, with some warm flatbreads or rice alongside.

SERVES FOUR
As a main

PORTOBELLO STEAKS AND BUTTER BEAN MASH

PORTOBELLO STEAKS

8 medium to large portobello mushrooms (about 650g), stems removed

10 garlic cloves, peeled

1 onion, peeled and cut into 6 wedges (150g)

1½ tbsp chipotle chilli flakes

1 red chilli (15g)

4 tsp cumin seeds, roughly crushed in a pestle and mortar

1 tbsp coriander seeds, roughly crushed in a pestle and mortar

2 tbsp tomato paste

400ml olive oil

BUTTER BEAN MASH

1 × 700g jar of good-quality cooked large butter beans, drained (500g) (we use Brindisa Navarrico large butter beans, but you can, of course, use tinned or cook your own)

1½ tbsp lemon juice

1 tbsp olive oil

flaked sea salt

We're not mad about calling vegetables a 'steak' or 'burger' or 'schnitzel', because it feels like you are trying to pass them off as something else, something superior. Vegetables are great simply as they are. In fact, they are the best! Sometimes, though, using a meaty name helps you understand what's going on and how delicious it is. Our portobellos aren't trying to be a steak, they are simply as good as any steak (with mash), if not better; in just the same way as our Romano pepper schnitzels (p. 146) are as delectable as any other schnitzel. What gives the mushrooms their verve is the chillies and spices and all the flavoured oil that coats them. You'll make more oil than you need here; keep it refrigerated in a sealed container to spoon over grilled vegetables, noodles, meat or fish. Serve this with some sautéed greens, if you like.

1. Preheat the oven to 150°C fan.

2. Put all the ingredients for the steaks and 1 tablespoon of flaked salt into a large ovenproof saucepan, for which you have a lid. Arrange the mushrooms so they are domed side up, then top with a piece of parchment paper, pushing it down to cover all the ingredients. Cover with the lid, then transfer to the oven for 1 hour. Turn the mushrooms over, replacing the paper and lid, and return to the oven for 20 minutes more, or until the mushrooms are very tender but not falling apart. Use a pair of tongs to transfer the mushrooms to a chopping board, then cut them in half and set aside.

3. Use a spoon to remove the onion, garlic and chilli (discarding the stem) – don't worry if you scoop up some of the spices and oil. Put them into the small bowl of a food processor and blitz until smooth. Return the blitzed onion mixture to the saucepan, along with the mushroom halves, and place on a medium-high heat. Cook for about 5 minutes, for all the flavours to come together.

4. While the mushrooms are cooking, make the mash by putting the beans into a food processor along with the lemon juice, olive oil, ½ teaspoon flaked salt and 2 tablespoons of water. Blitz until completely smooth. Transfer to a medium saucepan and cook on a medium-high heat for about 3 minutes, stirring, until warmed through.

5. To serve, divide the butter bean mash between four plates. Top with four mushroom halves per plate and spoon over a generous amount of the oil and its accompanying aromatics (you won't need all of it, though – see intro).

PRODUCE

What you do to a vegetable and what you pair it with are two of the ways in which you amplify its flavour. In some cases, though, there's so much going on *within* the ingredient itself that it can pretty much do all the work on its own. Sure, it may still need baking or toasting or frying or roasting to tease out its deliciousness, but this will more often be a case of releasing what's inherent within the ingredient rather than having to rely on pairing it with something else or somehow transforming its character through process.

There are all sorts of ingredients which do this: ingredients which have the capacity to carry a dish through their sheer 'oomph' and depth of flavour, or the interesting textural contrast they bring. These are often intensely savoury foods, all rich in the fifth sense, umami. After the first four senses – sweet, sour, salty and bitter – umami roughly translates from the Japanese as something like 'deliciousness' or 'savouriness'. Umami is the result of flavour compounds called glutamates. Unlike monosodium glutamate (which gets a bad rep from being chemically manufactured and liberally sprinkled over many a takeaway, to make it taste generically 'good'), there are many natural sources of glutamates. Parmesan or anchovies, for example, tomatoes or fermented pickles, soy sauce, seaweed, Marmite, ketchup. And mushrooms, the first of our four ingredients that we celebrate here.

MUSHROOMS

Play the 'word association' game with mushrooms and, chances are, the next word to come along will be something like 'earthy' or 'woody'. There's a good reason for this. Unlike plants, which grow above the ground, thereby harnessing energy from the sun, mushrooms – which are fungi – do all their growing underground. As mushrooms don't have the chlorophyll they'd need to get their energy from the sun, they go in search of nourishment elsewhere. Different mushrooms do this in different ways. Some live off plants, others live off plant remains and decay. They feed off whatever they can find. We don't see this network of fibres pushing through the soil to gain the nutrients they need to grow, and neither is this the part of the mushroom which we pick, cook or eat. They are, nevertheless, the reason they taste so earthy.

It's also the reason why the flavour of one mushroom can differ so wildly and wonderfully from the flavour of another. What they live off affects how they taste. Mushrooms growing under chestnut trees will taste of chestnut and soil. Mushrooms growing under pine trees will taste of pine and soil. Yotam will never lose the memory of foraging for mushrooms with his grandmother when he was growing up in Jerusalem. They found them under the pine trees in the hills surrounding the city. It was early autumn, after the first rains, and felt to Yotam a bit like magic, filling up sacks with mushrooms which appeared from one day (nothing!) to the next (everywhere!). What he didn't know at the time, of course, was how much of the work was being done out of sight, as the mushroom's network of fibres reached out underground, gathering energy and filling up with water. Returning home, it was always a shock, therefore, to witness just how much the booty in the sack shrank once cooked. The reward, on the other hand, was a concentrated essence of pine and soil, autumn and home.

As well as the location of the soil, the flavour, texture and colour of a mushroom is also affected by how long it's left in that soil. Pick a mushroom when it's young and it will be squeaky clean and relatively bland to taste. These are the little white closed-cup button mushrooms that make their way, very happily, into so many quick stir-fries and omelettes. Leave that same mushroom in the soil for a few more days or weeks, and they become bigger, browner, with a flavour

YOTAM WILL NEVER LOSE THE MEMORY OF FORAGING FOR MUSHROOMS WITH HIS GRANDMOTHER

that's more complex and 'earthy'. These are the nutty chestnut mushrooms that we love to use in our cooking: grilled and marinated and sitting on top of a bowl of warm HUMMUS, for example (P. 234), or bringing depth and body to the veritable mushroom party that is our SPICY MUSHROOM LASAGNE (P. 228). Here, mushrooms fill every conceivable party role: host and guest, DJ and dancer. Leave them a few days longer and they become even browner, earthier and more robust, as they open to display their inky gills. These are portobello mushrooms, perennially happy to be sat on a baking tray, gill side up, dotted with cheese which will melt under the grill, before being placed inside a brioche bun. Veggie burger sorted, since time immemorial.

Squeaky white buttons, nutty brown chestnuts, wide-capped portobellos: these are all common field mushrooms, also known as 'agaric' mushrooms. Mushrooms in this group can be identified by looking under their caps: if they have fine gills radiating outwards from the top of their stem, you are in the right field. It's the gill tissues which generate so much of the aroma of fresh common mushrooms. Those with immature, unopened caps – the baby white buttons, for example – won't have nearly as much flavour as the umbrella-

THE WORLD IS NOT ONLY GOING TO BE YOUR OYSTER BUT ALSO YOUR PORCINI AND YOUR SHIITAKE AND YOUR WILDEST OF ALL FLAVOUR-BOMB DREAMS

wide portobellos, which have been allowed to develop and mature more. Agaric mushrooms feed on plant remains and decay (rather than needing a living tree to grow under), so they can, as a result, be widely cultivated. The reason we have so many little white button mushrooms on our supermarket shelves is that they're really easy to produce.

The other category of mushrooms – the 'boletes' – do need the soil beneath a tree as a home. These are the porcini (ceps) and the carotene-orange girolles, for example, and the pearly-white oysters. Rather than having a firm stem, separate cap and distinct gills, these mushrooms are more a spongy mass of gills. Boletes form a symbiosis with living trees, in which both partners benefit: the mushrooms gather soil minerals and share them with tree roots, which in turn share the tree's sugars with the mushrooms. It's because of this – the fact that these mushrooms need living trees, that intensive production requires a forest and that they're still largely gathered from the wild – that these sorts of mushrooms are still relatively rare and expensive. It's because of this, as well, that their taste is so wonderfully transporting, rich and earthy.

For our purposes, in *FLAVOUR*, we've kept things relatively simple, using only six different types of mushrooms: three fresh and three dried. Given that the water content of mushrooms is high – about 80–90% – the difference in potential for the fresh vs. dried mushroom to soak up flavours is going to be fairly great. Sure, fresh mushrooms love to be thrown into a pan with some oil and garlic and hard herbs, thirstily taking on the flavours they are paired with, but, first, they'll have to release much of their liquid before they can do this. Thankfully, this transference is pretty rapid because mushrooms, with their thin outer cuticle, can shed liquid as quickly as they can let it in. Just make sure you are not overcrowding the pan – they need space so that the liquid released can evaporate rather than form a soggy puddle – and you'll be five minutes away from a simple, tasty meal.

Start with dehydrated mushrooms, though, and you're going to have a veritable sponge on your hands once they're submerged in a liquid. Dial up the flavour of that liquid with soy sauce, sugar and apple cider vinegar and the world is not only going to be your oyster but also your porcini and your shiitake and your wildest of all flavour-bomb dreams. When rehydrating mushrooms, always keep the liquid they've been soaking in, after they've been strained. Just as the mushrooms have taken on all the flavours in the stock, so the stock will take on the earthy flavour of the mushrooms. Combining the two in the making of our MUSHROOM KETCHUP, for example (P. 227), will take your appreciation of ketchup as the definitive 'umami-rich sauce' to a whole new level.

And there's another whole approach with dried mushrooms: rather than rehydrating them and taking it from there, they can be blitzed while still dry to form a mushroom powder. It's when armed with a jar of this, all set to sprinkle through our BROWN RICE AND SHIITAKE CONGEE, for example (P. 237), that the case against manufactured MSG can really be made, largely on the grounds of irrelevance. With a pot of dried, blitzed and now powdered shiitake mushrooms, ready to spread their umami depth throughout the porridge-like congee, you won't need anything more to help boost the flavour. Magical mushroom dust indeed.

ALLIUMS

Behind so many delicious dishes, there's often an onion or two at work. Chopped and added to the pan with some oil, the smell of an onion – or its relatives, shallot or leek – being cooked is one of expectation and promise: a meal is under way! If this all sounds a bit much, it wouldn't be the first time we've been accused of onion-shaped hyperbole. Yotam once wrote in the *Guardian:* 'Every time we chop an onion and sweat it in oil, it changes from being something that makes us cry to something that makes us smile with joy.' A reader responded. 'Every time?' wrote Brian Smith from Berlin. 'Don't be daft!' We couldn't help but giggle. Brian clearly had a point – it's a lot to put on a little white onion – but we *do* stand by our strength of feeling. The transformation of onions from raw to cooked – from harsh and sulphurous to meltingly soft and sweet – does feel, to us, just a little bit like alchemy.

Peek behind the velvet curtains of the magic show, though, and there's a fair amount of solid science and practical process at play. Unlike other vegetables, the onion family accumulates energy stores not in starch but in chains of fructose sugars, which long, slow cooking breaks down to produce a marked sweetness. The longer and slower the cooking of the onions, either in

BEHIND SO MANY DELICIOUS DISHES, THERE'S OFTEN AN ONION OR TWO AT WORK

the oven or in a pan on the stove, the sweeter and the more caramelised these sugars become. This gives rise to glutamic acid. And it's this acid which gives rise to the big, yummy umami taste we're so often in search of in *FLAVOUR*.

So much of this work – providing the sweet, caramelised base to many dishes – is what's going on when onions are behind the scenes, playing a background role. They're always there in the sofrito or mirepoix base: the diced onions, celery and carrots or peppers which are so often sweated down as the first step to a stew or soup. But this everyday way of using onions isn't why they get a section all to themselves here. What we find so thrilling are all the instances in which *onioniness* becomes the 'thing' a dish is all about. These are the thick ONION RINGS WITH BUTTERMILK AND TURMERIC, for example (P. 255), or the charred red milder Tropea onions bulking out a summery GREEN GAZPACHO starter (P. 242). They're the SWEET AND SOUR ONION PETALS stealing the side show to anything they're plated up with (P. 245), or the yellow onions, simply peeled and halved, baked with miso and butter until melting (P. 258). If anything, we're thinking we need to be laying on a bit *more* hyperbole, Brian – not less! – to do justice to the onion.

The same is true of garlic. A caramelised garlic tart from *PLENTY* was probably our first dish to be so clearly and unapologetically all about the garlic. More followed, often using a head or two of garlic in a single dish, cooked in different ways. Our freedom to use such lavish quantities totally relies on a breathtaking transformation of flavour which happens in the cooking: from something harsh, almost metallic, to something utterly sweet and mellow. One raw crushed garlic clove might be enough to make a salad dressing sing; *three whole garlic heads*, cloves separated and peeled, went into that garlic tart, making it the absolute sweetest of all savoury tarts.

Again – as with onions – it's the impact of long, slow cooking on the chains of fructose sugars in the garlic which is being seen here. The harsh notes – those which can linger on the breath when garlic is eaten raw – are the result of sulphurous compounds contained within each clove. The more a garlic clove is crushed and minced, when raw, the more the cell membranes are broken down and the more activated and released these compounds are. This is why one raw garlic clove, finely minced or crushed, goes a long way in a dressing. Gently crush that same clove, though, with the flat side of a big knife, or roast it whole, and no such activation takes place. Anyone in need of further convincing of the benign qualities of huge quantities of garlic needs to try the THREE-GARLIC BUTTER on P. 246, which sees 100 grams of butter being able to handle one whole head of roasted garlic, one small raw garlic clove and four black garlic cloves mashed in. Do a taste check, followed by a breath check, and *then* cast your vote.

The black garlic in this butter is something that anyone in search of deep umami flavour will adore. Rather than having to enact the transformation yourself in the kitchen, through the application of heat, black garlic is an ingredient where the work has already been done for you. Starting off as regular white cloves, the effect of time, heat treatment and fermentation is to change them so that they become the liquorice-black, wine-gum-soft-and-squishy cloves that they are. Thinly sliced, the cloves can be added to all sorts of rice dishes – any risotto, for example, or our DIRTY RICE on P. 252 – or we like to blitz them up in a yoghurt-based sauce.

It's not just black garlic cloves that can be thinly sliced to great effect. Several of the other dishes in this chapter – like the gently cooked LEEKS (P. 257) or the platter of 'meaty' chunks of roasted AUBERGINE (P. 251) – showcase the way in which a sliver of fried pale golden garlic can bring with it a welcome crunch and pop of un-fiery flavour that adds yet another layer of allium-ness. Being thinly or 'cleanly' sliced (as opposed to being minced or mashed when crushed), the process of activating the sulphurous compounds

WHISTLING, WEARING GOGGLES: YOU CHOOSE. US? WE JUST THINK OF THE JOY AS WE CHOP

is relatively contained. As such, the garlic can turn crisp and crunchy and golden – thanks to its natural sugars – without being troubled by the acid enzyme. It's these same sugars which can, at the same time, see slices of garlic pass from being warm and sweet to burnt and bitter in a matter of seconds, though, so keep a close eye on them in the pan and remove them from the oil to a plate lined with kitchen paper just seconds before you think they're ready. As always, with alliums, it's a fine balance you need to strike to tease all the sweetness out of those bulbs. It takes some attention, applying judgement and keeping an open eye – all small efforts for the sake of those magical flavours.

Of course the opposite of the joy alliums can bring – whether they are chopped or sliced – is the tears they can produce. These tears are the result of volatile compounds within the onion or garlic which are only released when they're cut. The best way of minimising the release of these compounds is to start with a really sharp knife. This will lead to as 'clean' and 'neat' a break in the cell wall as possible, thereby reducing the level of volatile compound activation. Other recommendations abound. Some swear by putting onions into the freezer for 10 minutes before chopping, and/or sticking a piece of bread in between your teeth as you work. Whistling, wearing goggles: you choose. Us? We just think of the joy as we chop – the expectation! the promise! – and smile, daftly, on.

NUTS AND SEEDS

If mushrooms, onions and garlic are all about body and depth, nuts and seeds can all too easily be seen as sprinkle, surface and light. And with their crunchy texture and nutty aroma, this can, clearly, be the case. As with our other categories of produce, though, nuts and seeds can also be about body and depth. They perform both roles – substance and surface – fantastically well.

First, though, some nuts and bolts. Strictly speaking, nuts – alongside grains (wheat, barley, rice, etc.) and legumes (beans and peas) – fall under the umbrella term 'seeds'. This broad definition, however, doesn't capture the way we use the words 'nuts' and 'seeds' as ingredients in the kitchen. For cooks, the definition relies on a couple of factors. One is that, when dry, they're ready to eat as they are: unlike a dried pulse, for example, you can snack on and crack on with a nut without any soaking or cooking or any other sort of -ing. Toasting them teases

OUR LIST OF THE WAYS IN WHICH TAHINI CAN BE ADDED TO A DISH COULD BE VERY LONG INDEED

out the flavour, sure, but it's not a necessary part of making them edible or digestible. They taste, well, nutty, and are full of rich and fatty oils. This makes them not only edible but, also, super satisfying and very delicious.

It's useful to spell out what makes a nut a nut because it's these factors – their 'being ready to be eaten as they are', their 'nuttiness' and their 'fattiness' – which, precisely, makes them so good at bringing body and depth to a dish. Nut pastes, of which tahini is our favourite, are a marvellous manifestation of these three factors. To state what might seem like an obvious point, nut pastes are simply pastes made from blitzing nuts or seeds together. There is nothing else in tahini apart from sesame seeds! All the nutty flavour, rich oil and fatty smoothness is sitting right there in the seeds, waiting to be released once the hulls are blitzed together. Our list of the ways in which tahini can be added to a dish to bring it substance could be very long indeed. From the obvious

HUMMUS (P. 234) at one end via ROAST POTATOES (P. 276) to the less obvious CUCUMBER (P. 113) at the other, a dribble or drizzle or spoon of tahini can turn unassuming vegetables, such as chickpeas, potatoes and cucumber, into something rich and substantial.

As well as being rich and substantial, though, tahini also has the ability to be nutty and light. It's this that we really love about it. Tahini is happy to be thinned down as much as a dish requires. This allows the sauce to work well with vegetables without their flavour being subsumed. This dilution can happen with all sorts of things – again, depending on what the dish requires. Lemon juice and water work really well, for example, as do tamarind or soy sauce by themselves, or soy sauce mixed with honey.

If dilution is one approach to lightening up the nuttiness, mixing the nut paste with another fat altogether is another, very different approach. An Italian pesto is a familiar example, in which pine nuts, olive oil and Parmesan are mixed to a paste (along with basil leaves and garlic). The nuttiness is broken down and, at the same time, complemented by other rich and fatty flavours, giving us a brilliantly complex experience. This same dynamic can be seen in our pumpkin seed and butter paste, for example, into which our CORN RIBS (P. 264) are dipped. The butter both moderates the pumpkin seed flavour and, at the same time, enriches it. It also, rather wonderfully, melts nicely into the grooves between the corn kernels to give them a good coating.

In both these examples – the pesto and the pumpkin seed butter – we've mixed crushed nuts or seeds with dairy. We love to do this – it's a win-win! – but the dairy factor is not always necessary. Indeed, and thankfully – for vegans who want to experience the milky sensation without eating dairy – the cross-over between nuts and seeds on the one hand and milk and eggs on the other is fairly direct. Take a small handful of seeds and nuts and see this for yourself: take your time chewing them and, as you'll see, you'll get a genuinely milky sensation in your mouth.

Even if you're not vegan or don't think of nut pastes as alternatives to milk or eggs, we have found a natural tendency, in *FLAVOUR*, to use them in places where, otherwise, a dollop of soured cream or a spoonful of mayonnaise would have made an appearance (see our CUCUMBER SALAD, P. 113, and our ROAST POTATOES, P. 276, respectively). More often than not, though, vegans use the natural creaminess of nuts consciously to make rich sauces which are normally impossible to achieve without eggs or dairy.

Coconuts are famously popular and very effective in giving depth, body and smoothness to vegan soups and stews. We use coconut cream to achieve this in our STUFFED AUBERGINES (P. 152) and there's also a COCONUT ICE CREAM (P. 286) which has a similar dairy-free creaminess. With a little more effort, a comparable texture and body can be achieved with other nuts too. Soaking or boiling almonds or cashews, for example, in water, then blitzing them smooth, is the basis for the frothy nut milks some like to pour into their cappuccinos. It's also a great way to get a splendidly creamy and rich sauce in which you can submerge your favourite roasted vegetable or our TOFU MEATBALLS (P. 268).

As well as having an uncanny talent for disguising themselves as milk, nuts are also naturally 'meaty', thanks to the high levels of fat and protein they contain. This quality has, however, led to what we think of as an unfortunate consequence: it's called the Nut Roast. Though we hear that there are versions of nut roasts out there which people swear by and love, we are yet to be convinced. From our experience, they are never as good as a good meatloaf

AS WELL AS HAVING AN UNCANNY TALENT FOR DISGUISING THEMSELVES AS MILK, NUTS ARE ALSO NATURALLY 'MEATY'

(which is what they are modelled on), nor are they a great showcase for nuts, being soggy and often bland. As a vegetarian or vegan stand-in for the star turkey at the holiday table, we'd far rather have a whole roasted cauliflower, or our CELERIAC STEAKS WITH CAFÉ DE PARIS SAUCE (P. 60), with protein coming from side dishes with lentils, chickpeas or soya beans.

However, for anyone still craving nuts as the main star at the holiday table, we have our TURNIP CAKE (P. 270). Steamed, fried, then sprinkled with clusters of shiitake mushrooms, nuts and seeds which are flavoured with soy sauce, garlic and maple syrup, this vegan take on a dish from a Chinese dim sum spread is a glorious centrepiece in both looks and complex flavour.

Our turnip cake is also an example of a dish which showcases the second role that nuts and seeds can play in a dish. If we've looked at all the ways these can bring body and depth, the last-minute smattering of nuts here shows how effective their 'surface and light' role can be as well. This is the case as much for an involved dish such as the turnip cake as it is for dishes which are simply and quickly assembled – our TOMATO AND PLUM SALAD (P. 267), for example, or the KOHLRABI 'NOODLE' SALAD (P. 260).

There are all sorts of ways to achieve this sprinkle and crunch. The simplest is to take one kind of nut, roughly chop it up and go from there. The impact of the almonds in our POTATO SALAD (P. 275), for example, is a case in point. The fact that you can easily buy already smoked, roasted and salted almonds makes this almost a cheat's way of disseminating a cluster of little flavour bombs throughout a dish.

Starting with plain peeled nuts (sometimes also called 'raw' nuts), then adding layers of flavour oneself, is also an easy win. The unsalted blanched peanuts in our RADISH AND CUCUMBER SALAD, for example (P. 263), confidently steal the salad's show once they've been coated in a mix of chilli, golden syrup, salt, lime and olive oil. At this point they're also, incidentally, the bar snack of all bar snacks.

Putting together a combination of seeds and nuts – rather than just starting with the almonds or peanuts, for example – is also a simple option which can yield disproportionate results. Individually, a tablespoon or two of sesame seeds or half a teaspoon of chilli flakes might not seem too exciting. Combine them,

though – with a bit of flaked sea salt and half a sheet of blitzed, umami-rich nori seaweed, as we do in our TOMATO SALAD (P. 267), and you suddenly have something that punches well above the little sesame seeds' weight.

A couple of practical notes, to end on. The first is to always taste your seeds and nuts before you use them. The same oils that make nuts so appealing also make them go rancid quite easily. Walnuts, cashews and peanuts are particularly prone to spoilage. Have a nibble and if they taste rancid or floury, get yourself some more. Unfortunately, no amount of toasting or blitzing is able to *undo* rancid or floury! Second, even if a recipe does not call for nuts or seeds to be toasted, we tend to always give them a little bit of time spread out on a baking tray in a 160°C fan oven. Doing this draws out the oil in the nut or seed and just makes them taste a bit 'nuttier' and 'seedier'. You can toast them in a pan on the stove, instead, if you prefer: just be sure to stir them very frequently and keep a close eye on them. Also, remove them from the pan a little bit before they are done: they keep on browning once off the heat. Don't get distracted, or you'll be cursing your half-raw, half-burnt pine nuts before the fun has even started.

SUGAR: FRUIT AND BOOZE

When we say that particular types of ingredients – mushrooms, onions, nuts and sugar being the four we have identified – have a unique ability to carry a whole dish by themselves and give it its particular edge, sugar is probably the simplest example. How the natural umaminess in mushrooms is key to making a vegetarian lasagne taste meaty is not an intuition we all have. The fact that puddings need sweetness in them, in one form or another, is a natural truth everyone understands.

For this reason, it is tempting to look at umami, sitting at the opposite end of the flavour spectrum to sweet, as being interesting, complex and nuanced in a way a dessert could never be, while dismissing sweetness as being one-dimensional. Sweetness equals sugar and sugar equals sweetness: the two get conflated in the mind. Sugar comes in a packet saying either 'caster', 'icing' or 'soft dark brown', and we all know that we shouldn't eat too much of it. That's all there is to it, right?

But what about all the other ways sugar can be introduced into our cooking and baking – all the different places and produce it can be harnessed from or teamed with for its complexity of flavour? What about all the amazing varieties of honey we can use for our TAPIOCA FRITTERS (P. 280), for example? What about the natural sweetness of vanilla and star anise, or the smoky sweetness that happens when sugar is mixed with ancho chilli to make a FLAN (P. 278)? Or the perfumed sweetness of the orange blossom water used for POACHED APRICOTS (P. 282)? The sugar we get from a packet might be one thing, but there are so many more shades of sweetness. Rather than looking at sugar per se, it's here – in these sugary shades and shadows – that our interest lies. In our constant pursuit of flavour – big, nuanced, dialled-up flavour – it's here that we want to head.

If it's shades and shadows we're interested in, one of the best places to look is under a sun-dappled tree. A fruit-growing tree, specifically, which is our first stop at the sweet shop. Using fruit as a means to create all kinds of intricate and complex layers of sweetness is our absolute favourite way of getting sugar into our cooking, particularly when making dessert. All but one of our puddings, in fact, have fruit in them, in one form or another. Strawberries and watermelons bring the sweetness of summer to our WATERMELON AND STRAWBERRY SORBET (P. 283), and bananas, coconuts, lychees and passionfruit bring the taste of the tropics to our CRÊPES WITH ROASTED BANANAS AND BARBADOS CREAM (P. 290) and our COCONUT ICE CREAM (P. 286). Our favourite lemons, limes, oranges and tangerines are so often there,

THE SUGAR WE GET FROM A PACKET MIGHT BE ONE THING, BUT THERE ARE SO MANY MORE SHADES OF SWEETNESS

ensuring that sweetness comes also with a citrus tang. In some puddings this is happening in a big, look-at-me way: MAX AND FLYNN'S LEMON SORBET, for example (P. 289), is served inside a hollowed-out lemon, no less! But citrus fruit can be equally as important when playing a background role, serving mainly to pull back the sweetness from becoming too cloying.

Chopping, pulping, juicing and zesting: these are all some of the ways to get fresh, fruity sweetness into a pudding. Dig in and dig down, though, and you see the fruit at work in different ways, often in altogether different ingredients. Take our POACHED APRICOTS WITH PISTACHIO AND AMARETTI MASCARPONE (P. 282). The fresh apricots are there, of course, halved and pitted and ready to be poached. But then apricot stones have also been used to make the amaretto liqueur, which, in turn, is used in the making of amaretti biscuits, which are, in turn, crushed into the mascarpone. Look further into that mascarpone and, again, you see citrus fruit juice at work. Although lemon juice might not be listed as an ingredient in the recipe for poached apricots, it's what's added to whole milk in the first place, to activate the coagulation that needs to take place in the making of mascarpone. Fruit is playing every role here: out front in the foreground, in the middle with the pack, as well as in the background, offstage but still important.

The relationship between sweetness and ripeness in fruit is clear: the riper the fruit, the sweeter, softer and juicier it will be. What might be less obvious is the difference between climacteric and non-climacteric fruit. Climacteric fruit, such as bananas, apricots, tomatoes and melons store their sugar in the

IF WE HAD OUR WAY, EVERY DESSERT WOULD BE DRENCHED IN SOME SORT OF SWEET WINE

form of starch. Once picked, this starch is converted back into sweetness. This makes them forgiving and versatile to the home cook, who can either ripen them at home or enhance their sweetness through cooking. Non-climacteric fruit, on the other hand, is not so malleable. This category of fruit includes things like peaches, strawberries, grapes and citrus fruit. Their sweetness will not develop beyond the point at which they're picked. So, when we state the need for 300 grams of *ripe* strawberries for our watermelon and strawberry sorbet, then ripe-and-ready they need to be. Making a sorbet with unripe strawberries is never going to capture the essence of summer.

Second only to fresh fruit as our favourite means of bringing sugar to the pudding table in an interesting way, is fermented fruit in the form of sweet wine. If we had our way, every dessert would be drenched in some sort of sweet wine or other, with a boozy trifle being the definition of perfection. Sauternes, for example, the sweet French wine, has a wonderfully concentrated, honeyed, crisp, exotic, raisin-like taste. This is due to the 'noble rot' – or good fungus – which attacks the three grapes the wine is made from, adding flavour to and intensifying their natural sweetness. The fermentation we trumpeted so passionately in a savoury context in the ageing section (P. 33) is also a massive flavour-enhancing factor here.

It's not just sweet fruit which can be boozy and bottled as wine. Rum, for example, used in our BARBADOS CREAM (P. 290), is made from the fermenting and distilling of sugarcane molasses. Amaretto, the sweet Italian liqueur, is made from brown sugar, vodka (itself made from sweetcorn), almond extract and vanilla extract. The number of different and various sweet notes contained within just these three tipples – grassy, toasted, spiced rum, bitter almond amaretto and honeyed, raisiny Sauternes – points to quite how many very sweet directions in which recipes that use them can be taken. The idea that sweetness is one-dimensional becomes, after a few sips, very hard – quite literally – to sustain.

BROCCOLI WITH MUSHROOM AND NORI

600g broccolini or purple sprouting broccoli, trimmed and leaves removed
2 garlic cloves, crushed
3 tbsp olive oil
flaked sea salt and black pepper

MUSHROOM KETCHUP
20g dried porcini mushrooms, rehydrated in 400ml hot water for 20 minutes
30g caster sugar
3 tbsp light soy sauce
200g shiitake mushrooms, stems discarded and caps roughly chopped
2 tbsp apple cider vinegar
2 tbsp olive oil

NORI TOPPING
1 tbsp sesame seeds, toasted
2 tsp nori sprinkles (or finely blitz ½ sheet of nori in a spice grinder and use 2 tsp)
1½ tbsp crispy shallots (shop-bought), roughly crumbled
20g ready-roasted and salted peanuts, finely chopped
1 tsp Aleppo chilli flakes (or ½ tsp regular chilli flakes)

We suggest using either purple sprouting broccoli or broccolini to make this dish. Normal broccoli is fine as well, but you'll need to blanch the florets for 2–3 minutes, then drain and dry them well before you roast them in the oven. The mushroom ketchup is full of complexity and flavour. It's good spread on toast, or in any situation that calls for ketchup, so feel free to double the recipe. It will keep in a sealed jar in the fridge for up to a week.

1. Preheat the oven to 240°C fan.

2. First, make the ketchup. Reserving their liquid, drain the porcini mushrooms and roughly chop them.

3. Put the sugar into a medium saucepan and place it on a medium heat. Leave to cook, resisting the urge to stir, for about 12 minutes, or until the sugar is a light caramel colour. Carefully add the soy sauce and 3 tablespoons of the reserved porcini liquid and stir to combine; it will bubble and sizzle vigorously (don't worry if it seizes up a little; it will melt back down). Increase the heat to medium-high, add the shiitakes and cook for 4 minutes, or until the mushrooms have released their liquid and are well coated in the caramel. Add the rehydrated porcini mushrooms and 250ml of their soaking liquid, then bring to the boil and cook for 8 minutes, or until the sauce has reduced by half. Transfer the mixture to a food processor and blitz until quite smooth, about a minute. With the machine still running, add the vinegar, oil, ½ teaspoon of flaked salt and a good grind of pepper and blitz for another 2 minutes, until completely smooth, then set aside to cool (you want it at room temperature).

4. In a bowl, toss together the broccoli, garlic, oil, 1 teaspoon of flaked salt and a good grind of pepper. Transfer to a parchment-lined baking tray and roast for 8 minutes, or until cooked through and lightly charred.

5. While the broccoli is in the oven, make the nori topping by combining all the ingredients in a small bowl along with ½ teaspoon of flaked salt.

6. To serve, spread the mushroom ketchup on a platter, then top with the broccoli and a few spoonfuls of the nori topping, serving any extra alongside.

750g chestnut
   mushrooms, halved
500g oyster mushrooms
135ml olive oil, plus extra
   for greasing
60g dried porcini
   mushrooms
30g dried wild
   mushrooms
2 dried red chillies,
   roughly chopped
   (deseeded for less heat)
500ml hot vegetable
   stock
1 onion, peeled and
   quartered
5 garlic cloves, roughly
   chopped
1 carrot, peeled and
   quartered (90g)
2–3 plum tomatoes,
   quartered (200g)
75g tomato paste
130ml double cream
60g Pecorino Romano,
   finely grated
60g Parmesan, finely
   grated
5g basil leaves, finely
   chopped
10g parsley leaves, finely
   chopped, plus an extra
   tsp to serve
250g dried lasagne
   sheets (that's about
   14 sheets)
salt and black pepper

SPICY MUSHROOM LASAGNE

This lasagne contains one of two epic ragù recipes in this book – the other is the ultimate traybake ragù, p.101 – which, we believe, give any meat ragù a terrifically good run for its money.

This particular ragù pays homage to penne all'Aconese, the first dish that Ixta fell madly in love with. It's served at Ristorante Pizzeria Acone, a community-run restaurant in the Tuscan village of Acone, perched at the top of the mountain on which she spent her formative childhood years. The recipe is a closely guarded secret, but the complex, earthy and deeply umami flavour of dried porcini mushrooms is impossible to miss. This is our meatless take on that mythical sauce.

The ragù can easily be made vegan if you lose the cream. It can also be made ahead and refrigerated, ready to be served with pasta or polenta, saving yourself the trouble of constructing the lasagne if you're short on time.

Reduce the black pepper and lose the chilli for a child-friendly version. If you want to get ahead, the lasagne can be assembled, refrigerated and then baked the next day (once it's come back up to room temperature). *Pictured overleaf.*

1. Preheat the oven to 230°C fan.

2. Put the chestnut and oyster mushrooms into the large bowl of a food processor in three or four batches and pulse each batch until finely chopped (or finely chop everything by hand). Toss the chopped mushrooms in a large bowl with 3 tablespoons of oil and 1 teaspoon of salt and spread out on a large, 40cm x 35cm parchment-lined, rimmed baking tray. Bake for 30 minutes near the top of the oven, stirring three times throughout, until the mushrooms are golden-brown; they will have reduced in volume significantly. Set aside. Reduce the oven temperature to 200°C fan.

3. Meanwhile, combine the dried mushrooms, chillies and hot stock in a large bowl and set aside to soak for half an hour. Strain the liquid into another bowl, squeezing as much liquid from the mushrooms as possible to get about 340ml: if you have any less, top up with water. Very roughly chop the rehydrated mushrooms (you want some chunks) and finely chop the chillies. Set the stock and mushrooms aside separately.

4. Put the onion, garlic and carrot into the food processor and pulse until finely chopped (or finely chop everything by hand). Heat 60ml of oil in a large sauté pan or pot on a medium-high heat. Once hot, add the onion mixture and fry for 8 minutes, stirring occasionally, until soft and golden. Pulse the tomatoes in the food processor until finely chopped (or finely chop by hand), then add to the pan along with the tomato paste, 1 ½ teaspoons of salt and 1 ¾ teaspoons of freshly cracked black pepper. Cook for 7 minutes, stirring occasionally. Add the rehydrated mushrooms and chillies and the roasted mushrooms and cook for 9 minutes, resisting the urge to stir: you want the mushrooms to be slightly crisp and browned on the bottom. Stir in the reserved stock and 800ml of water and, once simmering, reduce the heat to medium and cook for about 25 minutes, stirring occasionally, until you get the consistency of a ragù. Stir in 100ml of the cream and simmer for another 2 minutes, then remove from the heat.

5. Combine both cheeses and both herbs in a small bowl. To assemble the lasagne, spread one-fifth of the sauce in the bottom of a round 28cm baking dish (or a 30cm x 20cm rectangular dish), then top with a fifth of the cheese mixture, followed by a layer of lasagne sheets, broken to fit where necessary. Repeat these layers three more times in that order, and finish with a final layer of sauce and cheese: that's five layers of sauce and cheese and four layers of pasta.

6. Drizzle over 1 tablespoon of cream and 1 tablespoon of oil, then cover with foil and bake for 15 minutes. Remove the foil, increase the temperature to 220°C fan and bake for another 12 minutes, turning the dish round halfway. Turn the oven to the grill setting and grill for a final 2 minutes, until the edges are brown and crisp. Set aside to cool for 5 or so minutes, then drizzle over the remaining tablespoon of cream and oil. Sprinkle over the remaining parsley, finish with a good grind of pepper and serve.

25g basmati rice
200g dried vermicelli
   rice noodles
300g French beans,
   trimmed and cut in
   half widthways
½ large cucumber
   (200g), quartered
   lengthways, deseeded
   and cut into 2mm-thick
   slices at an angle
2 red chillies (20g),
   deseeded and julienned
½ red onion (60g),
   peeled and thinly sliced
70ml shop-bought
   tamarind paste,
   or double if you're
   extracting it yourself
   from pulp (see p. 20)
60ml maple syrup
3 tbsp fish sauce
   (optional; use 2 tbsp
   light soy sauce, if you
   like)
2 tbsp soy sauce
75ml lime juice (from
   4–5 limes)
135ml groundnut oil
300g chestnut
   mushrooms, finely
   chopped
300g oyster mushrooms,
   roughly torn
1 tsp red chilli flakes
120g raw peanuts, lightly
   roasted and finely
   chopped
5g mint leaves
5g Thai basil leaves
10g coriander leaves
salt

NOODLE SALAD WITH MUSHROOM AND PEANUT LAAB

We use mushrooms and peanuts here for a vegan (if not including the fish sauce, which is optional) take on laab, a minced meat dish from Thailand and Laos. Our laab is mixed with rice noodles to create a fresh salad which is rich and complex enough to make a wholesome meal in itself.

The noodles and laab can be made up to 3 hours before, if you want to get ahead, but don't add the herbs or assemble until you're ready to serve.

1. Put the rice into a small pan on a medium heat and toast for 10 minutes, or until the rice begins to colour and smell nutty. Take off the heat and, once cool, grind to a fine powder in a pestle and mortar or spice grinder.

2. Put the noodles into a heatproof bowl, top with 1 litre of boiling water, then cover with a large plate or lid and leave to soften for 10 minutes. Drain, run under cold water, then drain again.

3. Meanwhile, bring a small pot of water to the boil. Add a teaspoon of salt, followed by the beans, and boil for 3 minutes. Drain and run under cold water, to stop the beans cooking more, then drain again.

4. In a large bowl, toss the drained noodles with the beans, cucumber, chillies, onion and ⅓ teaspoon of salt, and set aside.

5. In a separate bowl, whisk the tamarind, maple syrup, 2 tablespoons fish sauce (if using), 1 tablespoon of soy sauce, 3 tablespoons of lime juice and 90ml of groundnut oil and set aside.

6. Heat the remaining 3 tablespoons of oil in a large sauté pan on a high heat. Add the mushrooms and cook for 12 minutes, stirring occasionally, until all the liquid they produce has cooked away and the mushrooms have browned. Add the chilli flakes and cook for 2 minutes more. Off the heat, stir through the peanuts, ground rice, the remaining tablespoon each of fish sauce and soy sauce and the last 2 tablespoons of lime juice. Keep warm.

7. When ready to serve, add the herbs to the noodle salad along with half the tamarind dressing and toss to combine.

8. Pour the remaining dressing over the mushroom laab and mix well. Spread the laab out on a platter, then top with the noodles so the laab can still be seen around the edges.

As a side or as part of a
mezze spread

HUMMUS
2 heads of garlic, top
  fifth cut off to expose
  the cloves
2 tbsp olive oil
2 tbsp tahini
300g cooked chickpeas
  (see basic cooked
  chickpeas recipe,
  p. 79), or use good-
  quality jarred chickpeas
2 tbsp lemon juice
3 tbsp ice-cold water
salt, flaked sea salt and
  black pepper

MUSHROOMS
140g chestnut
  mushrooms, quartered
120g shiitake
  mushrooms, roughly
  torn in half
1 garlic clove, crushed
  with the side of a knife
60ml olive oil
1 lemon: finely shave the
  skin to get 3 strips, then
  juice to get 2 tbsp
5g thyme sprigs
1½ tsp maple syrup
1 dried cascabel chilli
1 tbsp dill, roughly
  chopped
½ tbsp parsley, finely
  chopped

CONFIT GARLIC HUMMUS WITH GRILLED MUSHROOMS

The hummus will last for up to 3 days in the fridge, covered with a little oil so the surface doesn't form a crust. The mushrooms, however, are best grilled on the day, as they become limp and less meaty when they spend time in the fridge.

1. Preheat the oven to 200°C fan.

2. Drizzle the heads of garlic with 1 teaspoon of oil and sprinkle with a little salt and pepper. Wrap tightly in foil and place in the oven for 40 minutes, until the cloves have softened and are golden-brown. Remove the foil and, when cool enough to handle, squeeze out the cloves, discarding the papery skins.

3. While the garlic heads are cooking, prepare the mushrooms. Heat a large griddle pan on a high heat and add the mushrooms, spread out (you may need to do this in batches, depending on the size of your pan). Grill for about 8 minutes, turning throughout until all sides have dark char marks. Add the mushrooms to a medium bowl with the crushed garlic, oil, lemon strips and juice, thyme and maple syrup, 1 ½ teaspoons of flaked salt and a generous grind of black pepper. Mix well.

4. Add the dried chilli to the griddle pan to cook for 4 minutes, until fragrant. Roughly chop the chilli and add it to the bowl with the mushrooms, along with its seeds, and set aside to marinate for 1–2 hours.

5. For the hummus, add the cooked garlic and ¾ teaspoon of flaked salt to a food processor with all of the remaining ingredients for the hummus. Blitz until smooth, scraping down the sides of the bowl as you go, if necessary.

6. Spread the hummus in a shallow bowl, creating a large well in the centre with the back of a spoon. Add the dill and parsley to the mushrooms, then spoon into the well, along with the oil and aromatics.

BROWN RICE AND SHIITAKE CONGEE

SERVES FOUR
As a main

80ml sunflower oil

6 spring onions, finely chopped (60g), plus 2 spring onions, julienned, to serve (20g)

40g fresh ginger, peeled and very finely chopped

6 garlic cloves, very finely chopped (20g)

180g short-grain brown rice

50g dried shiitake mushrooms, roughly chopped

150g rainbow or breakfast radishes, thinly sliced

2 tbsp rice vinegar

½ tsp caster sugar

50g crispy shallots, shop-bought or homemade

salt

RAYU

1 tsp Aleppo chilli flakes (or ½ tsp regular chilli flakes)

1½ tbsp red bell pepper flakes

1½ tbsp white sesame seeds, toasted

1 tbsp black sesame seeds, toasted

2½ tsp finely grated tangerine zest

2½ tbsp soy sauce

This congee – 'like an amazing mushroom risotto, but more exotic', to quote Claudine, our recipe tester – can be served for a weekend brunch or an autumn supper. Soft-boiled egg or grilled or smoked fish are great served on top, if you are looking for a more substantial meal, as well as sautéed Asian greens served alongside.

Rayu is a Japanese chilli oil often enjoyed with rice, ramen or gyoza. Our variation includes tangerine zest (you can use orange instead), which sweetens and enriches it. You can make it even if you are not preparing the congee, and keep it in the fridge for whenever you need a bit of additional spice over your food. If you choose to do that, use all the sautéed spring onion, ginger, garlic and oil mixture and stir it together with double the rayu ingredients, along with another 60ml of warm sunflower oil. It will keep in a sealed jar in the fridge for up to 2 weeks.

Make the congee the day before, if you want to get ahead. You may need to add a splash of water to it, to loosen it when you reheat.

1. Put the oil, chopped spring onions, ginger, garlic and ¼ teaspoon of salt into a large, high-sided sauté pan on a medium heat. Fry for about 12 minutes, stirring often, until soft and very aromatic. Turn the heat down if the spring onion mixture begins to colour or sizzle too much. Remove from the heat and strain through a sieve, reserving the oil. Return half the spring onion mixture to the pan. Put the oil and the remaining spring onion mixture into a small bowl and set aside.

2. In two batches, blitz the brown rice in the small bowl of a food processor, pulsing until the grains become roughly broken, but not powdery. Set aside.

3. Add the shiitake mushrooms to a spice grinder (or food processor) in two or three batches, and pulse until chopped into roughly 1cm pieces. Add the rice and shiitake to the pan of spring onion mixture and return it to a medium-high heat. Add 1½ litres of water and 1¼ teaspoons of salt, bring to a simmer, then lower the heat to medium. Cook the rice for 30 minutes, stirring often, until the rice is soft and the consistency of a wet porridge.

4. While the rice is cooking, put the radishes into a small bowl with the vinegar, sugar and ¼ teaspoon of salt and set aside to lightly pickle.

5. Add all the ingredients for the rayu to the reserved spring onion and oil mixture, and stir to combine.

6. When the rice is cooked, divide it between four bowls and top each with the rayu. Garnish with the pickled radishes, julienned spring onions and crispy shallots, and serve.

OYSTER MUSHROOM TACOS WITH ALL (OR SOME OF) THE TRIMMINGS

_____

700g oyster mushrooms, roughly torn

2 garlic cloves, crushed

3 tbsp soy sauce

1½ tbsp maple syrup

105ml olive oil, plus extra for shaping

1 tsp cumin seeds

4 dried cascabel chillies, stalks removed and roughly broken

½ tsp allspice berries

125g masa harina (or more, if needed)

2 limes, cut into wedges, to serve

salt

PICKLED ONIONS

1 red onion, finely sliced into rounds on a mandolin, if you have one, or by hand (150g)

2 oranges: finely shave the skin to get 6 strips, then juice to get 60ml

2 hibiscus tea bags, or 5g dried hibiscus flowers (optional)

10 allspice berries

60ml white wine vinegar

1 tsp caster sugar

AVOCADO CREMA

1 medium avocado, peeled and pitted

90g coconut cream

10g coriander, roughly chopped

PICKLED KOHLRABI

1 small kohlrabi (or a large radish), peeled and cut into wide matchsticks (120g)

1½ tbsp lime juice

A tacos meal has an elasticity to it which appeals both to diners, who get to 'make' their own food as they assemble their tacos, and to the cook, who can choose how much effort he or she would like to put in. Here, you can prepare your own tortillas, for example, which take no technical skill, really, but still make you feel as if you'd conquered a substantial Mexican summit, or use shop-bought corn tortillas instead. Jarred pickles and a tub of guacamole are reasonable alternatives to our homemade (yet super-quick) versions. The only essential bit, which you won't regret adding to your repertoire, is the roasted oyster mushrooms, which are crispy, chewy and soft all at once, and soak up flavours like little sponges. The mushrooms also pair wonderfully with our fresh corn polenta (p. 140) or Esme's rough squash mash (p. 136).

The pickles can be made the day before, as can the tortillas. The tortillas should be kept covered with a tea towel and warmed through in a pan or a hot oven just before you serve. *Pictured overleaf.*

1. Preheat the oven to 200°C fan.

2. Mix all the ingredients for the pickled onions in a small serving bowl with ¼ teaspoon of salt and set aside.

3. Put all the ingredients for the crema into the small bowl of a food processor, with ¼ teaspoon of salt and 1 teaspoon of water. Blitz until smooth, scraping down the sides of the bowl as you go. Transfer to a small serving bowl and set aside.

4. Mix the kohlrabi with the lime juice and ¼ teaspoon of salt in a small serving bowl and set aside.

5. In a large bowl, mix the mushrooms with the garlic, soy sauce, maple syrup, 75ml of the oil and ¾ teaspoon of salt. Blitz the cumin, cascabel chillies and allspice to a powder in a spice grinder or a pestle and mortar. Put 1½ teaspoons of the spice mix into a small bowl with the remaining 2 tablespoons of oil and set aside, to serve. Add the rest of the spice mix to the bowl of mushrooms.

6. Transfer the mushrooms to two large, parchment-lined baking trays, spread out as much as possible, and roast for 20 minutes. Combine all the mushrooms on one tray, mix well and continue to roast for another 8 minutes, until crisp and browned.

7. While the mushrooms are roasting, make the tortillas. Put the masa harina and a good pinch of salt into a medium bowl and pour in 250ml of boiling water, stirring with a spatula until the dough comes together. Once cool enough to handle, knead into a smooth ball that has the texture of playdough (this should take less than a minute). The dough shouldn't be wet or come off in your hands, so you may need to add another 10–20g of masa harina depending on the brand you are using, as they can absorb water differently. Divide the dough into 12 pieces weighing about 30g each. With lightly greased hands, roll each piece into a smooth ball. Keep any dough you're not working with covered with a clean damp cloth.

8. Get a clean tea towel ready and cut out six squares of greaseproof paper measuring 14cm, which you'll need to help you press the dough. Place a large, non-stick frying pan on a high heat. Place one piece of dough between two sheets of paper, then, using a heavy-based pan (or a tortilla press, if you have one), press down evenly and firmly on the dough to spread it out into a circle 10–12cm wide. Remove the top sheet of paper and use the bottom sheet to transfer the tortilla to the hot pan. Cook for 90 seconds until nicely browned, then flip and cook for another minute to brown the other side. Transfer the cooked tortilla to the tea towel, fold it over to cover, then repeat with the remaining dough (cook as many tortillas at a time as will fit in the pan).

9. Warm the mushrooms in a hot oven for a few minutes if they have cooled, then pile on to a large platter and drizzle over the chilli oil you set aside earlier. Serve with the tortillas, lime wedges, crema and pickles (discarding the tea bags from the onions) alongside.

SERVES SIX TO EIGHT
As a starter

NEIL'S GRILLED ONIONS WITH GREEN GAZPACHO

8 Tropea onions, papery outer layers removed, trimmed, halved lengthways, leaving the shoots intact (or 4 red onions, peeled and quartered)
20ml olive oil
2 tsp lemon juice
120g feta, roughly broken
80g Greek-style yoghurt
20g croutons, homemade or shop-bought, roughly chopped
¼ tsp nigella seeds
salt and black pepper

GREEN GAZPACHO
2 green peppers, halved lengthways and deseeded (240g)
½ small cucumber, roughly chopped (200g)
1 green chilli, roughly chopped
20g chives
5g tarragon leaves
10g coriander leaves
5g parsley leaves
1½ tbsp apple cider vinegar
1 tbsp olive oil

This elegant starter was created by Neil Campbell, the charming and creative head chef at ROVI, as a true celebration of the humble onion. When we can, we use Calabrian Tropea onions in the restaurant, which are light red, sweet and wonderfully mild, but other varieties of mild onion are fine too, including regular red onions.

The green gazpacho will keep for 3 days in a sealed container in the fridge, as will the whipped feta yoghurt, if you want to get ahead. You'll make more gazpacho than you need. Whatever's left, serve in shot glasses to kick-start a summery supper.

Serve as part of a mezze spread (see p. 304), or as an elegant starter, individually plated.

1. Preheat the oven to 220°C fan.

2. First, make the gazpacho. Place the green peppers on a parchment-lined tray, skin side up, and roast for 25–30 minutes, until the skin has blackened a little. Transfer to a small bowl, cover with a plate and leave for 20 minutes, then peel off and discard the skin. Put the peppers into a blender with the remaining ingredients for the gazpacho, 2 tablespoons of water and ¼ teaspoon of salt. Blitz for a few minutes, until you get a smooth, green sauce, then refrigerate until needed. Reduce the oven temperature to 180°C fan.

3. Heat a large, non-stick frying pan on a high heat. Toss the onions with 2 teaspoons of oil, the lemon juice, ¼ teaspoon of salt and some pepper. Place the onions, cut side down, in the hot pan, then turn the heat down to medium-high. For the halved Tropea onions, cook for 5–6 minutes, undisturbed, until the cut side is well charred. If using quartered red onions, cook for 5–6 minutes on each cut side, until well charred. Place the onions in a baking dish, cover with foil, and bake until the onions are soft and cooked through, but still holding their shape. This can take anywhere between 30 and 40 minutes, depending on the type of onion.

4. Put the feta and yoghurt into the small bowl of a food processor and blitz until as smooth as possible (some small lumps will probably remain, which is fine).

5. Spread the whipped feta on a large platter, creating a dip in the middle with the back of a spoon. Pour about a quarter of the gazpacho into the dip, then arrange the onions haphazardly on top. Finish with the croutons and nigella seeds, drizzle with the remaining 2 teaspoons of oil, and serve.

SERVES FOUR

As a starter or part of a mezze spread

500g golf-ball-sized red onions (about 12), peeled, then halved lengthways

75ml olive oil

400ml pomegranate juice (100% pure)

10g chives, finely chopped

70g young and creamy rindless goat's cheese, broken into 2cm pieces (optional)

⅔ tsp Urfa chilli flakes (or another variety of chilli flake if you can't get them)

salt

SWEET AND SOUR ONION PETALS

These onions – sweet inside, charred at the edges and swimming in a tart pomegranate syrup – started their life at Testi, a north London Turkish restaurant that we love, where a similar dish is made by charring onions next to lamb on the grill, then tossing them in şalgam, a juice made from the sour-salty brine of fermented purple carrots and turnips, and finally sweetening them with pomegranate molasses. The bitter-sweet onions are served alongside the meat, cutting through its fattiness like a sharp knife.

Our onions are made with reduced pomegranate juice instead of molasses and şalgam. They would obviously sit well alongside grilled meats, but we find them totally delicious also in a vegetarian context, with or without the goat's cheese, which is optional. They will go really well with hummus, for example (like our hummus with lemon, fried garlic and chilli, p. 79), an aubergine salad (see aubergine with herbs and crispy garlic, p. 251) and some bread.

1. Preheat the oven to 200°C fan.

2. Heat a large non-stick frying pan on a high heat until very hot. Toss the onions with 2 tablespoons of oil and ¼ teaspoon of salt and place them, cut side down and spread apart, in the hot pan. Place a saucepan on top to weigh the onions down and create an even char, then turn the heat down to medium-high and cook, undisturbed, for about 6 minutes, or until the cut sides are deeply charred. Transfer the onions to a parchment-lined baking tray, charred side up, and bake for about 20 minutes, or until softened. If your onions are larger than golf-ball size, this may take longer. Set aside to cool.

3. Meanwhile, put the pomegranate juice into a medium saucepan on a medium-high heat. Bring to the boil, then simmer for about 12 minutes, or until the liquid has reduced to about 70ml and is the consistency of a loose maple syrup. Set aside to cool; it will thicken as it sits.

4. Combine the chives with the remaining 45ml of oil and a good pinch of salt, and set aside.

5. Pour the pomegranate syrup on to a large platter with a lip and swirl it around to cover most of the plate. Use your hands to loosely separate the onions into individual petals, then place them haphazardly over the syrup. Dot over the goat's cheese, if using, spoon over the chive oil, and finish with the Urfa chilli flakes.

OLIVE OIL FLATBREADS WITH THREE-GARLIC BUTTER

2 ripe plum tomatoes
2 black garlic cloves, thinly sliced
1 tsp picked thyme leaves
1 tsp picked oregano leaves
salt, flaked sea salt and black pepper

FLATBREADS
200g strong white bread flour
1 tsp fast-action dried yeast
1 tbsp olive oil, plus extra for greasing and drizzling
120ml lukewarm water

THREE-GARLIC BUTTER
1 head of garlic, top fifth cut off to expose the cloves
1 small garlic clove, roughly chopped
4 black garlic cloves, roughly chopped
10g parsley, finely chopped
1½ tsp caraway seeds, toasted and crushed
100g unsalted butter, softened

Some things are impossible to resist and, indeed, shouldn't be resisted. The three-garlic butter is the best example we can think of. Made with mellow slow-roasted garlic, sweet black garlic and pungent raw garlic, it is totally glorious and you'll want it over everything. Luckily, the recipe makes more butter than you'll need here (and we'd even make double). It will keep in the fridge for 2 weeks, ready to be smothered on toast, melted over roasted vegetables or stuffed into baked potatoes.

On top of the layer of butter, we also spoon freshly grated tomato, which adds freshness and acidity to the flatbreads and turns them into a very good standalone snack. Without the tomatoes, however, they can be served alongside lots of dishes in the book, such as the spicy berbere ratatouille with coconut salsa (p. 209) and the tofu meatball korma (p. 268), to name just two.

Wrapping a whole head of garlic in foil and roasting it, as we do here, is an accelerated way of getting results close to confit garlic. It's a nifty trick we use to add sweet-savoury depth to lots of other dishes, such as our butternut, orange and sage galette (p. 132), barley, tomato and watercress stew (p. 68), Romano pepper schnitzels (p. 146) and charred peppers and fresh corn polenta (p. 140). Roast three or four heads at a time, if you like: squeeze the cooked cloves into a jar and cover them with olive oil – they'll keep in the fridge for up to 2 weeks. The soft garlic is great to ramp up your soups, stews and sauces and the fragrant oil can be used to finish dishes.

Make the dough up to 2 days in advance and keep it refrigerated in a large, sealed container, if you want to get ahead. *Pictured overleaf.*

1. Preheat the oven to 200°C fan.

2. First, make the dough for the flatbreads. Put the flour, yeast, oil and ½ teaspoon of salt into a large bowl. Pour in the water and use a spatula to combine the mixture. Transfer to a lightly oiled work surface and then, with lightly oiled hands, knead the dough for 5 minutes until it's soft and elastic. You may need to add more oil if the dough starts to stick to your work surface. Return to the bowl, cover with a slightly damp clean tea towel and leave to rise in a warm place for at least 1 hour (preferably 2 hours), until nearly doubled in size. Cut the dough into four equal pieces and set aside, covered with a clean tea towel.

3. While the dough is rising, make the garlic butter. Drizzle the head of garlic with 1 teaspoon of oil and sprinkle with a little salt and pepper. Wrap tightly in foil and bake for 40 minutes, until the cloves have softened. Remove the foil and when cool enough to handle, squeeze out the cloves, discarding the papery skin. Increase the oven temperature to 240°C fan.

4. Put the cooked, raw and black garlic into a pestle and mortar with 1 ½ teaspoons of flaked salt and a generous grind of pepper. Pound to a rough paste, then transfer to a bowl with the parsley, caraway seeds and softened butter. Mix everything together and set aside.

5. Coarsely grate the tomatoes, discarding the skin. Transfer the tomatoes to a sieve set over a bowl and set aside to drain a little.

6. Place a large baking tray on the middle shelf of the oven to heat up.

7. Transfer the dough balls to a lightly oiled work surface and use your hands to stretch each piece into a rough circle, about 18cm wide and ½cm thick.

8. Bake two flatbreads at a time. Remove the hot tray from the oven and quickly place each flatbread on the tray, spaced apart. The dough will be very thin but should have enough elasticity not to break. If you do get a hole in the dough, don't worry; this just adds to the homemade look.

9. Quickly return the tray to the oven for about 7–8 minutes, until the dough is golden-brown and crisp. Continue with the other two flatbreads in the same way.

10. Spread each flatbread with about 1 tablespoon of the garlic butter and top with the drained, grated tomatoes and the black garlic slices. Sprinkle over the herbs and finish with a drizzle of oil, a generous pinch of flaked salt and a good grind of pepper.

SERVES SIX
As a side or part of a
mezze spread

4 medium aubergines
    (1.2kg)
175ml olive oil
6 garlic cloves, finely
    sliced on a mandolin,
    if you have one, or by
    hand
2½ tbsp white wine
    vinegar
1 green chilli, finely
    chopped
15g mint leaves, finely
    sliced
15g coriander leaves,
    finely sliced
15g dill, finely chopped
1 tsp lemon juice
salt and black pepper

AUBERGINE WITH HERBS AND CRISPY GARLIC

_____

This is somewhere between a salad and a condiment, perfect as part of a spread, or equally delicious stuffed into sandwiches and wraps. You'll have some oil left over from frying the garlic, which can be happily tossed through pasta or salad.

The aubergine can be prepared up to the point where the herbs are added the day before, if you like, finishing with the herbs, lemon juice and crispy garlic when you're ready to serve.

1. Preheat the oven to 210°C fan.

2. Cut the aubergines into 3cm chunks and put them into a large mixing bowl with 100ml of oil, ¾ teaspoon of salt and a good grind of pepper. Toss together and spread out over two large, parchment-lined baking trays. Roast for 35 minutes, stirring the aubergines and swapping the trays halfway through so they cook evenly, until a dark golden-brown. Remove from the oven and leave to cool.

3. While the aubergines are roasting, heat the remaining 75ml of oil in a small saucepan on a medium-high heat and line a plate with kitchen paper. Once the oil is very hot, fry the garlic, stirring to separate the slices, until pale golden, about 1 minute. Watch that you don't cook it further, or it may burn and go bitter. Use a slotted spoon to transfer the garlic to the paper-lined plate, reserving the oil. Sprinkle the fried garlic with a little salt and set aside.

4. Put the aubergine into a large bowl with the vinegar, chilli and 3 tablespoons of the garlic-frying oil. Toss together, then add the herbs and mix well. Transfer to a serving plate, drizzle over the lemon juice and serve with the fried garlic scattered on top.

SERVES FOUR
As a side

DIRTY RICE

200g basmati rice
75ml olive oil
7 garlic cloves, peeled,
    4 finely sliced and
    3 crushed
50g unsalted butter (or
    another 50ml olive oil,
    to keep it vegan)
3 onions, finely chopped
    (350g)
**180g ready-cooked and
    peeled chestnuts,**
    finely chopped
25g black garlic, finely
    chopped
**1½ tbsp Cajun spice
    blend** (we use Bart's)
**150ml vegetable stock
    or water**
10g parsley, finely
    chopped
1 tbsp lemon juice
salt

Yotam first fell in love with dirty rice in New Orleans, where the famous Herbsaint restaurant does an insanely delicious version of this Cajun dish. With the help of Rebecca Wilcomb, chef de cuisine at Herbsaint at the time, we then recreated it in London. Rebecca taught us the importance of getting bits stuck to the bottom of the pan in order to boost the flavour and get the 'dirty' look, which is also helped by the ground meat and offal that are part of the original dish. In this meat-free version we use deeply caramelised onions, black garlic and chestnuts to create a similar effect. We think, hand on heart, that it is just as good as the real thing.

Cajun spice blends vary in levels of heat, so you may need to adjust how much you add, according to your taste. Some will also contain salt as the first ingredient, so do bear that in mind when seasoning the dish.

The rice can be made up to 2 days before, but don't add the parsley, garlic slices, lemon juice or reserved oil until you are ready to serve.

1. Put the rice, ¼ teaspoon of salt and 400ml of hot water into a medium saucepan, for which you have a lid, on a medium-high heat. Bring to the boil, then turn the heat to low, cover the pan and leave to cook for 12 minutes. Remove from the heat and leave, covered, for 10 minutes, then fluff up with a fork.

2. While the rice is cooking, heat 3 tablespoons of the oil in a very small pan on a medium heat. Once hot, fry the sliced garlic (not the crushed!), stirring to separate the slices, until pale golden, about 2–2 ½ minutes. Watch that you don't cook it further, or it may burn and go bitter. Use a slotted spoon to transfer the garlic to a plate lined with kitchen paper, reserving the oil. Sprinkle the fried garlic with a little salt and set aside.

3. Add the butter (or oil), the remaining 2 tablespoons of olive oil, the onions and crushed garlic to a large, non-stick sauté pan on a high heat. Fry for about 12 minutes, resisting the urge to stir too often, until the onions are a very deep golden-brown – the onions should catch on the bottom of the pan every now and then, but shouldn't burn, so turn the heat down if necessary. Reduce the heat to medium-high, then add the chestnuts, black garlic, Cajun spices and ½ teaspoon of salt and continue to fry for 7 minutes, stirring every now and then, until the whole thing is a deep, dark brown, but not burnt.

4. Stir the rice into the mixture until fully combined and increase the heat to high. Once the rice at the bottom of the pan begins to crisp up a little, about 2–3 minutes, add the stock and cook, undisturbed, until the liquid has evaporated, about another 2 minutes. Remove from the heat, stir through the parsley, fried garlic slices, lemon juice and reserved garlic oil, and serve.

SERVES FOUR
As a snack

250ml buttermilk
2½ tbsp white wine
    vinegar
25g fresh turmeric,
    peeled and finely
    grated (or ½ tsp
    ground turmeric)
325g plain flour
2½ tbsp nigella seeds
1½ tbsp caraway seeds
1 lime: finely grate the
    zest to get 2 tsp, then
    cut into wedges, to
    serve
1 onion, cut into 2cm-
    thick pinwheels,
    then separated into
    individual rings (150g)
10 spring onions,
    trimmed
900ml sunflower oil, for
    deep-frying
salt and flaked sea salt

DIPPING SAUCE
¼ garlic clove, peeled
5g fresh turmeric, peeled
    and roughly chopped
2½ tbsp mirin
1 tbsp lime juice
1 red chilli, finely chopped

FRIED ONION RINGS WITH BUTTERMILK AND TURMERIC

Fried onion rings are an irresistible treat and we found out that fried spring onions are equally delicious, so we added some here. We serve them – to kick-start a party or as a fine snack – with a dipping sauce made with turmeric, mirin and lime. This punchy combination is perfect with the rich fried onions, but you can easily do without it and serve them with just wedges of lime.

A couple of suggestions. Marigolds or kitchen gloves are useful when grating the turmeric, to prevent stubborn yellow marks. Have your dipping sauce prepped, your vegetables battered and your work surfaces ready before you start frying, so you don't get distracted away from the frying pan and can tuck in as soon as you're done.

1. For the dipping sauce, pound the garlic, turmeric and ⅛ teaspoon of flaked salt to a rough paste in a pestle and mortar. Transfer to a small serving bowl, stir in the mirin, lime juice and chilli, and set aside, to serve.

2. In a medium bowl, mix the buttermilk, vinegar and turmeric and set aside.

3. Mix the flour, nigella and caraway seeds, lime zest and 1 teaspoon of salt together in a high-sided tray or a wide container.

4. Set up two large racks on baking trays, lining one rack with plenty of kitchen paper.

5. Working in batches, coat the onion rings and spring onions first in the flour mixture, then in the buttermilk mixture. Lift them out, shaking off any excess batter, then coat once more in the flour and place, spaced apart, on the rack without the kitchen paper.

6. Heat the oil in a large, high-sided sauté pan on a medium-high heat. Once hot (180°C if you have a temperature probe), fry the rings and spring onions in three or four batches for 2–3 minutes, turning them over halfway, until crisp and golden. Use a slotted spoon to lift them from the oil and on to the paper-lined rack. Sprinkle with plenty of flaked salt, then arrange on a platter and serve with the dipping sauce and the lime wedges alongside.

LEEKS WITH MISO AND CHIVE SALSA

SERVES FOUR
As a starter

12 medium leeks (2.1kg)
300ml sunflower oil, for deep-frying
1¼ tsp cornflour
4 garlic cloves, finely sliced on a mandolin, if you have one, or by hand
1 tbsp olive oil
salt and flaked sea salt

MISO AND CHIVE SALSA
15g fresh ginger, peeled and roughly chopped
1½ tbsp mixed black and white sesame seeds, very well toasted
15g chives, finely chopped, plus an extra tsp to serve
1½ tbsp white miso paste
60ml mirin
¾ tbsp rice vinegar

The punchy salsa is the star here, pairing wonderfully well with the mild sweetness of the leeks. You can also use it to dress new potatoes, or to drizzle over tofu, fish or chicken. The fried leek tops and garlic add aroma and crunch, but, if you want to avoid deep-frying, you can easily leave them out and simply serve the leeks with the salsa. They will go well with the turnip cake (p. 270), for example, or alongside fried tofu or roasted meats.

The salsa can be made up to 3 days ahead and kept in a sealed jar in the fridge. Don't steam the leeks too long before serving, as they can lose their colour.

1. Remove and discard the tough outer layers of the leeks then wash the leeks well to remove any grit. Cut off and reserve the darker green tops of the leeks so each leek is about 22cm long.

2. Finely slice 60g of the reserved green leek tops into 8cm-long, thin strips. Rinse very well to remove any grit, then dry thoroughly and set aside.

3. For the salsa, pound the ginger and ¼ teaspoon of flaked salt into a paste using a pestle and mortar (or with the side of a knife). Put into a small bowl along with all the remaining salsa ingredients, stir well to combine, and set aside.

4. Half fill a pot (large enough to fit the length of the leeks lying down) with lightly salted water and place on a medium-high heat. Once simmering, add the leeks and reduce the heat to medium. Place a lid smaller than the saucepan on top of the leeks, weighing them down so they don't float above the surface of the water. Simmer gently for 20 minutes, or until a knife goes through easily but they still hold their shape. Transfer the leeks to a colander and stand them vertically so they drain thoroughly.

5. While the leeks are draining, put the sunflower oil into a medium, high-sided saucepan on a medium-high heat and line a plate with kitchen paper. Toss the dried, sliced green leek tops with 1 teaspoon of cornflour. Once the oil is very hot (170°C if you have a temperature probe), add the leek tops and fry for about 2 minutes, stirring with a fork, until golden and crispy. Transfer to the paper-lined plate with a slotted spoon and sprinkle with some flaked salt. Toss the garlic with the remaining ¼ teaspoon of cornflour and fry for about a minute, stirring frequently to separate the slices, until crisp and golden-brown. Add to the fried leeks and sprinkle with flaked salt.

6. Arrange the leeks on a large plate and spoon over the miso salsa. Drizzle over the olive oil and top with the fried leeks and garlic. Sprinkle with the extra chives and serve.

MISO BUTTER ONIONS

8 regular-sized onions
  (1.2kg)
100g unsalted butter,
  melted
100g white miso paste

These onions are a bit of a revelation, and the very definition of low effort/high impact, where just three ingredients come together to create something truly spectacular.

Still, the effort we save you on mise en place we take back by asking for a roasting tray which is *just* the right size. This is important. The tray should be just big enough to fit the halved onions in a single layer, without them overlapping. The onions will then shrink as they cook, creating the space the sauce needs to evaporate and thicken into a glorious gravy. If your tray isn't big enough to fit eight onions (that's sixteen halves), then roast fewer, decreasing the rest of the ingredients proportionally (the cooking method and time stay the same).

It's also important to saturate each onion half very well every time you baste, spooning the sauce over several times so the cut sides remain moist. This is to ensure that the onions caramelise, rather than burn.

These are best eaten straight out of the oven, but if you are making them ahead, warm the sauce up before serving, letting it down with a bit of water. Serve spooned over toast, rice or mashed potatoes. Roasted chicken, predictably, is also a great match.

1. Preheat the oven to 240°C fan.

2. Halve the onions lengthways, discarding the papery skin, as well as the layer beneath if it is tough or dry. Trim the tops, and a little off the bottom (not too much – you want to ensure the onion halves stay held together at the base).

3. Whisk the melted butter, miso and 1 litre of warm water together until fully combined.

4. Place the onion halves, cut side down and spaced apart, in a 40cm x 28cm high-sided baking tray or dish and pour over the miso water. Cover tightly with foil and bake for 35 minutes, then remove the foil and turn the onions over so they are cut side up (take care to ensure they remain intact). Baste the onions very well, then return to the oven, uncovered, for another 45–50 minutes, basting every 10 minutes, until the onions are very soft, deeply browned on top, and the sauce has reduced to a gravy consistency.

5. Carefully transfer the onions to a platter, pouring the sauce over and around them, and serve at once.

KOHLRABI 'NOODLE' SALAD

SERVES FOUR
As a side

1 tbsp white or black sesame seeds, or a mixture of both, toasted

1 tsp poppy seeds, toasted

1 tsp nori sprinkles (or finely blitz ½ sheet of nori in a spice grinder and use 1 tsp)

1½ tsp Aleppo chilli flakes (or ¾ tsp regular chilli flakes)

½ tsp Szechuan peppercorns, finely crushed

1 tbsp ready-roasted and salted peanuts, roughly chopped

2–3 medium kohlrabi, trimmed and peeled (570g)

3 tbsp lime juice

20g fresh ginger, peeled and roughly chopped

1 tbsp rice vinegar

6 spring onions, finely chopped (60g)

60ml sunflower oil

flaked sea salt

Heat, acidity and the numbing effect of ginger and Szechuan pepper create an intensity in this salad which can flavour an entire meal. We would serve it with a bowl of rice and some simply fried tofu (see cardamom tofu with lime greens on p. 172 for how best to fry tofu), seafood or meat.

The nut-seaweed-chilli-seed sprinkle is very special, so make extra to sprinkle over salads, noodles and rice. It will stay crunchy in a sealed container for up to 3 days.

If you can't get kohlrabi, this will also work with a large radish, such as daikon, or with green papaya. The salad can discolour and get a bit soggy, so best to toss it together just before serving.

1. Put the first six ingredients into a small bowl with ½ teaspoon of flaked sea salt.

2. Slice the kohlrabi as thinly as possible, on a mandolin if you have one (or use the appropriate attachment on a food processor). Stack the slices on top of each other in manageable piles and slice into 2cm-wide strips (to resemble short flat noodles). Put into a bowl with the lime juice and 1 teaspoon of flaked sea salt, toss together and set aside for 10 minutes.

3. Meanwhile, put the ginger and ¾ teaspoon of flaked sea salt into a pestle and mortar and pound to a paste. Place in a small bowl with the vinegar and two-thirds of the spring onions. Heat the oil in a small pan on a medium heat until warm, and add to the bowl of ginger and spring onions. Set aside for 20 minutes for the flavours to meld.

4. Drain the kohlrabi to get rid of most of the liquid that will have collected, then toss with the oil and ginger mixture. Transfer to a platter, sprinkle over the mixed seeds and nuts, and finish with the rest of the spring onions.

SERVES FOUR
As a side

RADISH AND CUCUMBER SALAD WITH CHIPOTLE PEANUTS

———————

1 cucumber, cut into ¼cm-thick half-moons, on a mandolin, if you have one, or by hand (300g)

1 daikon, peeled and cut into ¼cm-thick half-moons, on a mandolin, if you have one, or by hand (300g)

50g breakfast radishes, thinly sliced, on a mandolin, if you have one, or by hand

20g coriander, leaves picked with some of their stalks

1 garlic clove, crushed

¼ jalapeño, deseeded and finely chopped (5g)

1 tsp cumin seeds, toasted and roughly crushed in a pestle and mortar

2–3 limes: finely grate the zest to get 1 tsp, then juice to get 3 tbsp

2 tbsp olive oil

flaked sea salt and black pepper

CHIPOTLE PEANUTS

1 dried chipotle chilli, stem discarded (or ½ tsp chipotle chilli flakes)

90g unsalted blanched peanuts

a pinch of cayenne pepper

1¼ tbsp golden syrup

2 tsp lime zest

1½ tsp lime juice

1½ tsp olive oil

If you're in the mood for an all-out Mexican feast, serve this salad alongside the cheese tamales (p. 158) or the oyster mushroom tacos with all (or some of) the trimmings (p. 238), or indeed both (see our Mexican feast, p. 303)! Less taxing would be pairing it with just the roasted mushrooms from the tacos recipe, making this a meaty salad fit for a midweek supper. Jicama, a crunchy Mexican root, can happily replace the daikon if you can get your hands on it.

Double up on the chipotle peanuts, if you like. They are very snack-friendly and will stay crunchy in a sealed container for up to 3 days. The salad, however, will lose its crispness if it sits around for too long, so is best served at once.

1. For the chipotle peanuts, blitz the dried chilli in a spice grinder until you have a fine powder, or finely crush in a pestle and mortar. Measure out ½ teaspoon (reserving the rest for another recipe) and place in a small sauté pan along with the peanuts, cayenne, golden syrup, ⅓ teaspoon of flaked sea salt, the lime zest, lime juice and oil. Place the pan on a medium-high heat and cook, stirring often, for about 8 minutes, or until the peanuts are sticky and well coated. Transfer to a parchment-lined baking tray and leave to cool completely. Break apart into bite-size pieces and set aside.

2. Put the cucumber, daikon, radishes and coriander into a large bowl. Separately, in a small bowl, combine the garlic, jalapeño, cumin, lime zest, lime juice, olive oil, 1¼ teaspoons of flaked salt and a good grind of black pepper. Whisk well and pour this mixture over the vegetables. Transfer to a large serving platter and top with half the peanuts, serving the rest in a bowl alongside.

CORN RIBS

3 whole corn on the cob, husks removed (700g)
1.3 litres sunflower oil, for deep-frying
1½ tsp runny honey
flaked sea salt

BLACK LIME AND PUMPKIN SEED BUTTER
25g pumpkin seeds
60g unsalted butter, very well softened
1–2 dried black limes (see p. 18), roughly broken, then finely blitzed in a spice grinder to get 2¼ tsp (alternatively, use grated lime zest)

We got the idea for corn-as-ribs for our restaurant ROVI from Max Ng and the team at Momofuku Ssäm, New York. These deep-fried corn quarters, which magically curl up to look like ribs, worked phenomenally well at ROVI, with its ethos of treating vegetables like meat. So much so, that a few diehard fans cancelled their reservations abruptly when corn went out of season and we had to take it off the menu.

For home cooks who aren't endowed with the muscles or the knives of our hardy chefs, the biggest challenge is preparing the corn, cutting through its hard core. Make sure you start with a big sharp knife and make decisive, powerful cuts (keeping fingers well away). A blunt knife won't do the job and is more likely to cause an accident.

Double up on the black lime and pumpkin seed butter. It's seriously delicious spread on toast with a drizzle of honey, and will keep in a sealed jar in the fridge for up to a week.

1. Preheat the oven to 160°C fan. For the black lime butter, place the pumpkin seeds on a small baking tray and toast in the oven until they are fragrant and golden-brown and the skins are beginning to split, about 10 minutes. Coarsely blitz the toasted pumpkin seeds in a spice grinder (or finely chop them) and leave to cool for 10 minutes.

2. In a medium bowl, use a spatula to whip the butter together with 2 teaspoons of the ground black lime, the finely chopped pumpkin seeds and 1 teaspoon of flaked salt, until fully combined. Keep refrigerated, if getting ahead, removing it from the fridge 30 minutes before it's needed, to soften.

3. Use a large, sharp knife to carefully cut the corn in half widthways, then cut each half lengthways into quarters. This is easiest with the corn standing upright, so you don't squash the kernels.

4. Heat the oil in a medium, high-sided saucepan on a medium-high heat. Once very hot (around 180°C if you have a temperature probe), test the heat by lowering in the end of one of the pieces of corn; it should sizzle but shouldn't brown straight away.

5. Fry the corn in three batches for 6–7 minutes (take care, the oil may spit!), turning them a few times until they have curled slightly and turned golden-brown. Remove from the oil using a slotted spoon and set aside on a tray lined with kitchen paper while you continue with the rest in the same way. Transfer to a bowl and toss with the honey and 1½ teaspoons of flaked salt.

6. Pile on to a platter and serve the butter alongside, sprinkled with the remaining ground black lime.

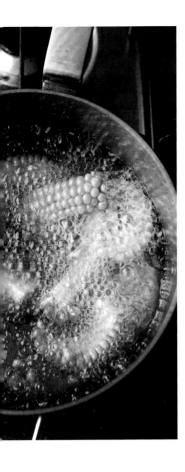

TOMATO AND PLUM SALAD WITH NORI AND SESAME

SERVES SIX

800g mixed ripe
   tomatoes (beef, plum,
   tiger, green, yellow and
   cherry), large ones cut
   into 1cm-thick wedges,
   cherry tomatoes halved
   or quartered
3 ripe plums, pitted
   and cut into 1cm-thick
   wedges (250g) (or more
   tomatoes instead, see
   introduction)
4 spring onions, finely
   sliced
5g coriander leaves,
   roughly chopped
flaked sea salt

DRESSING
1¼ tsp fish sauce
   (optional)
2 tsp caster sugar
2 tbsp rice vinegar
2 tsp soy sauce
2 tbsp groundnut oil
5g fresh ginger, peeled
   and julienned
½ garlic clove, crushed
¼ tsp finely grated
   orange zest

NORI AND SESAME SALT
½ sheet of nori seaweed
1½ tbsp white or black
   sesame seeds, or a
   mixture of both, toasted
½ tsp chilli flakes

It's very 2020 to ditch crisps and snack on dried nori sheets instead. This can only be a good thing, because they are delicious and nutritious and because it means you can get them easily and use them to ramp up the flavour in all kinds of dishes, from roasted vegetables and salads to rice and noodles. So double (or quadruple!) the amount of nori and sesame salt, if you like, and keep as handy seasoning for all these instances.

The plums are glorious with the tomatoes but, if they aren't in season, substitute them with more tomatoes; the salad will still taste great without them. Toss the tomatoes and plums together with the herbs and dressing just before you're ready to serve, so the salad doesn't become too soggy.

1. Whisk all the ingredients for the dressing together with ½ teaspoon of flaked salt and leave to infuse while you prepare the rest of the salad.

2. Roughly break up the nori sheet, then blitz to a rough powder (a spice grinder is best for this). In a small bowl, mix the nori with the sesame seeds, chilli flakes and ½ teaspoon of flaked salt.

3. In a large bowl, toss the tomatoes together with the plums, spring onions, coriander and the dressing. Transfer to a platter, sprinkle over the nori and sesame mix, and serve.

½ **red onion,** thinly sliced
(60g)
2 tbsp lemon juice
40g cashews
20g blanched almonds
6 cardamom pods, shells
discarded and seeds
removed
2 tsp cumin seeds
2 tsp coriander seeds
3 tbsp olive oil
1 onion, roughly chopped
(150g)
4 garlic cloves, crushed
15g fresh ginger, peeled
and grated
1 green chilli, deseeded
and finely chopped
1 cinnamon stick
¾ tsp ground turmeric
2 plum tomatoes, grated
and skins discarded
(180g)
2 tbsp coriander leaves,
finely sliced, to serve
salt and black pepper

TOFU MEATBALLS
2 tbsp olive oil, plus extra
for shaping
**250g chestnut
mushrooms,** sliced
½cm thick
200g extra-firm tofu,
patted dry and then
roughly crumbled into
large chunks
3 garlic cloves, crushed
150g silken tofu
2 tbsp tahini
1 tbsp soy sauce
30g panko breadcrumbs
½ tbsp cornflour
5 spring onions, thinly
sliced (75g)
10g coriander, finely
chopped

TOFU MEATBALL KORMA

If you don't have time to make the meatballs here, you could just make the sauce to serve with roasted cauliflower or sweet potato. It will keep for 3 days in the fridge and up to a month in the freezer. The meatballs can be cooked the day before, just warm them together with the sauce in a pan before serving.

The flatbreads on p. 246 will make an excellent side here, outshining any shop-bought garlic naan. Both the korma and the flatbreads make up part of our korma feast (see p. 303), if you're up to the challenge.

1. Preheat the oven to 200°C fan. Combine the red onion, lemon juice and ⅛ teaspoon of salt in a small bowl and set aside while you make the meatballs and sauce, or leave overnight.

2. Put the cashews and almonds into a small saucepan on a medium-high heat. Cover with water, bring to the boil, then lower the heat to medium and simmer for 20 minutes. Drain and set aside.

3. For the meatballs, heat the oil in a large sauté pan on a high heat, then add the mushrooms and firm tofu and cook until lightly golden, about 8 minutes. Stir in the garlic for 30 seconds, then remove from the heat. Place in a food processor and pulse until roughly chopped. Transfer to a large mixing bowl with all the remaining ingredients for the meatballs, ¾ teaspoon of salt and a good grind of black pepper. Mix very well to combine. With oiled hands, form into 16 ping-pong-sized balls, about 40g each, compressing them as you go so they hold together. Place them on a parchment-lined baking tray, spaced apart, and bake for 25 minutes until lightly golden. Set aside.

4. While the meatballs are in the oven, make the sauce. Finely crush the cardamom, cumin and coriander seeds in a pestle and mortar and set aside. Put 1½ tablespoons of oil into a large sauté pan, for which you have a lid, on a medium-high heat. Add the onion and cook for 10 minutes, or until softened and deeply browned. Transfer to a blender along with the nuts and 200ml of water, and blend until completely smooth, about 2 minutes.

5. Put the remaining 1½ tablespoons of oil into the same pan on a medium-high heat. Add the garlic, ginger and green chilli and cook for 1 minute, then add the spices and cook for 1 minute more. Add the tomatoes and cook for 4 minutes, stirring occasionally, until thickened. Add the puréed onion and nut mixture, another 500ml of water, 1½ teaspoons of salt and a good grind of black pepper. Bring to a simmer, then lower the heat to medium and cook for 25 minutes, until reduced by a third. Add the meatballs to the pan of sauce, then cover with a lid and heat for 5 minutes, until the meatballs are warmed through. Sprinkle over the coriander and sliced red onion.

SERVES FOUR

As a main

SOY MAPLE NUTS

15g dried shiitake mushrooms, soaked in boiling water for 20 minutes

30g pine nuts, roughly chopped

50g ready-cooked and peeled chestnuts, roughly chopped

1 tbsp white or black sesame seeds, or a mixture of both

1 small garlic clove, crushed

¼ tsp fresh ginger, peeled and finely grated

3 tbsp soy sauce

60ml maple syrup

salt

TURNIP CAKE

130g Thai white rice flour (not interchangeable with the glutinous variety, or with regular rice flour)

1 tbsp cornflour

2½ tsp caster sugar

1 small garlic clove, crushed

¼ tsp fresh ginger, peeled and finely grated

2 tsp sesame oil

1–2 large daikon, trimmed, peeled and roughly grated (600g)

105ml sunflower oil, plus extra for greasing

TO SERVE

40ml soy sauce

20ml maple syrup

1 tsp toasted sesame oil

1½ tbsp finely chopped chives

TURNIP CAKE

A mild obsession and a pet peeve came together here, in a dish which we are especially proud of. The obsession is turnip cake – which isn't really a cake and isn't made of turnips but of daikon – served as part of Chinese dim sum. The pet peeve is nut roast, the traditional centrepiece offered to vegans and vegetarians at Christmas when no one can think of anything better to serve them. The challenge was to combine both, to create a festive vegan dish which is both special and truly satisfying. We like to think that our cake, in which the traditional Chinese sausage and dried shrimp are replaced with sweet and salty clusters of shiitake mushrooms, pine nuts, chestnuts and sesame seeds, can sit respectfully both at the centre of any holiday feast (see p. 304) and on the tables of the best restaurants in Chinatown.

If you don't have a 30cm x 23cm high-sided tin, use another dish or tin with a similar surface area; the main objective is that the cake is 2cm thick. The dish or tin needs to be high-sided as it needs to sit in a water bath, and you don't want the water spilling over the sides.

Make the cake the day before, to get ahead, and keep refrigerated, ready to be fried just before serving. Keep the soy-maple-nut mixture loosely covered at room temperature, if you've made it the day before as well. The cake is best pan-fried on both sides but, to save time, you can brush the slices with oil and grill them in a very hot oven for about 7 minutes, or until golden-brown on top. *Pictured overleaf.*

1. First, make the soy maple nuts. Drain the mushrooms, squeezing them until dry, then finely chop and set aside.

2. Put the pine nuts and chestnuts into a large, non-stick frying pan and place on a medium-high heat. Toast for 3–4 minutes, stirring, until golden and fragrant, then add the sesame seeds for 1 minute, followed by the chopped mushrooms, garlic, ginger, soy sauce, maple syrup and ⅛ teaspoon of salt. Continue to cook, stirring, until the liquid bubbles, reduces and coats the nuts and mushrooms, 4–5 minutes. Spread out on a parchment-lined tray and set aside.

3. For the turnip cake, whisk together the first six ingredients with 240ml of water and 1 teaspoon of salt in a large bowl until smooth, then set aside while you prepare the rest.

4. Place a large sauté pan on a medium heat with the 600g of grated daikon and 2 tablespoons of water and cook for 15 minutes, stirring every now and then, until all the liquid has evaporated (take care not to brown the daikon). Leave to cool for 10 minutes.

5. Preheat the oven to 220°C fan. Line and grease a 30cm x 23cm high-sided baking tin or baking dish and set aside.

6. Transfer the daikon to the bowl of rice flour mixture, along with 80g of the soy maple nuts, and stir together. Spoon the mixture into the prepared tin, smoothing the top as you go, then seal tightly with foil and place the tin in a high-sided baking tray that is slightly larger than the tin. Pour enough boiling water into the baking tray to rise three-quarters of the way up the sides of the tin of turnip cake – and bake for 35 minutes. Remove the tin from the water bath, discard the foil and set aside to cool. Transfer to the fridge for 40 minutes, or overnight, until completely chilled.

7. Turn the cake out on to a chopping board, then cut into eight even slices. Brush the turnip cakes on each side with 4 tablespoons (total) of the oil.

8. Heat a large, non-stick frying pan on a medium-high heat, then add 1 ½ tablespoons of sunflower oil. Fry the slices in two batches (or more batches, if you can't fit four slices into the pan), spread apart, for 2–3 minutes on each side, until crisp and golden brown. Keep the first batch warm while you fry the rest with the remaining 1 ½ tablespoons of sunflower oil.

9. Put all the serving ingredients (except the chives) and 80ml of water into a small saucepan on a medium-high heat and warm through, about 3 minutes.

10. Arrange the turnip cake slices on a large platter, overlapping each other. Pour over half the sauce, then sprinkle over the chives and the rest of the nuts and seeds. Serve at once, with the remaining sauce on the side.

POTATO SALAD WITH THAI BASIL SALSA

600g small to medium
salad potatoes (or
1.1kg, if you're not using
Jerusalem artichokes),
peeled and cut into
3–4cm pieces

600g Jerusalem
artichokes, peeled and
cut into 3cm pieces
(500g) (optional)

75ml olive oil

50g breakfast radishes,
thinly sliced on a
mandolin, if you have
one, or by hand

3 limes: finely grate the
zest to get 1¼ tbsp, then
juice to get 3 tbsp

1 small garlic clove,
roughly chopped

15g fresh ginger, peeled
and roughly chopped

20g Thai basil, roughly
chopped, plus 8g picked
leaves to serve

1 large green chilli, finely
sliced into rounds

30g smoked, ready-
roasted and salted
almonds, roughly
chopped (or regular
ready-roasted almonds,
instead)

salt and flaked sea salt

This is as fresh as a potato salad will get, thanks to the large quantities of lime, garlic, chilli and Thai basil that are poured over it. It will make a good light supper with the broccoli two ways (p. 186), for example, and will also partner really well with salmon or roasted chicken.

If you can't get hold of Thai basil, an equal combination of coriander and regular basil is a very good alternative. The salsa won't stay bright green for long, so make it just before you're ready to serve.

When Jerusalem artichokes are in season, we like to roast them and add them to this salad. We appreciate, however, that not everyone is a fan, so you can easily substitute them with the same amount of potatoes (in which case they'll all be boiled, so no need to turn on the oven).

1. Preheat the oven to 210°C fan (if roasting Jerusalem artichokes).

2. Put the potatoes into a large saucepan, cover with cold, salted water, bring to a simmer, then cook for around 10 minutes, or until the potatoes are cooked through but still holding their shape. Drain and set aside to cool for 15 minutes.

3. Meanwhile, mix the Jerusalem artichokes (if using) with 1 tablespoon of oil and ½ teaspoon of flaked salt, and spread them out on a parchment-lined baking tray. Bake for 18–20 minutes, tossing them halfway through, until golden-brown and cooked through. Leave to cool for a few minutes, then put into a large bowl with the cooled potatoes.

4. While the artichokes are roasting, mix the radishes with 1 tablespoon of lime juice and ¼ teaspoon of flaked salt and set aside.

5. In a spice grinder or the small bowl of a food processor, blitz the lime zest, garlic, ginger and 20g of Thai basil with 1 teaspoon of flaked salt and the remaining 60ml of oil to get a bright green paste. Scrape into the bowl of potatoes, along with the remaining 2 tablespoons of lime juice. Gently stir through the radishes (including the liquid) and the picked Thai basil leaves. Finish with the chilli and almonds and serve.

SPICY ROAST POTATOES WITH TAHINI AND SOY

900g roasting potatoes, skin on and cut into 2½–3cm cubes

50g rose harissa (adjust according to the brand you are using; see p. 20)

1 garlic clove, crushed

3 tbsp olive oil

1½ tbsp chives, finely chopped

1½ tbsp black or white sesame seeds, preferably a mixture of both, toasted

salt and black pepper

TAHINI AND
SOY DRESSING

60g tahini (stir very well before using, to combine the solids and fat)

2 tbsp soy sauce

1½ tbsp mirin (or maple syrup)

1½ tbsp rice vinegar

There are different schools of roast potatoes. The English school, which calls for peeling, parboiling and roasting in scalding fat, is one which Yotam proudly endorses and Ixta strongly opposes. We both, however, come together in adoration of the Italian school, which involves minimal faff and maximum olive oil (two good things), yet still gives a great crisp result. The toppings here – tahini, soy, sesame and chives – may seem a little unorthodox, but add a nutty savouriness that the potatoes love.

Double or triple the tahini and soy dressing, if you like; it's great as a salad dressing (see cucumber salad à la X'ian Impression, p. 113), drizzled over rice and noodles, or as a dipping sauce for tofu or chicken skewers. It will keep in a jar in the fridge for up to 2 weeks.

1. Preheat the oven to 240°C fan.

2. In a large bowl, mix the first four ingredients with ¾ teaspoon of salt and a generous grind of pepper until well combined. Transfer to a large parchment-lined baking tray and spread out as much as possible, then cover tightly with foil and roast for 15 minutes.

3. Remove the foil, reduce the heat to 200°C fan and roast for another 25 minutes, uncovered, stirring halfway through, until the potatoes are cooked through and nicely browned.

4. While the potatoes are roasting, whisk all the ingredients for the dressing together with 1 tablespoon of water until smooth.

5. Transfer the potatoes to a large, shallow serving bowl and drizzle over the tahini dressing. Finish with the chives and sesame seeds and serve.

TANGERINE AND ANCHO CHILLI FLAN

120g caster sugar
1 tbsp tangerine juice

CUSTARD
1 large dried ancho chilli, soaked in boiling water for 10 minutes then drained (and deseeded if you prefer less heat)
270g condensed milk
100ml double cream
400ml whole milk
3 eggs
1 tsp vanilla bean paste, or vanilla extract
1 tsp finely grated tangerine zest
a generous pinch of flaked sea salt

Flan is the most traditional Mexican dessert, consisting of caramel with custard set on top (or below, once flipped). The method here couldn't be simpler: once you've made the caramel, all the custard ingredients are thrown into a blender and blitzed until smooth. It's as easy as that.

This recipe was originally developed with blood oranges, which pair wonderfully with ancho chilli. If they are in season, do use them instead. And by all means experiment with other dried chillies and fruit juices!

The flan will keep for up to 3 days in the fridge, if you want to get ahead.

1. Preheat the oven to 150°C fan. Place a 20cm x 20cm non-stick square tin, or a similar-sized ovenproof dish, in the oven to keep warm until required. Make sure your tin is not spring-form; you don't want the caramel to escape.

2. For the caramel, put the sugar into a large pan on a medium heat and cook for about 8 minutes: resist the urge to stir, and instead swirl the pan until the sugar has melted. Continue swirling slowly until the sugar turns dark amber, then carefully and quickly remove the tin from the oven and pour in the caramel, tilting the tin as you go so the caramel covers the base evenly. Leave the caramel to set while you make the custard.

3. Squeeze the chilli very well to remove any liquid. Discard the stalk, then put the chilli, its seeds and all the remaining ingredients for the custard into a blender and blitz on high speed for about 30 seconds, until well combined.

4. Tap the caramel to make sure it has set hard, then place a fine-mesh sieve over the tin. Pour the custard through the sieve into the tin, discarding any larger bits of chilli that collect in the sieve.

5. Transfer the tin carefully to a larger, high-sided baking dish and place in the oven, keeping the oven door open. Carefully pour enough boiling water into the larger dish to come halfway up the sides of the flan tin. Bake for 40–50 minutes, or until the surface is set and golden-brown, but the flan still has a good wobble to it (it will set in the fridge). Remove from the water bath and set aside to cool slightly, then refrigerate for at least 3 hours, or overnight.

6. Remove the flan from the fridge 30 minutes before you want to serve it. Carefully run a small knife around the edges of the flan to release it. Place a large plate (larger than your flan dish, and with a lip to catch the liquid caramel) on top of the flan tin. Holding both the plate and the tin together, quickly flip the whole thing over. Gently lift off the tin – the flan should have released itself on to the plate. Drizzle the tangerine juice over the flan and serve at once.

TAPIOCA FRITTERS WITH ORANGE SYRUP AND STAR ANISE

90g small pearl tapioca
420ml whole milk
120ml double cream
1 tsp vanilla bean paste
   or vanilla extract
½ tsp ground star anise
3 tbsp caster sugar
⅓ tsp flaked sea salt
1 egg, separated, plus
   1 extra yolk
3 oranges: finely grate
   the zest to get 1½ tsp,
   then juice 2 oranges to
   get 80ml
75g runny honey
2 whole star anise
15g tapioca flour
500ml sunflower oil, for
   deep-frying
10g icing sugar, for
   dusting

Even if you think that you don't like tapioca, please try these fritters. They are sweet, soft, crisp and very difficult to stop eating once you get started. They can be prepared a day in advance up until the stage when you chill the raw mix, ready to fry when you need them. The sauce can also be prepared a day ahead.

1. Put the first five ingredients into a medium, heavy-based saucepan and leave to soak for 20 minutes. Place the pan on a medium-high heat and bring to a simmer. Add the sugar and salt, then lower the heat to medium and cook for another 12 minutes, stirring often, until the tapioca has become translucent and chewy and the pudding has thickened. Whisk the egg yolks together with 3 tablespoons of the tapioca mixture in a small bowl, then add this to the saucepan. Switch off the heat and stir continuously for about a minute, until the yolks have blended into the pudding but have not scrambled. Stir in the orange zest and transfer the mixture to a bowl to cool.

2. Beat the egg white until medium-firm peaks form. Fold this into the cooled pudding, then cover the surface with cling film to prevent a skin from forming. Transfer to the fridge to set, about 1½ hours or overnight.

3. Using a sharp knife, trim the top and tail off the remaining unjuiced orange. Cut down along its round curves, removing the skin and white pith. Slice between the membranes to release the segments, then cut each one in half. Set aside until needed.

4. For the syrup, put the orange juice, honey, 30ml of water and star anise into a small saucepan and place on a medium-high heat. Leave to bubble away for about 10–12 minutes, or until it has reduced by half. Remove from the heat, stir in the orange segments and set aside to cool completely.

5. Stir the tapioca flour into the pudding mixture until well combined.

6. Heat the oil in a medium saucepan on a medium-high heat. Once hot, pick up about 35g of the tapioca mixture with your hands, shaping it into a rough ball the size of a small golf ball; the mixture will be very sticky, so you might want to use gloves. Gently drop the ball into the hot oil and continue in this way, working quickly, frying about five balls at a time, until deeply golden on the outside and warmed through the centre, about 4–5 minutes. Transfer them to a tray lined with kitchen paper while you continue with the rest. You should make fifteen in total.

7. To serve, divide the syrup between four plates, top each with three of the fritters (saving any extra for seconds) and dust the tops with icing sugar.

SERVES FOUR

POACHED APRICOTS WITH PISTACHIO AND AMARETTI MASCARPONE

80g pistachios
80g amaretti biscuits
  (the hard variety),
  roughly crumbled
2 tbsp caster sugar
120g mascarpone
120ml double cream
1 tsp finely grated lime
  zest

POACHED APRICOTS
100ml Sauternes, or
  another light dessert
  wine
1 lime: finely shave the
  skin to get 3 strips, then
  juice to get 1 tbsp
¼ tsp vanilla bean paste
  or vanilla extract
60g caster sugar
6 medium apricots,
  halved and pitted
  (280g)
1 tsp orange blossom
  water

Pesche ripiene – stuffed peaches – is a typical dessert from Piemonte, Italy. It is a lesson in simplicity, where just a few great ingredients – namely ripe peaches, amaretti biscuits, mascarpone, sugar and eggs – are needed to create something quite spectacular. Perhaps because it is so easy, it was one of the first desserts Ixta ever made, from the first recipe book she ever had, *Italy: The Beautiful Cookbook* by Lorenza de' Medici. A few Ottolenghi twists and turns later, we have this recipe, inspired by pesche ripiene, using apricots instead of peaches, and with the addition of pistachios, orange blossom and lime zest.

   This dessert is both rich and wonderfully refreshing, and requires very little effort. Make sure, though, that you use apricots that are at their very best. If your apricots aren't ripe, add them to the saucepan of hot syrup *before* you take it off the heat, allowing them to simmer gently for a couple of minutes before setting the pan aside. You can poach them the day before serving, if you want to get ahead. The amaretti cream can also be made a day ahead; the biscuits in it will soften a bit, but that's okay – you'll get the crunch factor from the remaining biscuits with which you'll top the dessert. *Pictured overleaf.*

1. For the apricots, put the Sauternes, 40ml of water, lime strips and juice, vanilla and the 60g of caster sugar into a medium saucepan on a high heat and cook until the sugar has melted and the liquid is simmering. Take off the heat and place the apricots in the hot liquid, cut side down. Leave them to poach in the residual heat until they are soft but still hold their shape, anywhere between 20 and 40 minutes depending on how ripe the fruit is. Remove the apricots and discard the lime strips, then cover the apricots to prevent discolouration and set aside. Return the saucepan of syrup to a medium-high heat and simmer until reduced to 70ml, 5–6 minutes. Stir in the orange blossom water and set aside at room temperature until needed.

2. Preheat the oven to 170°C fan. Place the pistachios on a baking tray and roast for 10 minutes until very fragrant.

3. Once cool, finely chop the pistachios and put them into a bowl with the amaretti and the 2 tablespoons of sugar.

4. Put the mascarpone and cream into the bowl of a stand mixer with the whisk attachment in place, or use an electric handheld whisk, and whip for 1–2 minutes until smooth and fluffy (take care not to over-whip). Fold through three-quarters of the amaretti and pistachio mixture, and set aside.

5. To serve, divide the apricots and the amaretti cream between four bowls. Pour the syrup over the apricots and sprinkle the remaining amaretti and pistachio crumble over the cream. Finish with the lime zest, and serve.

WATERMELON AND STRAWBERRY SORBET

SERVES EIGHT

1 small watermelon
(1.4kg), rind and seeds
removed and flesh cut
into 2cm chunks (to get
700g of flesh)

300g ripe strawberries,
hulled and roughly
chopped

**10g fresh kaffir lime
leaves,** stalks removed
and leaves blitzed in
a spice grinder or very
finely chopped (or
3 rooibos tea bags)

250g glucose

8 limes: finely grate the
zest to get 4 tsp and
juice to get 90ml, then
cut the remainder into
wedges to serve (you'll
need an extra tsp of lime
zest if using roiboos tea)

60ml vodka

1¼ tbsp caster sugar, to
serve

This sorbet is made without an ice cream machine but it's still remarkably smooth. You can thank the vodka and glucose for that; they work together to prevent large ice crystals forming.

You can choose to flavour your sorbet with fresh lime leaves or rooibos tea. Though very different, they both work really well. Fresh kaffir lime leaves, which are becoming more readily available in supermarkets, deliver an intense citrus fragrance that pairs wonderfully with the watermelon and strawberry.

If you can't find lime leaves, or want to try something different, we found that rooibos tea – made from the leaves of the South African 'red bush' – is an equally wonderful flavour pairing, bringing with it floral and ever-so-slightly bitter notes. If you're going with rooibos, which is readily available in any supermarket, simply steep three tea bags in the warm glucose, in place of the lime leaves. You can then use a teaspoon of regular lime zest in the finishing sugar, rather than the fresh kaffir lime leaves.

Take the sorbet out of the freezer 5–10 minutes before serving, to make it easier to scoop. It will keep in the freezer for up to a month. *Pictured overleaf.*

1. Put the watermelon chunks and strawberries into a large container that will fit in your freezer, and freeze until solid – about 2 hours.

2. Meanwhile, put two-thirds of the lime leaves (or all the rooibos tea bags) into a medium saucepan with the glucose, lime zest, lime juice and vodka and gently heat on a medium heat until the glucose has melted and is warm. Set aside for 30 minutes to infuse, then pour through a sieve set over a blender, discarding the aromatics. Add the frozen fruit to the blender and blitz until completely smooth and slushy.

3. Transfer to a wide freezer-proof container, cover with a lid and freeze until set, about 5 hours.

4. Mix the remaining lime leaves (or an extra teaspoon of lime zest if using rooibos) with the sugar. Divide the sorbet between eight glasses or bowls and serve with some of the sugar sprinkled on top and the lime wedges alongside.

SERVES SIX

COCONUT ICE CREAM WITH LYCHEE AND PASSION FRUIT

180g coconut flakes
560g coconut cream
300g caster sugar
1 tsp vanilla bean paste
  or vanilla extract
¾ tsp ground star anise
1 tsp flaked sea salt
140ml aquafaba (i.e.
  the liquid drained from
  a 400g tin of chickpeas;
  use the chickpeas
  to make orecchiette
  puttanesca, p. 139)
15 fresh lychees, peeled,
  pitted and roughly torn
  in half (tinned is also
  fine, 250g)
90g passion fruit pulp
  (that's 4–5 passion fruit)
3 tbsp lime juice

This is a dessert to impress and it doesn't even require an ice cream machine. It gets its volume and smooth texture from aquafaba – the viscous water you find in a tin of chickpeas – which can (incredibly) be whipped up like egg whites.

You'll make enough ice cream and coconut chips (dubbed coconut 'crack' in the test kitchen, for reasons that will become quite obvious when you make them) for around twelve portions. Both will keep for a good while, so you can always go back for more. The fruit will be enough to serve six, so increase or decrease depending on how many mouths you're feeding.

The ice cream melts very quickly, so take it out of the freezer just before you serve, and return it to the freezer very soon afterwards.

1. Preheat the oven to 180°C fan. Spread the coconut flakes on a large tray and bake for 7 minutes, stirring halfway, until golden-brown and fragrant.

2. Put the coconut cream into a medium saucepan on a medium heat with the sugar, vanilla and star anise. Bring to a simmer and cook until the sugar and cream dissolve, about 5 minutes. Remove from the heat, add the toasted coconut flakes and leave to steep for at least 1 hour. Drain the liquid into a large bowl, compressing the flakes with a spoon to ensure all the liquid goes through. Transfer the strained coconut flakes to a large, 40cm x 30cm parchment-lined tray with the flaked salt. Mix well, and spread them out as much as possible. Set aside at room temperature for at least 2 hours. If making the day before, cover loosely with parchment paper, but do not refrigerate.

3. Put the aquafaba into the bowl of a stand mixer with the whisk attachment in place (or use a hand-held electric whisk). Whisk on high speed for about 8 minutes, until you get semi-stiff peaks. Gently fold the aquafaba into the bowl of coconut cream, until well combined. Pour the mixture into a large container, then cover with a lid or wrap tightly with cling film and freeze for 5 hours, or overnight, stirring the mixture two or three times during that time.

4. Preheat the oven to 160°C fan. Bake the reserved coconut flake mixture for 15 minutes, stirring twice, until deeply golden. Set aside for 10 minutes, to cool and crisp up.

5. Mix the lychees, passion fruit and lime juice together in a medium bowl.

6. Scoop about 70g of ice cream into each of six bowls, spoon over the fruit mixture, and finish with a small handful of coconut chips.

MAX AND FLYNN'S LEMON SORBET

SERVES EIGHT

8 large, unwaxed lemons
200g caster sugar
3 hibiscus tea bags
   (or 10g dried hibiscus
   flowers)
10g mint, stalks and leaves

Some might think this hibiscus and lemon sorbet served in a lemon is a little garish – the sorbet is such a bright shade of pink from the hibiscus – but we love both the colour and the old-school Italian presentation. Yotam's sons Max and Flynn proclaimed it the best dessert they'd ever had, 'better than custard'. It was probably the colour that so enchanted them, but it is undeniably delicious, albeit very sour, in a wholly enjoyable, face-inverting kind of way.

Feel free to set the sorbet in a regular container if you don't want to carve out the lemons. If you don't have an ice cream machine, churn by pouring the unfrozen sorbet into a plastic container and freezing it over a few hours, breaking down the ice crystals with a fork every now and then. The filled lemons will keep in a sealed container in the freezer for up to a month.

1. Cut the top third off each lemon. Juice both parts to give you 350g of juice and pulp combined. Use a spoon to hollow out the lemons, discarding the remaining flesh and pith and being careful not to puncture the skins. Don't worry if you can't get it all out. Shave a little off the bottom half of each lemon so they can sit upright (again, taking care not to puncture the skin) and arrange them in a tray, open side up, so they are snug and balanced. Freeze the bottoms and their lids on separate trays, while you make the sorbet.

2. Put the juice and pulp, discarding the pips, into a medium saucepan with the sugar, hibiscus (tea bags or dried flowers) and 350ml of water. Place on a medium-high heat and simmer for about 6 minutes, stirring occasionally, until the sugar has melted and the liquid is hot. Remove from the heat, add the mint and leave to steep for 15 minutes, until the liquid is bright pink.

3. Strain the liquid through a sieve into a wide container and discard the aromatics. Refrigerate until completely chilled. Pour the chilled liquid into an ice cream machine and churn for 25–30 minutes, or until frozen and smooth. Transfer the sorbet into a piping bag or a Ziploc bag and seal it closed. Freeze for 3–4 hours until firm, crushing the bag with your hands a couple of times to break the ice crystals.

4. Remove the tray of hollowed-out lemon bottoms from the freezer. Cut the tip of the piping bag or Ziploc bag to create a 2–3cm-wide opening. Pipe the sorbet into the lemons to come up about 5cm above the rim (you may need to hold the piping bag with a tea towel, as it gets very cold). Top each with a lemon lid, pushing them down so they are stable, and return to the freezer for at least an hour before serving.

SERVES FOUR

CRÊPES WITH ROASTED BANANAS AND BARBADOS CREAM

_____

CRÊPES
50g plain flour
1 tsp soft light brown sugar
1 large egg
150ml whole milk
25g unsalted butter, for frying
20g flaked almonds, lightly toasted
salt

BARBADOS CREAM
100g mascarpone
150g extra-thick Greek-style yoghurt (such as Total)
½ tsp vanilla bean paste or vanilla extract
1 tbsp spiced dark rum
35g soft light brown sugar

ROASTED BANANAS
30g unsalted butter
2½ tbsp soft light brown sugar
¼ tsp ground ginger
4 ripe bananas, peeled, halved widthways and then lengthways

Barbados cream, introduced to us by Ixta's aunt Rose (via Nigella Lawson), is extremely dangerous: creamy, boozy, sweet and, with the sugar stirred into the rum just before serving, crunchy as well.

You'll make enough batter for about seven crêpes, three more than you will actually need. These are to account for those 'missing in action', when the cook just can't resist temptation. Make the crêpe batter the day before if you want to get ahead, or, like Yotam, triple the batter, fry lots of crêpes and keep them in the freezer, separated with baking parchment, ready to be quickly defrosted whenever you have a hankering. The cream mixture can also be made the day before, but hold off on roasting the bananas and mixing the rum with the sugar until just before serving. *Pictured overleaf.*

1. Preheat the oven to 230°C fan. For the crêpes, whisk the flour in a medium bowl with the sugar and ⅛ teaspoon of salt. Add the egg and whisk together, then add the milk gradually, whisking until you have a smooth, thin batter. Set aside to sit for 20 minutes.

2. For the Barbados cream, mix together the mascarpone, yoghurt and vanilla until smooth and set aside.

3. For the bananas, place a medium, ovenproof frying pan on a medium-high heat and add the butter. Once melted, add the sugar and ginger and stir until melted and combined, 1–2 minutes. Remove from the heat, add the bananas and gently mix so they are coated, then arrange so they are cut side up. Transfer to the oven for 12 minutes, or until softened and browned. Sprinkle with a little salt.

4. Put 5g of the butter for the crêpes into a medium frying pan and place on a medium-high heat. Once melted and bubbling, add about 3½ tablespoons of the batter, swirling the pan to form a thin crêpe about 16cm in diameter. Cook for 1–2 minutes, then, using a spatula, flip over. Cook for another 30–60 seconds, until nicely browned on both sides, then set aside. You may need to lower the heat to medium if the pan gets too hot. Continue with the remaining butter and batter until you have four good crêpes (the first few may not be perfect). Cover and keep warm.

5. Just before serving, stir together the rum and sugar in a separate small bowl.

6. To serve, divide the crêpes between four plates, then top each with a quarter of the bananas. Fold the crêpe over and spoon some of the Barbados cream alongside. Drizzle over the rum sugar, finish with the almonds and serve.

COFFEE AND PANDAN PUDDINGS

SERVES FOUR

50g fresh pandan leaves, roughly cut into 4cm pieces (or 1 vanilla pod, halved lengthways)
300ml whole milk
300ml double cream
15g cornflour
1¼ tsp instant espresso powder
5 egg yolks
50g caster sugar
1 tsp cocoa powder
¼ tsp flaked sea salt
25g unsalted butter, at room temperature, cut into 1cm cubes
30g salted macadamia nuts, well roasted and roughly chopped

COFFEE SYRUP
150ml strong brewed coffee
50g caster sugar

Brilliantly fragrant, pandan leaves are used in Asian cooking to flavour all sorts of sweet and savoury dishes. Their aroma is somewhere between grass and vanilla, and they work particularly well with tropical fruit, in cakes and when paired with coffee, as we have here. They are easily found in Asian supermarkets, but if you can't get hold of them, substitute with a whole vanilla pod.

The coffee syrup can be made a day ahead of time, but it tends to seep into the pudding if it is left to sit, so be sure to pour it on just as you serve. It takes 2 hours to infuse the milk with the pandan and about 6 hours for the puddings to set, so you'd probably want to make them a day ahead as well. *Pictured overleaf.*

1. Put the pandan leaves (or vanilla pod), milk and cream into a medium saucepan, for which you have a lid, and place on a medium heat. Cover and leave to gently heat and steam, pressing down on the leaves a few times to release their flavour, about 20 minutes. Remove from the heat and leave to infuse, covered, for at least 2 hours. Strain through a sieve set over a bowl, pushing down to extract as much liquid as possible, discarding the leaves (or pod). Measure out 80ml of the milk into a medium bowl and add the cornflour, whisking until smooth. Pour the remaining strained milk back into the saucepan, add the espresso powder and whisk to combine. Set aside until needed.

2. Meanwhile, make the coffee syrup by putting the coffee and sugar into a small saucepan on a medium-high heat. Bring to the boil and leave to bubble away for 6–7 minutes, or until it has reduced by about half and is the consistency of maple syrup. Set aside to cool; it will thicken more as it sits.

3. In a medium bowl, whisk together the egg yolks, sugar, cocoa powder and salt until smooth.

4. Return the saucepan of infused milk to a medium heat and bring to a simmer. Temper the eggs by slowly pouring half the warm milk mixture into the egg yolk bowl, whisking continuously until the bowl is warm to the touch. Add the cornflour and milk mixture and whisk until smooth. Slowly pour the now tempered mixture back into the saucepan and whisk continuously, until it's the consistency of a thick but pourable custard, about 5 minutes. Remove from the heat and whisk in the butter until incorporated.

5. Divide the pudding between four martini glasses (or something similar) and leave to cool slightly before covering with cling film and refrigerating until set; about 6 hours or overnight.

6. To serve, top each pudding with 2 teaspoons of coffee syrup, then sprinkle with the macadamia nuts, serving any extra syrup alongside.

SERVES SIX

BERRY PLATTER WITH SHEEP'S LABNEH AND ORANGE OIL

————————

900g sheep's yoghurt, or cow's yoghurt as an alternative

½ tsp salt

100ml good-quality olive oil

10g lemon thyme sprigs, plus a few extra picked thyme leaves to serve

1 orange: finely shave the skin to get 6 strips

200g blackberries

250g raspberries

300g strawberries, hulled and halved lengthways (or quartered if they're larger)

50g caster sugar

1 lime: finely grate the zest to get 1 tsp, then juice to get 1 tbsp

200g blueberries

150g cherries, pitted

This display of the season's best can double up as a light dessert or as a brunch centrepiece. You can make your own labneh but it requires draining the yoghurt for a good 24 hours, or you can make everything easily on the day using shop-bought labneh or some Greek-style yoghurt mixed with a little double cream. The berries you use are totally up to you, depending on what's good and not too expensive. You can use fewer types, or some frozen berries, if you like, especially for those which get blitzed in the recipe. You'll make more oil than you need; store it in a glass jar to drizzle over salads or lightly cooked vegetables.

1. Put the yoghurt and salt into a medium bowl and mix well to combine. Line a colander with a piece of muslin large enough to hang over the sides and place the colander over a bowl. Transfer the yoghurt to the muslin and fold over the sides to completely encase the yoghurt. Place a heavy weight over the muslin (a few tins or jars will do), and transfer to the fridge to drain for at least 24 hours (and up to 48).

2. Meanwhile, put the oil into a small saucepan, for which you have a lid, on a medium heat. Heat gently for about 7 minutes, or until tiny air bubbles form. Remove from the heat, add the thyme and orange strips, then cover with a lid and leave to infuse, ideally overnight, though half an hour will also do the job.

3. The next day, put 50g of blackberries, 100g of raspberries and 100g of strawberries into the small bowl of a food processor along with the sugar and lime juice and blitz until completely smooth. Put all the remaining berries and the cherries into a large bowl along with the blitzed fruit and gently combine. You can serve it straight away or leave it in the fridge for a few hours, bringing it back to room temperature before serving.

4. Spread the labneh out on a large platter. Spoon over the berries, then sprinkle with the lime zest. Drizzle with 2 tablespoons of the infused oil, along with a couple of the orange strips and the extra picked thyme leaves.

FLAVOUR BOMBS

We had various working titles for *FLAVOUR* throughout the course of writing it. One of them was 'The Ottolenghi F-bomb'. It was never going to fly, we knew, but the idea of 'the flavour bombs' is one which was with us every step of the way. Stocked up with a little arsenal of flavour-packed condiments, sauces, pickles, salsas, infused oils and so forth, a meal full of flavour will only ever be just a few steps away. This list is our arsenal. They're all recipes-within-recipes from the book but useful to have here as well, to see how standalone and versatile they can be. You don't need to make all of them, but having one or two or three in your fridge at any one time is really useful. Five-minutes-made scrambled eggs will never be the same again once you've drizzled them with smoked cascabel oil or served them with a bit of charred chilli salsa alongside.

A couple of practicalities: if you are making a batch of something for a recipe, it's often worth doubling or tripling the quantities so that you have some at the ready. Shelf lives and keeping notes vary depending on what you are making, so see each recipe for details. If you are scaling up a recipe, you'll probably need to increase pan or bowl size and cooking time accordingly. We always give a visual description of what you are looking for, so use this as a guide, if quantities have been increased, rather than sticking religiously to times given. As always, trust your instincts and have the confidence to be your own judge. If you think something is looking, smelling and tasting delicious and ready, then, chances are, it *will* be.

Oils, butters and marinades

1. Chilli oil (P. 159)
2. Numbing oil (P. 196)
3. Smoked cascabel oil (P. 41)
4. Rayu (P. 237)
5. Black lime and pumpkin seed butter (P. 264)
6. Three-garlic butter (P. 246)
7. Lime leaf butter (P. 50)
8. Chilli butter (P. 205)
9. Fenugreek marinade (P. 63)

Sauces, salsas and dressings

10. Blood orange nam jim (P. 202)
11. Charred chilli salsa (P. 45)
12. Coriander chutney (P. 193)
13. Nam prik (P. 44)
14. Quick chilli sauce (P. 151)
15. Sweet tamarind dressing (P. 193)
16. Chamoy (P. 187)
17. Tahini and soy dressing (P. 113)

Condiments and pickles
18. Marie Rose sauce (P. 146)
19. Curry leaf mayonnaise (P. 89)
20. Date barbecue sauce (P. 59)
21. Hibiscus pickled onions (P. 158)

Nuts and sprinkles
22. Chipotle peanuts (P. 263)
23. Nori and sesame salt (P. 267)

MEAL SUGGESTIONS AND FEASTS

Vegetable-focused meals are flexible by their very nature. There isn't a natural hierarchy or a clear order in which things need to appear at the table. The notion of a main course and sides, on which so many of us rely, simply doesn't lend itself so easily to a meal in which meat or fish don't occupy centre stage. Though we aren't big fans of any form of fixed meal structure, even when we serve meat or fish, we are aware that the freedom that comes with the plurality of options of a veggie menu can bring with it some confusion.

To help a little with choosing how to put together meals from *FLAVOUR*, we have come up with some suggestions. These are there as ideas only, seeds we plant in your head so you can navigate between dishes you've never cooked before. We encourage you to pick and choose from our menus. They are not set in stone. Add if you need more in your meal, take away if you think it's too much.

We would also love you to serve our dishes alongside your old favourites. Cooking a new dish is a challenge, cooking two is double the challenge. Make your life easier by taking single steps, if you need to.

In fact, cooking a single dish from the book and serving it with one or two 'sides' is something we recommend wholeheartedly. Most of the dishes in *FLAVOUR* were designed with big flavours in mind. The 'simple salad', 'sautéed greens' or 'simple rice' we mention below are all code for your favourite dishes from the raw veg, cooked veg or starch families. Make them to go with one of our more substantial dishes, and that's all you'll need.

Lastly, make ahead! Whenever we can we give you an idea about which parts of a recipe can be prepared in advance; often it's the dish in its entirety. Please take advantage of this. There is nothing better than getting a meal on the table in a matter of minutes and with (what looks like) very little effort. It leaves you stress free and with all the time in the world to enjoy your hard-earned efforts.

Everyday Cooking

ONE PAN, READY IN 30 MINUTES OR LESS

Potato and gochujang braised **eggs** (P. 99) + simple **salad**

Za'atar cacio e pepe (P. 104) + simple **salad**

One-pan **orecchiette** puttanesca (P. 139) + simple **salad**

Cardamom **tofu** with lime **greens** (P. 172) + sticky **rice**

Super-soft **courgettes** with harissa and lemon (P. 204) + **pasta** or **rice**

ONE PAN, READY IN 1 HOUR

Bkeila, **potato** and **butter bean** stew (P. 75) + simply grilled **tofu** or **fish**

Polenta with fresh corn and braised **eggs** (P. 163) + simple **salad**

The ultimate traybake **ragù** (P. 101) + pasta or polenta and simple **salad**

READY IN 1 HOUR

Steamed **aubergines** with charred chilli salsa (P. 45) + **noodles** or **rice**

Spring vegetables in Parmesan broth with charred lemon salsa (P. 109) + **pasta** or **noodles**

Chickpea **pancakes** with mango pickle yoghurt (P. 91) + simple **salad**

Kimchi and Gruyère **rice fritters** (P. 166) + simple **salad**

Udon **noodles** with fried **tofu** and orange nam jim (P. 202)

Noodle salad with mushroom and peanut **laab** (P. 233)

Mafalda and roasted **butternut** in warm yoghurt sauce (P. 151) + sautéed **greens** or simple **salad**

Brown **rice** and shiitake **congee** (P. 237) + soft-boiled **egg** or grilled **tofu** and sautéed **greens**

Spicy berbere **ratatouille** with coconut salsa (P. 209) + **rice** and/or **flatbreads**

Coconut and turmeric **omelette** feast (P. 145) + fried **tofu** or **prawns**

Sweet potato in tomato, lime and cardamom sauce (P. 131) + **rice** and sautéed **greens**

LOW-EFFORT/HIGH-IMPACT MEALS

Curry-crusted **swede** steaks (P. 63) + **rice** or **flatbreads**

Sweet and sour **sprouts** with chestnuts and grapes (P. 93) + grilled **tofu** and **rice**

Cauliflower roasted in chilli butter (P. 205) + **rice** and sautéed **greens**

Portobello steaks and butter bean mash (P. 210) + sautéed **greens** or simple **salad**

LOW-EFFORT/HIGH-IMPACT SIDES

Cucumber salad à la Xi'an Impression (P. 113)

Oven **chips** with curry leaf mayonnaise (P. 89)

Tomato salad with lime and cardamom yoghurt (P. 164)

Braised **greens** with yoghurt (P. 175)

Sweet and sour **onion** petals (P. 245)

Miso butter **onions** (P. 258)

Grilled **figs** with Shaoxing dressing (P. 110)

Tomato and **plum salad** with nori and sesame (P. 267)

Kohlrabi 'noodle' **salad** (P. 260)

Spicy roast **potatoes** with tahini and soy (P. 276)

Roasted **carrot** salad with chamoy (P. 187)

MAKE-AHEAD MEALS

The ultimate traybake **ragù** (P. 101) + **pasta** or **polenta**

Rainbow **chard** with tomatoes and green olives (P. 183) + **rice** or **pasta**

Spicy **mushroom lasagne** (P. 228) + simple **salad**

Stuffed **aubergine** in curry and coconut **dal** (P. 152) + **rice** and/or **flatbreads**

Aubergine dumplings alla parmigiana (P. 156) + **pasta** and sautéed **greens**

Tofu meatball korma (P. 268) + **rice** and/or flatbreads and simple **salad**

Brown **rice** and shiitake **congee** (P. 237) + soft-boiled **egg** or grilled tofu and sautéed **greens**

Spicy berbere **ratatouille** with coconut salsa (P. 209) + **rice** and/or **flatbreads**

Portobello steaks and butter bean mash (P. 210) + sautéed **greens** or simple **salad**

Feasts

BRUNCH SPREADS

Potato and gochujang braised **eggs** (P. 99) or Coconut and turmeric **omelette** feast (P. 145) + Radish and cucumber **salad** (P. 263) + **Crêpes** with roasted bananas and Barbados cream (P. 290)

Polenta with fresh corn and braised eggs (P. 163) + **Tomato** salad with lime and cardamom yoghurt (P. 164) + **Butter beans** in smoked cascabel oil (P. 41) + Super-soft **courgettes** with harissa and lemon (P. 204)

THREE-COURSE MEALS

Pappa al pomodoro with lime and mustard seeds (P. 85) + **Za'atar cacio e pepe** (P. 104) + Poached **apricots** with pistachio and amaretti mascarpone (P. 282)

Corn ribs (P. 264) + Swede **gnocchi** with miso butter (P. 94) + Coconut **ice cream** with lychee and passion fruit (P. 286)

Roasted and pickled **celeriac** with sweet chilli dressing (P. 55) + Cardamom **tofu** with lime greens (P. 172) and simple **rice** + **Coffee** and pandan puddings (P. 291)

Herb and burnt **aubergine soup** (P. 42) + One-pan **orecchiette** puttanesca (P. 139) + Max and Flynn's lemon **sorbet** (P. 289)

ROVI SPREAD

Tempura stems, leaves and herbs (P. 184) + Hasselback **beetroot** with lime leaf butter (P. 50) + Charred **peppers** and fresh corn polenta (P. 140) + Rainbow **chard** with tomatoes and green **olives** (P. 183) + Tangerine and ancho chilli **flan** (P. 278)

KORMA FEAST

Tofu meatball korma (P. 268) + Spicy berbere **ratatouille** with coconut salsa (P. 209) or Curry-crusted **swede** steaks (P. 63) + Olive oil **flatbreads** with three-garlic butter (without the tomatoes) (P. 246) or simple **rice**

MEXICAN FEAST

Cheese **tamales** with all (or some of) the trimmings (P. 158) or Oyster **mushroom tacos** with all (or some of) the trimmings (P. 238) (or both) + Radish and cucumber **salad** with chipotle peanuts (P. 263) + Tangerine and ancho chilli **flan** (P. 278)

EAST ASIAN FEAST

Cabbage with ginger cream and numbing oil (P. 196) + Asparagus and gochujang **pancakes** (P. 102) + Fusion caponata with silken **tofu** (P. 135) + Cucumber **salad** à la Xi'an Impression (P. 113) + **Coffee** and pandan puddings (P. 291)

FESTIVE SPREADS

Turnip cake (P. 270) + Sweet and sour **sprouts** with chestnuts and grapes (P. 93) + **Leeks** with miso and chive salsa (P. 257) + Esme's rough **squash mash** (P. 136) + Dirty **rice** (P. 252)

Cauliflower roasted in chilli butter (P. 205) + Lime and coconut **potato gratin** (P. 72) + Roasted **carrot** salad with chamoy (P. 187) + Slow-cooked charred green **beans** (P. 49) or simple steamed green **beans**

SUNDAY ROAST

Celeriac steaks with Café de Paris sauce (P. 60) + Cucumber, za'atar and chopped lemon **salad** (P. 191) + Oven **chips** (without the curry leaf mayonnaise) (P. 89)

OUTDOOR SUMMER FEAST

Melon and buffalo mozzarella salad with kasha and curry leaves (P. 80) + **Tomato** and plum **salad** with nori and sesame (P. 267) + **Potato salad** with Thai basil salsa (P. 275) + Olive oil **flatbreads** with three-garlic butter (P. 246) + Super-soft **courgettes** with harissa and lemon (P. 204)

MEZZE

Aubergine with herbs and crispy garlic (P. 251) + Sweet and sour **onion** petals (P. 245) or Neil's grilled **onions** with green **gazpacho** (P. 242) + Confit garlic **hummus** with grilled mushrooms (P. 234) + **Tomato** salad with lime and cardamom yoghurt (P. 164) + Olive oil **flatbreads** with three-garlic butter (P. 246)

DIPS

Hummus with lemon, fried garlic and chilli (P. 79) + Mashed **sweet potatoes** with yoghurt and lime (P. 192) + White **bean mash** with garlic aïoli (P. 76) + Curried **carrot mash** with brown butter (P. 67)

A

B

ACKNOWLEDGEMENTS

I am often asked how I carry on creating new recipes for home cooks after more than a decade of publishing cookbooks. The answer is that I don't. What I did create (with many others) is an environment that I am tremendously proud of: the test kitchen that sits under a railway arch in Camden, north London, and the Ottolenghi restaurants, including NOPI and ROVI. These are the places where new dishes are shaped and it's the people who work in them that come up with the ideas that find themselves, in print, on people's kitchen counters.

In Camden, alongside Ixta and Tara, Team Test Kitchen is blessed with Noor Murad, who grew up in Bahrain and is the unofficial expert in Middle Eastern feasts, tamarind and everything rice related, amongst countless other talents. I am also immensely grateful to Gitai Fisher, who's good at everything, and is often the one with the clever idea that helps us crack a 'troublesome' dish.

Other constant contributors are Calvin Von Niebel, Verena Lochmuller, Paulina Bembel, Neil Campbell, Helen Goh and Esme Howarth. I am grateful to them all. I am also grateful to Claudine Boulstridge for her priceless appraisals.

I would like to thank Jonathan Lovekin and Caz Hildebrand, my long-standing creative partners, for being so incredibly good at their jobs, Wei Tang for the props and honesty and Nishant Choksi for the clever illustrations. Thanks also to Sam Carroll and Sytch Farm Studios.

Thanks to Felicity Rubinstein for standing by my side, often having to hold my hand, through old challenges and new, and to Lizzy Gray for her intelligence and infinite patience.

A massive thank you to Noam Bar for his continual presence behind every single project, to Cornelia Staeubli for her unconditional support and to Sami Tamimi for his friendship.

I am also extremely grateful to the team at Ebury: Joel Rickett, Sarah Bennie, Celia Palazzo, Stephenie Naulls, Catherine Wood, Vanessa Forbes and Catherine Ngwong. Across the Atlantic, my deepest thanks to Kim Witherspoon, Aaron Wehner, Lorena Jones, Kate Tyler, Windy Dorresteyn, Sandi Mendelson, Jane Chinn, Kelly Booth, Emma Rudolph, Doug Ogan, Mari Gill, Robert McCullough, Lindsay Paterson, and Carla Kean.

Thanks also to Mark Hutchinson and Gemma Bell and her team and to Bob Granleese and Tim Lusher.

Finally, but most importantly, thank you to the love of my life, Karl Allen, and to the two monkeys, Max and Flynn. Thanks also to Michael and Ruth Ottolenghi; Tirza, Danny, Shira, Yoav and Adam Florentin; Pete and Greta Allen, Shachar Argov, Garry Chang, Alex Meitlis, Ivo Bisignano, Lulu Banquete, Tamara Meitlis, Keren Margalit, Yoram Ever-Hadani, Itzik Lederfeind, Ilana Lederfeind and Amos, Ariela and David Oppenheim.

YOTAM OTTOLENGHI

Thank you to my parents, Nicolas Belfrage and Maria Candida De Melo, for love that knows no bounds, and for the unforgettable adventures through Brazil, Mexico and Italy that shaped the cook that I am today.

To my sister Beatriz Belfrage, for wisdom and support I can always turn to.

To my cousin Moby Pomerance, for nurturing a love of food in me.

Thanks to Claudia Lazarus, my partner in crime in most food-related endeavours outside of Ottolenghi. Thanks to NOPI restaurant, where I met Claudia across a crowded kitchen, and where my Ottolenghi adventure began.

Thank you to Alex Intas, for his unwavering love and support, but more importantly for his unwavering willingness to eat.

Thanks to Lauren and Felipe Gonzalez, for giving me a copy of *Plenty More* all those years ago with a message in it to the tune of 'follow your dreams'. I could never have dreamt of this!

To Noor Murad, thank you for being a constant source of light and inspiration.

To Jonathan, Lizzy, Celia, Annie, Caz, Wei and Nishant, thank you for helping make this first venture into the world of book-making a joyous one.

And, most importantly, thank you to Yotam for the opportunity of a lifetime, and for being a fiercely patient, intelligent and kind teacher.

IXTA BELFRAGE

10 9 8 7 6 5 4 3 2

Ebury Press, an imprint of Ebury Publishing,
20 Vauxhall Bridge Road,
London, SW1V 2SA

Ebury Press is part of the Penguin Random
House group of companies whose addresses
can be found at
global.penguinrandomhouse.com

Penguin
Random House
UK

First published by Ebury Press in 2020

www.penguin.co.uk

A CIP catalogue record for this book
is available from the British Library

Publishing Director: Lizzy Gray
Project Editor: Celia Palazzo
Design: Here Design
Photography: Jonathan Lovekin
Illustrations: Nishant Choksi
Prop styling: Wei Tang
Production: Catherine Ngwong

ISBN: 978-1-785-03893-8

Colour origination by Altaimage Ltd, London
Printed and bound by Graphicom S.r.l

Penguin Random House is committed
to a sustainable future for our business,
our readers and our planet. This book is
made from Forest Stewardship Council®
certified paper.

MIX
Paper from
responsible sources
FSC® C018179

FLAVOUR

Yotam Ottolenghi
Ixta Belfrage

THE PERFECT INTERACTIVE COMPANION TO THE BOOK

A GIFT FROM YOTAM AND IXTA

All of the recipes at your fingertips, wherever you are

BROWSE

Access all the recipes online from anywhere

SEARCH

Find your perfect recipe by ingredient or browse through the chapters

FAVOURITES

Create your own list of go-to recipes and have them at your fingertips, whether shopping on the way home or looking for recipe ideas during a weekend away

TO UNLOCK YOUR ACCESS VISIT BOOKS.OTTOLENGHI.CO.UK AND ENTER YOUR UNIQUE CODE: WTAJ-JG58-MEYC-HA33

SHOP ONLINE

From our list of FLAVOUR's 20 Ingredients, we've put together a selection that captures the spirit and essence of the recipes in this book. An exciting mix of new additions to the Ottolenghi pantry, as well as some of our old favourites.

We have also included a tote bag, so you can take FLAVOUR with you wherever you go.

GO TO OTTOLENGHI.CO.UK/FLAVOUR-INGREDIENTS

Aleppo Chilli Flakes, Ancho Chilli, Black Garlic, Whole Black Lime, Cascabel Chillies, Gochujang, Hibiscus, Masa Harina, White Miso, Red Bell Pepper Flakes, Rose Harissa.

OTTOLENGHI